To:
HENRY

May you continue to
have success with making
HR a Strategic
Contributor!

Best Wishes!

Jon
1/4/2006

HIGH-IMPACT HUMAN CAPITAL STRATEGY

HIGH-IMPACT HUMAN CAPITAL STRATEGY

ADDRESSING THE 12 MAJOR CHALLENGES TODAY'S ORGANIZATIONS FACE

Jack J. Phillips and Patricia Pulliam Phillips

American Management Association
New York • Atlanta • Brussels • Chicago • Mexico City •
San Francisco • Shanghai • Tokyo • Toronto • Washington, D.C.

Bulk discounts available. For details visit:
www.amacombooks.org/go/specialsales
Or contact special sales:
Phone: 800-250-5308
E-mail: specialsls@amanet.org
View all the AMACOM titles at: www.amacombooks.org
American Management Association: www.amanet.org

This publication is designed to provide accurate and authoritative information in regard to the subject matter covered. It is sold with the understanding that the publisher is not engaged in rendering legal, accounting, or other professional service. If legal advice or other expert assistance is required, the services of a competent professional person should be sought.

Library of Congress Cataloging-in-Publication Data

Phillips, Jack J., 1945–
    High-impact human capital strategy : addressing the 12 major challenges today's organizations face / Jack J. Phillips and Patricia Pulliam Phillips.
        pages cm
    Includes bibliographical references and index.
    ISBN 978-0-8144-3606-6 (hardcover)—ISBN 0-8144-3606-4 (hardcover)—ISBN 978-0-8144-3607-3 (ebook)—ISBN 0-8144-3607-2 (ebook) 1. Manpower planning. 2. Human capital. 3. Personnel management. 4. Strategic planning. I. Phillips, Patricia Pulliam. II. Title.

    HF5549.5.M3P52 2015
    658.3'01—dc23   2015007532

About AMA
American Management Association (www.amanet.org) is a world leader in talent development, advancing the skills of individuals to drive business success. Our mission is to support the goals of individuals and organizations through a complete range of products and services, including classroom and virtual seminars, webcasts, webinars, podcasts, conferences, corporate and government solutions, business books, and research. AMA's approach to improving performance combines experiential learning—learning through doing—with opportunities for ongoing professional growth at every step of one's career journey.

Printing number
10 9 8 7 6 5 4 3 2 1

Contents

Preface

This new book focuses directly on how to develop a human capital (HC) strategy in today's turbulent and changing environment. Too often, HC strategy encompasses a classic and traditional approach to human resources (HR): recruiting the best people, preparing them for assignments, motivating them for high performance, and retaining them for several years. While this is all necessary, it is more helpful to have a strategy that fits into the current environment and context. An HC strategy must effectively address the demographic changes in the workforce, current skill shortages and mismatches in labor markets, societal and structural shifts in organizations, the persistent energy crisis, globalization, and important environmental challenges. At the same time, the strategy must be feasible, actionable, measurable, and implemented with remarkable success. This book addresses twelve forces that must be addressed in HC strategy.

Why This Is Necessary

No function, process, or issue in an organization is more important than the human capital managed by the HR department. HC strategies often make great companies, build great products, and deliver great services. Even in governments, a human capital strategy can make the difference between success and failure. A major part of the financial problem in Greece came from its HC issues, as the Greek government created more jobs than needed, paid far too much for them, and provided excessive benefits, making it easy to retire early with large pensions. At the same time, the accountability for the work went away. Every high school graduate wanted to work in a government job. The government grew, overshadowing the private sector as the dominant employer and leaving the country with a staggering debt that is still unraveling. Greece did not have an effective HC strategy.

The HR function is so important that some magazines (e.g., *CFO Magazine*) have suggested that it should be placed under the direction of the chief financial officer, because it represents the largest expenditure in an organization and has the most promise of creating a very successful and effective organization. Gartner Research has reported that this is now a trend.

While HC's importance has never been higher, the image of HR is still tarnished, and according to some, it is at a low point. For the most part, HC strategies are driven by the HR executive instead of the top executives. While this is helpful and important for action, it marginalizes the influence of the HR executive. In some organizations, the view of HR is often outdated, still perceived as an administrative, legal, and transactional process that is, at best, a necessary evil. Jack Welch, the former CEO of General Electric, has stated that many of his colleagues see HR as a "health and happiness sideshow."[1]

Typical HC strategy focuses on recruiting, selection, talent development, compensation, motivation, compliance, and maintenance. While these functions are obviously important, the dynamics of the environment where these processes occur is changing rapidly. Many forces contribute to an organization's health and its employees' well-being and success, and these must be addressed when developing HC strategy.

The HR function should be perceived as important, integral, and a contributing part of the organization. One of the best ways to improve the image of this function, increase its influence within the organization, and deliver unmistakable, credible results is to have an HC strategy that focuses on the following twelve goals:

1. Setting the optimal investment level for human capital and reviewing this expenditure periodically
2. Aligning HR programs to the business as they are initiated, developed, and implemented
3. Managing critical talent in the organization, ensuring that the appropriate number and quality of talented employees are available, addressing skills shortages, and ensuring that talent remains in the organization
4. Pursuing a program of employee satisfaction, commitment, and job engagement, so that employees are fully involved in their work, remain loyal to the organization, and help attract others to the organization
5. Creating a performance and innovation culture to achieve results in the organization with proper direction, roles, and motivations
6. Ensuring that employees are healthy and safe with proper healthcare and wellness opportunities
7. Addressing the current demographics and societal issues to ensure that a proper employee mix is available and included in processes to enhance productivity and innovation
8. Using technology to its fullest extent to unleash the creativity and potential of employees, while ensuring that it is driving productivity, innovation, and customer satisfaction
9. Addressing globalization in terms of how it effects employees in the present and will affect employees in the future, by having them actively engaged in every part of the process
10. Addressing environmental and energy issues as they relate to jobs, the organization, and society
11. Developing effective leaders who can operate successfully in a global, diverse environment
12. Implementing a system for accountability, including measuring success with analytics and big data, and delivering value that will be credible to top executives, including the chief financial officer

These imperatives are, at best, only casually mentioned in HC/HR strategy and execution books but represent critical processes needed to deliver value in medium and large organizations alike.

Who Will Benefit from This Book

HR executives, managers, and administrators—the individuals who must develop an appropriate strategy and present it to the executive team—will find this book to be a useful guide for developing the human capital strategy. An effective strategy will require several elements to be in place, and they are all described in this book. This book will be an indispensable tool for HR leaders to connect the HR function to key strategic issues in the organization and drive organizational value.

Senior executives, who must support HC strategy and take the lead in developing it, will find this book to be a helpful reference to what's possible. These executives need to be in harmony with the strategy to support it, provide resources for it, and constantly reinforce and adjust it.

HR specialists, coordinators, advisors, and consultants within the organization, who must align HR with the strategy, will benefit from this book as well. They have an important input into the strategic processes, and this book will help them understand why the strategy is necessary. It will also help them define their roles in the process, execute the strategy, and deliver results.

Finally, professionals who are external to organizations will also find this book to be a valuable resource. This includes professors, consultants, and researchers who are promoting, teaching, exploring, researching, and assisting with HC strategies. Consultants can use it as guide to help organizations, and professors can use it as a textbook in MBA or HRM courses at the senior and graduate levels. Researchers will find this book to be a useful guide for HC strategy research.

The Flow of the Book

This book begins with two introductory chapters that set the stage for the remainder of the book. Chapter 1 focuses on the importance of human capital, tracking some of the key issues that highlight how the concept of human capital has been a critical issue for top executives and is the main focus of the human resources function. Chapter 2 examines the approaches to human capital strategy, outlining what is classically covered and the strategic issues that are always contained in current strategy documents. At the same time, this chapter points to the shortcomings of those strategic documents, highlighting that there are twelve major forces that are often not addressed clearly and completely.

Throughout the rest of the book, the twelve forces that are affecting businesses, particularly in the human capital area, are addressed one chapter at a time. Each chapter starts by defining the force, particularly in the context of how it affects human capital and the business. Next, the force is detailed in terms of its elements, components, principles, issues, and challenges, including the effect it is having on organizations. Part of the discussion is about what the human resources function should consider or explore. The chapter then focuses on what strategic questions must be addressed and what strategic statements must be included in the human capital strategic plan.

Acknowledgments

Jack and Patti would like to acknowledge, first and foremost, all the human resources executives who really make a difference. HR executives have struggled to be fully accepted in the C-suite as an important part of the top executive team, but many have made this journey and are making great contributions. Far too many are not there yet, but they are working on it. We acknowledge those who have made it and those who are striving to make it, too numerous to mention here by name, and recognize that all of them are making great contributions.

We want to thank our editor, Stephen S. Power at AMACOM, who has been very patient with us as we developed this manuscript during a very hectic global travel schedule. Thanks, Stephen, for your patience and for taking on this project, our second book with AMACOM.

Jack would like to thank three of his former CEOs: Herbert Stockham, Carl Register, and B. K. "Skipper" Goodwin. All three allowed Jack to experiment with many of the concepts in this book. Our HR function was a laboratory, ahead of its time.

We also want to recognize our staff who have contributed their efforts to this book, particularly Hope Nicholas, director of publications, who always juggles many projects. Hope is our strategy when it comes to books. Her efforts to organize, edit, and deliver this manuscript have been outstanding. As always, the entire ROI Institute team provided excellent support and assistance when we wrote this book.

1

THE IMPORTANCE OF HUMAN CAPITAL

The Journey to Show the Value

This introductory chapter examines the importance of human capital and introduces several arguments for why human capital should be a reigning priority. It begins by examining the role of people in organizations and then explores issues such as how human capital is (or is not) valued. The role of human capital in highly successful organizations is highlighted in lists such as *Fortune*'s "100 Best Companies to Work For" and "Most Admired Companies." In almost all cases, logical arguments point toward the importance of the human part of the organization, which contributes most, if not all, of the organization's successes. The discussion emphasizes the value successful organizations place on their people and their reasons for doing so.

Are People Necessary?

The beginning point in the discussion about the importance of human capital is to think about the value people bring to an organization. This always brings up a question: Are people really necessary? Of course, in practice, we all realize that people are critical, but should the goal be to eliminate them or let someone else work with them? Is it possible to automate almost everything, as some companies attempt to do?

People Cause Problems

It's interesting to observe an automobile assembly line in a modern factory. There are no people to be seen—just expensive and impressive robots. Why would the company take this approach and replace humans with robots? Is it cheaper? Is it because of the problems employees create? Is it because of the difficulty in finding qualified workers? Maybe it's all these issues.

Some managers view the human aspect of organizations as an irritant, a burden, or perhaps a necessary evil. People cause most of the problems. It is the people who are dissatisfied, file grievances, have complaints, allege sexual harassment, get injured on the job, file workers compensation claims, go on strike, and create a host of other problems that not only take them out of service but take precious time and resources to resolve. Some executives have estimated that employee problems account for as much as 20 percent of the total cost of human capital investment. If the people could be removed, the problems would go away; there would be no complaints, charges, gripes, grievances, accidents, or work stoppages. For some executives, this would be Utopia, and they strive to achieve this scenario.

Technology Replaces People

The advancement of equipment, machines, and technology has enabled many organizations to automate parts of the job—and in some cases, all of the job. As technology evolves, is it possible to have a completely automated workplace? Is it possible to remove the human factor, at least for the most part? Consider something that would have been almost unheard of years ago: automated air travel. With available technology, airplanes could basically take off, fly to their destination, and land, completely automated. Much of the check-in, boarding, and logistics could be automated, as it is now to a certain extent. It may be possible for the entire process (from checking in to arriving at the desired destination) to be accomplished without any human interaction. To some, this seems like science fiction, but it could be a reality. Is this desired? Perhaps not. What happens if technology fails or there is a glitch in the automation? The dream becomes a nightmare. It may be impossible to remove the human factor in the short term, but this is a goal for many.

Automation Is Healthy

Regardless of your position on job automation, there are some jobs that should be eliminated; automation should be an essential and significant part of the strategy of deciding how much to invest in employees. Four types of jobs are ideal candidates for automation. First, the jobs that are considered very monotonous and boring should be eliminated. These jobs are routine and require little thought and concentration. Many assembly-line jobs fit into this category. If possible, these jobs should be automated; otherwise, the monotony leads to dissatisfaction, which leads to absenteeism, turnover, injuries, withdrawal, and sometimes even sickness. Employees can become sick solely because of the rote work they do.

Second, jobs that are highly dangerous should be automated. This is a critical issue in heavy industry, manufacturing, and mining—using technology to remove the employee factor so that injuries and deaths can be prevented. This is not only the cost-effective thing to do but the humane thing as well.

Third, transaction-based jobs should be automated. These jobs involve simple-step transactions that can be handled much more efficiently with technology. Consider the issue of booking an airline reservation—a very transaction-based process. A few years ago, it was all handled on the phone or face to face; now the majority of reservations are made on the Internet, thus eliminating many people who previously had to be involved in the process. Some airlines charge an additional fee when reservations are made via the phone, thus providing an incentive to reserve a seat via the Internet. The newer technology produces fewer errors and is quicker and less costly for the organization.

Fourth, jobs where it is difficult to recruit employees should be automated, if possible. Many organizations are automating processes, steps, and even entire functions. Consider the local service station and the job of fueling your automobile. Gone are the days when three attendants ran out to your car, filled the tank, checked the oil, washed the windshield, put air in the tires, and took your money. Today, the individual consumer is familiar with the gas pump. By following a few simple directions, the consumer fills the tank, pays with a credit card, and goes through an automatic car wash. These "modern" conveniences have enabled companies to provide more efficient delivery of their gasoline. If an attendant had to pump the gas and take the money, the associated cost would have to be passed onto the consumer—some estimate as much as 5–10 cents per gallon. This automation has eliminated jobs that are hard to fill and usually have high turnover. At the same time, there is increased efficiency and convenience. The hours of store operation are no longer a consideration; you can fuel your car at any time, any day of the week. Some service stations are open 24/7 with no people involved in the process.

People Are Still Necessary

With the previous discussion as a backdrop, several conclusions can be reached about the role of people in the workplace. First, minimizing the numbers is not necessarily a bad strategy. In the name of efficiency, employee welfare, and the desire to have motivating and challenging jobs, certain jobs need to be eliminated or minimized.

Second, human capital investment at some level is necessary. Even in a completely automated transaction, people are involved in making key decisions, solving problems, and ensuring that the processes work correctly. The investment still exists; it is just that it may be a smaller percentage of the operating expenses.

Third, in a highly automated workplace, people are still critical. Sometimes their skills are upgraded because of problems that arise when transactions, technology, or equipment fails. They are also needed to coordinate and implement the new technology in the first place. In an ideal situation, as jobs are eliminated, skills are upgraded so that the workforce is maintained or, in some cases, even grows. A firm that has both job creation (adding jobs) and significant automation (eliminating jobs) is adding tremendous value to the economy, which is the challenge of many organizations.

The Stock Market Mystery

When considering the value and importance of human capital, executives need to look no further than the stock market. Investors place a tremendous value on human capital in organizations. For example, consider San Diego–based QUALCOMM, a leader in developing and delivering innovative wireless communication products and services based on the company's CDMA (code division multiple access) digital technology. The company owns significant intellectual property applicable to products that implement any version of CDMA. QUALCOMM is included in the S&P 500 Index and is a Fortune 500 company traded on the NASDAQ stock market. QUALCOMM is a very profitable company, with revenues in 2013 of $44.9 billion and a net income of $6.9 billion.[1]

QUALCOMM reported total assets (tangible) on its balance sheet of $45.5 billion; however, its market value is much higher. The stock price in 2014 was $75 per share, and the company had a market value of $120.9 billion. In essence, tangible assets represented only 37 percent of the market value, even though they included not only the current assets of cash, marketable securities, accounts receivable, and inventories but also property, plants, equipment, and even goodwill.

Thus investors see something in QUALCOMM that has a value much greater than the assets listed on the balance sheet. This "hidden value," as it is sometimes called, comes from the intangible assets, which now represent a major portion of the value of organizations, particularly those in knowledge industries, such as QUALCOMM. It is helpful to understand what makes up intangible assets; human capital is certainly a big part of it.

A Brief History of Valuing Human Capital

The concern for the value of human capital can be traced back many years, but this concern gained popularity in the late 1960s and early 1970s in the form of human resources accounting.[2] Although interest diminished in the early 1980s, human resources accounting (HRA) enjoyed renewed emphasis in the late 1980s and continued strong throughout the 1990s. Human resources accounting was originally defined as a process designed to identify, measure, and communicate information about human resources in order to facilitate effective management within an organization. It was an extension of accounting principles—matching costs, revenues, and organizational data to communicate relevant information in financial terms. With HRA, employees are viewed as assets or investments for the organization. Methods of measuring these assets are similar to those of other assets; however, the process includes the concept of accounting for the condition of human capabilities and their value.

In the 1980s, organizations began developing case studies describing their application of HRA principles. For example, UpJohn used HRA to measure and forecast the return on investment in people. Even professional baseball teams began to use the concept to place a value on their talent. Three important questions placed HRA under scrutiny: Are human beings assets? What costs should be capitalized? What methods are most appropriate for establishing a value for employees with the eventual allocation of such values to expenses?[3]

In 1986, Karl Erik Sveiby, manager and owner of a Swedish-based publishing company, published *The Knowledge Company*, a book that explains how to manage these intangible assets.[4] It was one of the first books to focus on "intellectual capital," and it inspired other critical research in Europe. In Asia, the idea developed as firms attempted to show the value of their intangible assets. Japan's Hiroyuki Itami published an analysis of the performance of Japanese companies.[5] His study concluded that much of the difference in the performance of firms comes from intangible assets. In 1991, Skandia AFS, an insurance firm in Sweden, organized the first known corporate Intellectual Capital Office, naming Lief Edvinsson its first vice president for intellectual capital.[6] Edvinsson's mission was to learn how others were managing intellectual capital and using it to generate profits.

Major changes in the economy and organizations have created a tremendous interest in human capital. In the last century, the economy has moved from agricultural to industrial to knowledge-based, as shown in Figure 1.1.[7] The knowledge era is perhaps the most far-reaching and explosive of the economic eras.

During the agricultural era, the focus of production was on land and how to make it more productive. During the industrial age, which dominated much of the first half of the twentieth century, the focus of production was on how efficiency

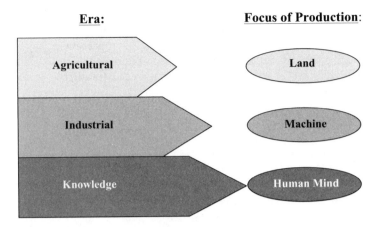

Figure 1.1. The shifting economic eras.

and profits could be generated through the use of machinery. In the knowledge economy, the focus of production is on the human mind and how knowledge is used to build a more productive and efficient economy. Some researchers have labeled the knowledge economy as the talent economy, dominated by talent organizations.

Talent organizations are those that have no or few natural resources and very little physical capital. In 1963, for example, there were only a handful of companies that met this category, such as IBM, Eastman Kodak, Proctor & Gamble, and RCA. By 2013, more than half of the top fifty companies were talent based, including three of the four biggest: Apple, Microsoft, and Google. Truly, this knowledge-based or talent-based economy is where the value of human capital really shines.[8]

When it comes to classifying intangible assets, there is no agreement on the specific categories; the assets are important and varied. A large technology company, such as QUALCOMM, has a market value far exceeding the actual book value that reflects its tangible assets. Important intangible categories make up this huge difference in value, and a big part of this is human capital.

The first step to understanding the issue is to clearly define the difference between tangible and intangible assets. As presented in Table 1.1, tangible assets are required for business operations and are readily visible, rigorously quantified, and represented as a line item on a balance sheet.[9] Intangible assets are key to enjoying a competitive advantage in the knowledge era and are invisible, difficult to quantify, and not tracked through traditional accounting practices. With this distinction, it is easier to understand the different categorizations.

Intellectual capital was earlier defined as the intangible assets that could be converted to profit. This concept has created a tremendous interest in understanding the impact of the knowledge contribution of successful organizations. Although there are more than a dozen ways to classify intangible assets, some categories are common between the groupings; three variations are presented here. A widely

Table 1.1.   Comparison of tangible and intangible assets.

Tangible assets *Required for business operations*	Intangible assets *Key to competitive advantage in the knowledge era*
Readily visible	Invisible
Rigorously quantified	Difficult to quantify
Part of the balance sheet	Not tracked through accounting practices
Produce known returns	Assessment based on assumptions
Easily duplicated	Cannot be bought or imitated
Depreciate with use	Appreciate with purposeful use
Finite in application	Multiapplication does not reduce value
Best managed with "scarcity" mentality	Best managed with "abundance" mentality
Best leveraged through control	Best leveraged through alignment
Can be accumulated	Dynamic (short shelf life when not in use)

accepted grouping is contained in Figure 1.2, where the enterprise is divided into tangible assets, intellectual capital, and financial capital.

In this arrangement, intellectual capital is divided into customer capital, human capital, and structural capital. Thomas Stewart, Leif Edvinsson, Hubert Saint-Onge, and many others support this division. Figure 1.3 shows the elements of intellectual capital offered by another researcher/practitioner in the field.[10] This categorization includes research and development, intellectual assets, and knowledge, with knowledge being divided into tacit knowledge and codified knowledge.

Still another definition comes from Thomas Stewart,[11] who suggests that human capital has three elements:

- *Collective skills.* These represent the talents of individuals, colleagues, and teams. This essentially reflects the capability to build on the skills of others.
- *Communities of practice.* Organizations are made up of communities, and these communities of professional practice have become a recognized part of business life. The nature of knowledge will require companies to foster communities where there is a high level of candor and where corporate doublespeak has no place.
- *Social capital.* What transforms workers into colleagues is social capital. It is the stock of active connections among people—the trust, mutual understanding, and shared values and behaviors that make cooperative action possible.

Whatever the definition, human capital is a significant part of intellectual capital, and intellectual capital is an important part of intangible assets. For organizations—especially knowledge-based organizations—intangible assets are often far greater than tangible assets. The bottom line is that we are in the knowledge era. Knowledge comes from humans—not machines, financial resources, or natural resources.

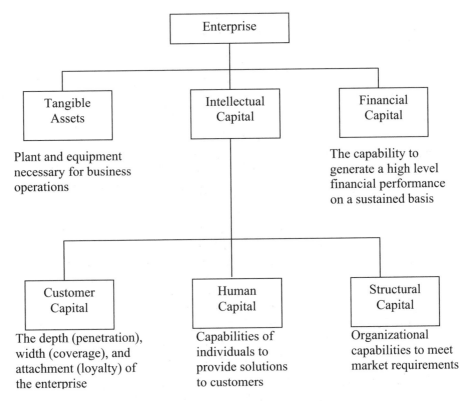

Figure 1.2. Categories and relationship of intellectual capital.

The Accounting Dilemma

One of the problems of attempting to place a value on human capital stems from accounting standards. Both financial accounting (which appears in annual reports) and management accounting (which enables managers to take action) are inadequate for current organizations. Although there has been much discussion, the general accepted accounting principles (GAAP) offered by the Financial Accounting Standards Board (FASB) are inadequate for placing a value on intangible assets, particularly human capital. Even Alan Greenspan, former chairman of the Federal Reserve Board, complained that accounting was not tracking investments of intellectual assets and that technology change has muddied the crucial distinction between capital assets and ordinary expenses. FASB indicates that accounting's fundamental purpose is to provide information that is useful in making rational investment, credit, and disposal decisions. That is not happening. If the books were communicating stories that investors found useful, then a company's market value would correlate with the value accountants place on it. The QUALCOMM example illustrates the tremendous difference between market value and book value.

Professor Baruch Lev, who specializes in valuing trademarks and patents, conducted a series of in-depth comparisons of corporate asset values (book values) and

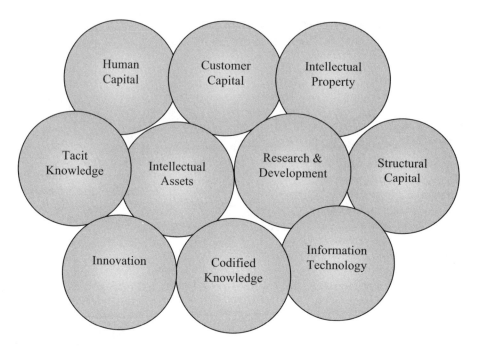

Figure 1.3. Elements of intellectual capital.

share prices.[12] He concluded that the financial reporting methods used by nearly all corporations—the methods codified by the FASB and required of public companies by the Securities and Exchange Commission (SEC)—were giving "exactly the wrong impression" of the real comparative worth of corporations. In growth industries, in particular, the accounting numbers consistently overstated the value of physical assets (like buildings and machinery) and consistently underestimated other assets, especially the intangibles that were, in the early 1990s, just coming to be seen as critical sources of corporate competitiveness. The debate will continue as the accounting profession tries to adjust to the new economy.

The Expanded Role of Human Capital

The press is exploding with coverage of human capital. The number of documents produced containing the term *human capital* increased from almost 700 in 1993 to more than 8,000 in 2003 to well over 25,000 in 2013. This growth in coverage emphasizes the importance of human capital in the management of organizations.

In the 2013 "Conference Board CEO Challenge," 729 CEOs provided input on their most pressing issues.[13] Human capital was the number-one issue from a global perspective. An earlier study conducted by IBM in 2012, "Leading Through Connections: Insights from the Global Chief Executive Officer,"[14] also identified human capital as the number-one issue. A total of 1,700 CEOs were involved in this study. Even though the term *human capital* is commonplace in organizations, management's role in this important resource is often unclear. This lack of clarity lends to the mystery of human capital, where investment in this resource now commands much executive time and attention.

The management community has a broader view of human capital. For example, *The Human Resources Glossary* defines *human capital* as the return an organization gains from the loyalty, creativity, effort, accomplishments, and productivity of its employees.[15] It equates to, and may actually exceed, the productive capacity of machine capital and investment in research and development.

Human capital represents the relationship between what organizations invest in employees and the organization's emerging success. The relationship to success is the mystery. Imagine this scenario: The CEO of a $5-billion-revenue company proposes to its board of directors that the company make an investment of $1.8 billion for the coming year. When describing the investment, the CEO is optimistic that the returns will follow, although he does not know how much of a return will be realized and cannot estimate it reliably. However, he is confident that the investment is needed and that it will pay off for the company. The executive explains that this investment, which represents almost 40 percent of the company's revenues, is based on benchmarked data that show other firms are making similar investments. Even when the investment is made and the consequences are realized, the CEO suggests that the value of this investment may still be unknown. Nevertheless, he asks for the money.

The investment in question is the investment in human capital. As extreme as it may seem, this scenario plays out in organizations each year as they invest in their workforce. Budget approvals are granted on faith, assuming that the requested investment will pay off. Far too much mystery shrouds the connection between the investment in employees and the success that follows. Human capital analytics can make this connection.

Struggles of the Human Resources Function

Despite the importance of human capital—and likely due to the ambiguity surrounding investment in it and the lack of progress in measuring it properly—the human resources function has had its share of criticism in recent years. Almost two decades ago, a major article in *Fortune* essentially said the HR function was irrelevant.[16] Thomas Stewart, the respected *Fortune* editor who wrote the article, said that the HR function should be eliminated and the essential transactions should be performed by other functions or outsourced altogether. As the author bluntly described the situation, "Chances are its leaders are unable to describe their contribution to value added except in trendy, unquantifiable, and wannabe terms. . . . I am describing your human resource department and have a modest proposal: Why not blow it up?" Stewart reached this conclusion, in part, because HR had failed to show its value.

Although some may argue that this view is extreme, the article served as a wake-up call for HR executives looking for a better way to show value in the organization—that is, to show the contribution of the human resources function.

As critics ask for more measurement and accountability, the HR function has been under pressure, internally, to show value. Because the investment is quite large, many top executives ask HR executives to show the contribution to avoid budget cuts. In some cases, managers must demonstrate contribution in order to increase the budget or fund specific projects. When funding occurs, executives want to see the actual return. However compassionate executives are about people and the role of people in the organization, they are also driven by the need to generate profits; enhance resource allocation; build a successful, viable organization; and survive in the long term. The philosophy of caring for employees and striving for results appears, to some, to be counterintuitive. It is not. Caring and accountability work together, as will be demonstrated many times in this book.

The typical human resources reaction to this movement toward HR account-ability has been unimpressive. HR functions have resisted the call for additional accountability in many ways. Some argue that people are not widgets, so they cannot be counted in the same way as products. Some consider the issue of accountability inappropriate and maintain that we should not attempt to analyze the role of people with financial concepts. They argue that the issues are too "soft," and much of what is invested in human capital will have to be taken on faith; investments must be made based on intuition, logic, and what others have invested. Still other executives simply do not know how to address this issue. They are not as familiar with the organization as they should be, lack the necessary knowledge in operations and finance, and are unprepared for this type of challenge. Their backgrounds do not include assign-ments in which measurement and accountability are critical to success. Some do not understand the measurement issue and what can and should be done.

The signs indicate that resistance is diminishing. The focus on human capital analytics is contributing to a paradigm shift as human capital measurement and investment take on a new life. Table 1.2 illustrates this paradigm shift from the

Table 1.2. Human capital perspectives.

Traditional view	Present view
Human capital expenses are considered costs.	Human capital expenditures are viewed as a source of value.
The HR function is perceived as a support staff.	The HR function is perceived as a strategic partner.
HR is involved in setting the HR budget.	Top executives are increasingly involved in allocating the HR budget.
Human capital metrics focus on cost and activities.	Human capital metrics focus on results.
Human capital metrics are created and main-tained by HR alone.	Top executives are involved in the design and use of metrics.
There is little effort to understand the return on investment in human capital.	The use of return on investment has become an important tool to understand cause-and-effect relationships.
Human capital measurement focuses on data at hand.	Human capital measurement focuses on the data needed.
Human capital measurement is based on what GE and IBM are measuring.	Human capital measurement is based on what is needed in the organization.
HR programs are initiated without a business need connected to them.	HR programs are linked to specific business needs before implementation.
Overall reporting on human capital programs and projects is input focused.	Overall reporting on human capital programs and projects is output focused.

traditional view of human capital to the present view. These shifts are dramatic for the human resources function. They underscore how the HR function is evolving to show the importance of human resources and its connection with business results. Human capital analytics makes this possible.

The Chief Financial Officer's Perspective

When investments are made, the chief financial officer (CFO) takes notice. Typically, the CFO is involved in investment decisions such as predicting them up front, auditing the success afterward, and reporting them to top executives, directors, and shareholders. However, the concept of human capital places the CFO in an awkward position. CFOs realize that companies make a heavy investment in this area, yet few finance or accounting executives understand it in any detail or know how the investment creates value for the business. Studies conducted by *CFO Magazine* show that less than 20 percent of companies surveyed say they have little more than a moderate understanding of the return on human capital investments.[17] In many organizations, traditionally accepted finance and accounting practices cannot be used for their largest investment, human capital. Despite the CFO's emerging role as the chief resource allocator who helps direct the resources to the most productive investment, human capital remains a vast area of spending where the finance function offers little insight beyond guidance on what the company can afford to spend. Here is where a human capital analytics function, sponsored or supported by the CFO, can make a difference.

The Last Major Source of Competitive Edge

Most executives realize the importance of human capital in some way. They understand the fact that the other sources of capital in the organization such as finance, technology, and access to markets are basically the same, regardless of the organization. One particular organization does not necessarily have unique access to the other types of capital. The differentiator of most organizations is human capital, thus making it the last source of competitive advantage. It is how the organization attracts, maintains, motivates, and retains the knowledge, skills, and creative capability of employees that drives organizational success. Without a doubt, human capital is critical, but in today's environment, a greater understanding of it is essential in order to make the appropriate investment.

Barriers to Change

Several major barriers prevent organizations from treating human capital as a true investment. First is the failure to "walk the talk." In brochures, handbooks, manuals, and HR programs, executives proudly proclaim employees as their greatest asset, but they do not necessarily walk the talk. They treat employees as expenditures and investments in employees as expenses in the organization, quickly trimming employee numbers to save costs and to drive revenue.

The second barrier is ownership: Who actually owns human capital management? For many years, it has been the human resources function. Executives have turned to HR to claim ownership for and make improvements in this important area. However, for the human capital investment to be successful, it must be owned by the entire organization and managed by the senior executives. HR managers and senior executives must take a role in ensuring that proper solutions are in place, the appropriate measures are tracked, and improvement is generated. It also means that chief financial officers and operating executives all have important roles in this process to ensure that it functions properly.

The third major barrier to change is the failure to consider the dynamics of the human capital investment. A variety of programs and projects are often implemented with little or no concern about how they will affect various parts of the organization. Sometimes, projects even work in conflict with each other. Too much focus has gone toward activities, programs, and projects and not enough attention has been given to outcomes, integration, success, and ultimate accountability.

The fourth major barrier is the lack of appropriate measurements. Executives who are concerned about the human capital investment do not have a clear understanding of what can be measured, what should be measured, and what is being measured. More important, they fail to recognize the connection between those measures and the success of the organization, or if a particular program or project is implemented to improve a particular measure, they do not know how to develop accountability around that project or program. A fully functioning human capital analytics team can help remove this barrier.

The fifth major barrier is a lack of effective and appropriate human capital strategy. A strategy provides direction, and the execution of the strategy drives the success of an organization. Human capital strategy has been reactive in its development and largely ineffective in meeting the challenges of facing the current environment. The relationship between the CEO and the chief human resources officer (CHRO) is not as effective as it needs to be. Most CEOs want CHROs to take a more strategic role and be proactive in their approach. The human capital strategy, when updated to reflect the current turbulent times and changing environment, can be the vehicle to build this productive relationship and drive the success that is needed.

Final Thoughts

The beginning point to understand the importance of human capital is to examine the history: how we got here. From all indications, human capital is extremely important to organizations and represents the last source of competitive edge. When managed properly, the results can be amazing. With the knowledge-based and talent-based economy continuing to dominate, human capital becomes even more critical. The problem is that it is often perceived as not being administered or managed properly in organizations. This book will provide the information necessary to ensure that human capital is a strategic force in the organization, designed to deliver value and make a tremendous difference in its success.

2	THE IMPORTANCE OF HUMAN CAPITAL STRATEGY AND THE ROLE OF THE CHIEF HUMAN RESOURCES OFFICER

The first step in examining the ability of the CHRO to create value for an organization is to revisit the strategy. This chapter explores a variety of issues involved in linking human resources to the strategy of the organization and includes current trends, processes, and successes. The focus throughout this chapter is how to develop a human capital strategy to create value, drive results for the organization, and prepare for the forces influencing organizations.

The Importance of Linking Human Resources to Strategy

Connecting HR to strategy has been a developing trend for many years. Human resources was originally initiated in organizations because business strategy determined that HR was necessary. The level of CHRO participation in the corporate strategic planning process has been increasing, and there is evidence to suggest that the CHRO's role as strategic planner will be increasingly important in the years to come.[1] This conclusion is based on how CHROs respond to five basic questions that surround the strategic planning process:

1. What is our business?
2. What will our business be?
3. What should our business be?
4. What forces will influence our success?
5. How will we address these forces?

Human resources is an important part of framing the appropriate responses to these questions. The CHRO, as part of top management's strategic planning effort, can provide the knowledge and vision necessary to make decisions and take action that will provide employees the opportunity to achieve success.

HR is being completely transformed in many organizations. The result is the creation of strategic, value-added, critical business processes within the organization. To achieve value, the human capital function is creating business results, assisting in strategy implementation, and helping in strategy formulation.

Influences

Although the connection of human resources to strategy seems to be a logical, rational evolution of the field, several important influences emerge. For HR to become more effective and produce the desired results, it must be closely linked to the strategic objectives of the organization. Otherwise, it may not add the appropriate value and move the organization in the desired direction. Thus providing the right opportunities at the right time for the right individuals to generate the desired results requires a close alignment with strategic business objectives.

At the heart of any strategic direction of an organization is change and change management. Change is the only constant in most organizations, and human resources is often seen as the driver for the change process. This requires the HR function to be more closely aligned with strategy as the CHRO organizes, coordinates, implements, evaluates, and leads organizational change.

Recent interest in accountability for human resources has brought more attention to the strategic connection. As senior executives and internal clients demand a measurable value, the HR function must initiate and design programs with specific business objectives. These objectives are derived from an analysis of the business needs of the organization, which are usually defined by the strategic direction. Thus the requirement to produce business results from HR is driven by business objectives, which come from business needs, which are connected to strategy. This chain of events links human resources to the key strategic objectives of the organization.

As the human resources function becomes more sophisticated, CHROs are planning strategically. HR functions have mission statements, vision statements, and their own strategic plans, which must support the strategic plan of the organization. Thus as the HR function plans strategically, it becomes more closely aligned with the organization's overall strategy.

Top executives recognize the importance of HR and the necessity to use it in a strategic role. In some situations, top executives are applying top-down pressure to link human resources to strategic direction. For example, some organizations have developed a strategy to transform customer service into a strategic and competitive weapon. HR programs are one of the most effective processes to achieve excellent customer service. Consequently, HR is an important tool to fulfill a major strategic objective.

Finally, with increased concern about intellectual capital, knowledge-based organizations, and human capital development, some top executives are realizing that to sustain their competitive advantage, they must acquire, develop, and retain effective human capital. To do so, the CHRO must connect human resources directly to the strategic direction of the organization.

Overall, these major influences have placed considerable pressure on organizations to connect HR more closely with strategy. The evidence is impressive, and the progress has been significant. However, there are still more advances to be made as more organizations attempt to make this dramatic shift.

Human Capital Is Critical

Perhaps no influence in the evolution of organizations and human resources and its connection to strategy is more pronounced than the growth of human capital.

Some argue that *human capital* is just another label for the traditional personnel function, just renaming the process to enhance its image. Others argue that human capital is much different—designed to imply more of a strategic approach than traditional "personnel."

The importance of human capital rests with four major issues:

1. In most, if not all organizations, the cost of employees is the largest single line-item expense. This tremendous cost brings human capital into the focus of executives with two concerns. They want to control the costs, but at the same time, they want to see it as an investment that can reap many returns in the future.

2. Human capital is the last source of competitive advantage. All organizations have relatively the same access to raw materials, financial resources, and technology. The key differentiator to developing a competitive organization is the human capital, and just like tangible assets from an accounting perspective, which are often called capital assets, the humans in the organization are considered to be important capital. Thus human capital becomes the number-one asset.

3. Human capital is the number-one differentiator in the success of organizations. The most admired companies, the most innovative organizations, the best places to work, and the most successful businesses all attribute their success to how their employees are engaged and drive value for the organization.

4. How human capital is actually employed, just like the employment of financial capital, is the critical issue. In some organizations, the employment of human capital is not very successful, and in others, it is highly successful. The challenge is to make sure that human capital is addressed from the acquisition phase all the way through to optimization.

The clear-cut differences between traditional HR and the human capital approach were presented in Chapter 1, as Table 1.2.

Strategic Roles

The CHRO is poised to assume several roles in developing and supporting organizational strategy. In some organizations, only one or two roles are developed, while in world-class HR teams, as many as five roles are defined to build a strong linkage with strategy.

The first important role for the CHRO is to develop a strategic plan for human resources. This brings strategy to the HR functional level. Beginning with a mission statement or business objective, this plan contains specific strategies that the learning and development staff members can understand and implement while staying connected to the organization. A major part of this book focuses on this effort.

In another role, the CHRO is often involved in developing the strategic plan for the organization. In this role, the CHRO has a "seat at the table" where strategy is developed and provides important input, raises critical issues, voices necessary concerns, and offers suggestions and solutions to shape the direction of the HR function. This is another critical role of human resources in its linkage to strategy. The material in this book helps ensure that the forces external to the organization that influence the availability and success of human capital are appropriately addressed in the organization's strategic plan.

A third role is in implementation. As different parts of the organization implement strategic plans, the CHRO is often involved in the implementation with specific programs, services, and processes. Almost every strategy implementation will include the need for HR programs and services, because people are essential to achieving the strategic objectives. When HR programs and services are successful, business results are produced—usually linked to strategic objectives. Thus the human resources function is operating strategically, as it drives the important operating and business performance measures.

A final role assumed by some HR functions is to teach the strategic planning and implementation process to others in the organization. A successful organization requires an adequate level of knowledge and skills with strategic planning and implementation processes. Every employee should understand some level of the processes, requirements, tasks, and outcomes of strategic planning. Through consulting services, rewards systems, and learning programs, the HR function can build the appropriate expertise.

Several operational frameworks are used to develop a strategic role for the human resources organization. A strategic role requires a major shift for HR with more focus on purpose and direction. As depicted in Figure 2.1, the early focus of the HR department was on products or programs. The HR staff developed as many products as possible. There was little concern about whether the programs were needed or actually worked. The goal was to have as many products as possible, used by as many groups and individuals as possible.

The shift to a service-focused HR function was an improvement, where the focus was on ensuring that products and services met the actual needs of the organization. The client concept entered the process, and customer service became extremely important. With various customers identified, the staff focused on ensuring that customers were pleased with the products and services delivered, usually through client surveys.

The HR function is now strategically focused, implementing products and services and meeting organizational needs that are linked to strategic objectives. The focus goes beyond client satisfaction, ensuring that the products and services are closely linked to important strategies in the organization and achieving desired results. This mindset helps ensure that the HR function is adding value to the organization and becoming an important business partner with the management team.

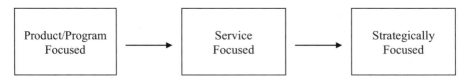

Figure 2.1. Thinking strategically.

Strategic Planning Process

Strategy is about value. According to strategy expert Ken Favaro, strategy boils down to three fundamental questions: First, how can you differentiate yourself from the competition in the way you create value? Second, what capabilities do you have that are distinct from those of your rivals and essential to your particular way of creating value? Third, what businesses should you be in, and what products and services should you offer, given your chosen approach to creating value and your particular set of distinctive capabilities?[2]

Most organizations fail to fully answer these questions—particularly in a fashion that views them as an integral whole. This leaves leaders without guideposts to navigate the most pivotal challenges of top management, including transformation, change, agility, and invention. As a result, instead of growth and innovation, there is only incoherence and inefficiency.

Several models are available that reflect the varied stages, processes, and steps of developing a strategic plan and process for the organization. From the perspective of creating value, the model shown in Figure 2.2 is the most useful and practical model. A few select parts of the model are described here.

Develop a Vision for Value

An important part of developing the strategic direction of the HR function is to develop an appropriate vision that reflects strategy and other shifts in the human resources function. At times, the vision starts with the value the organization places on its people. Although top executives *claim* that people are the most important issue, sometimes it needs to be more specific.

For example, at SABMiller, one of the world's largest brewing companies with operations in more than forty countries and beer brands in the world's top fifty (more than any other brewery), the efforts of the training institute are reflected in its initial value. According to the company, "Unquestionably, SABMiller believes in the value of people as a core element of business success. Today, SABMiller competes successfully in the global beer industry and is proud to acknowledge that one of our key points of differentiation is our Human Resource Proposition. Whilst

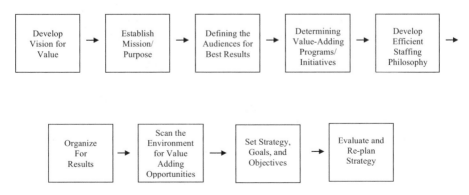

Figure 2.2. HR strategy for creating value.

virtually all our competitors leverage a brand-led or capital resource-led expansion strategy, our international expansion has been led by our people proposition. This proposition has established our reputation for attracting the most talented individuals." They go on to indicate that "a corporate university allows not only world-class skills development, but an opportunity to instill in employees the corporate culture, corporate ethics and the soul of the company. Leadership by examples is SAB's corporate brand essence and this is woven into the culture the corporate university imparts to all delegates."[3]

The following vision comes from a large healthcare chain and reflects HR's connection to strategy as the organization shifts from the traditional HR function to a human resources performance-consulting role.

> We will exceed the expectations of our business partners by providing world class HR performance and development processes, expertise, and tools driving superior performance. We will achieve this vision by:
>
> - Attracting and selecting the most capable and diverse employees
> - Consulting with our business partners to assess performance gaps, recommend improvement strategies, and shepherd ongoing performance improvement
> - Designing, developing, and delivering performance improvement programs for work processes and employees
> - Evaluating the impact of HR programs focused on the organization's strategic imperatives of achieving superior customer satisfaction, dominating market share, maximizing profitability, and promoting a culture of winning with highly motivated, well-informed, diverse associates

Establish Mission/Purpose

The next step of the model is to develop the specific mission or purpose for the organization, whether it is a learning and development position in a major department, division, unit, subsidiary, or the entire company. The mission statement describes why HR exists. It is usually simple, sometimes one sentence, and it serves as the reason for being.

Sometimes the mission statement is quite simple and very specific. As mentioned in Chapter 1, QUALCOMM is a leading developer in supplying digital wireless communication products and services and is the innovator of code division multiple access (CDMA), a technology that has become the world standard for the wireless communications industry. It is truly one of the most successful telecommunication and technology companies today. QUALCOMM's human resources mission statement is "We are committed to optimize employee performance and engagement providing HR opportunities linking overall business goals and professional development needs."

Part of the mission is defining the overall purpose of the HR function. The human resources function has been shifting from an activity-based process to a results-based process. This is a slow transition for some and a much quicker one for others. An HR function focusing on results with a desire to create value for the organization will quickly move to a results-based process. Figure 2.3 shows the shift

Activity-based programming	Results-based programming
• No business need for the programs/ solutions	• Programs/solutions linked to specific business needs
• No assessment of performance issues	• Assessment of performance effectiveness
• No specific measurable objectives	• Specific objectives for application and business impact
• No effort to prepare program partici- pants to achieve results	• Results expectations communicated to participants
• No effort to prepare the work environ- ment to support implementation	• Environment prepared to support implementation
• No efforts to build partnerships with key managers	• Partnerships established with key manag- ers and clients
• No measurement of results or benefit/cost analysis	• Measurement of results and benefit/cost analysis
• Planning and reporting is input focused	• Planning and reporting are outcome focused

Figure 2.3. The paradigm shift in human resources.

that has been occurring for some time. The focus on results is about more than just measuring success; it is creating value throughout the process from beginning to end. Programs and solutions are developed with the end in mind, described by very specific business needs. Performance issues and objectives are developed for application and business impact. Results and expectations are communicated to a variety of audiences, with the focus on learners. An environment is prepared to support the implementation. Partnerships are developed with all key managers and clients, and metrics are utilized, including a healthy dose of return on investment (ROI). More important, the planning and reporting is based on output, not input, as measured by number of programs, projects, involvement, costs, and processes. This, in essence, is the focus of much of this book: to show organizations how the CHRO is adding value along all these dimensions—and others—as the shift to value is occurring.

Define the Audiences for Best Results
In many organizations, the "clients" of the HR function are predetermined by exec- utives and may not be adjusted easily; the audience is usually all employees. How- ever, sometimes there is some flexibility. In most organizations, there are a variety of audiences that can be served by HR. Figure 2.4 shows the variety of audiences in a typical multiple-purpose organization.

Although human resources may be part of a division or subsidiary or even a business unit within a major organization, the same issues may be developed. The employees (or employee groups served) are at the core of any HR function. This key

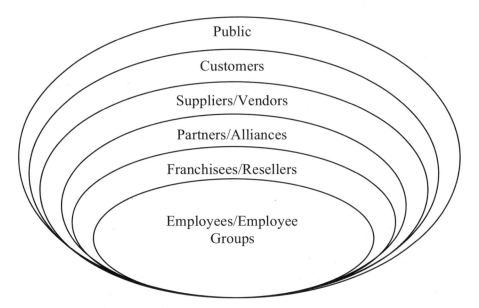

Figure 2.4. Target audiences.

target group has several subdivisions, ranging from professional staff, to sales staff, to manufacturing, to technical support, to research and development, and many others. Human resources should focus on all employee groups and levels, as this is the fundamental target for creating results.

The next logical progression is those groups closely aligned to the employee network. These are the franchise owners or resellers—individuals who are charged with selling the product or services. This is an excellent audience for leveraging results. Most HR program opportunities will focus on value-adding processes that are easily measured and should translate into sales growth and market share enhancement. A notable example of franchisee training is Subway Restaurants. The company provides HR advice and support to franchisees to recruit, select, train, compensate, engage, retain, and discharge employees. This provides a tremendous opportunity for improving sales, increasing profits, decreasing customer complaints, and preventing excessive employee turnover.

The next logical audience is partners or allies. These groups or organizations may represent joint ventures, alliances, or partnerships, both formal and informal. From the HR perspective, there is value in helping partners recruit, select, and develop skills and capabilities, although the payoff may not be as direct as with employees, franchisees, and resellers.

Another prospective audience is made up of suppliers and vendors. For some, it may seem unusual for a supplier or vendor network to participate in diversity and affirmative action programs. However, because of the need to have consistency in processes and focus on quality and standardization, some organizations provide learning opportunities for the supplier network. For example, many HR functions provide a variety of training and development programs for their suppliers and require them to meet compliance standards.

Another interesting audience group is the company's actual customer base. While not appropriate for every organization, some HR functions provide learning and development opportunities for their customers with the goal of enhancing the use and implementation of their products and services. For example, the learning center at Home Depot provides customer clinics, demonstrating how to use tools and processes to successfully complete home improvement projects. Microsoft Learning, through a variety of learning centers, provides all types of training and certification on the proper use of Microsoft products. Verizon Communications provides a similar service.

A final target audience is the public; companies target this audience by offering a variety of programs and opportunities for anyone interested in improving performance. These are usually developed after an HR function has established a reputation for being very successful in communicating innovative approaches and ideas. Several notable organizations have developed these types of programs. DuPont developed a tremendous reputation for safety and ultimately sold this service to an external, public company. Walt Disney designed the Disney Institute to provide customer service programs to a variety of organizations. These programs represent a great opportunity to generate results, as these HR programs are usually operated at profit centers, sometimes driving a significant amount of revenue for the organization while enhancing corporate image.

If there is flexibility, audiences should be selected for maximum results. Some audiences, such as those dealing directly with customers, the public, franchisees, and employees, represent some of the best opportunities for driving results. Usually those connected closely to the customer provide the best opportunities for adding value.

Organize for Results

When focusing on results, organizational structures are very important for the CHRO. Structure can sometimes make the difference between an inefficient, bureaucratic, and unresponsive learning center and an efficient, productive, and effective process. The first issue involves the actual reporting relationship of the CHRO. Figure 2.5 shows the potential reporting relationships. Where the CHRO is positioned in the organization often reflects the senior executives' view of HR. Ideally, the CHRO should report directly to the CEO, and this is common in some organizations. This placement ensures the proper support and direction from top management and sends a strong message throughout the organization that HR is important. However, in large organizations with many issues, functions, and priorities, the CHRO may report to other executives. A second choice is reporting to the chief operating officer (COO) or the equivalent role. Because HR mainly supports the operations of the organization, this provides a direct link to the leader of that function. A growing trend is for CHROs to report directly to operating units to ensure support, commitment, and direction from the customers that are most often served. One disadvantage to this is that service to nonoperating units may suffer on the priority list. Another disadvantage is the lack of corporate oversight of the function and alignment with the CEO and his or her direct staff.

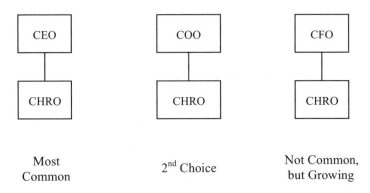

Figure 2.5. Potential reporting relationships.

A trend that has been developing in recent years is to have the CHRO report directly to the CFO. According to Gartner Research, the prevalence of this practice is growing, though slowly, and this is surprising to some HR observers. Gartner explains it this way: The human resources function manages the human capital strategy of the organization. The largest single expense is human capital. Previously, the HR function had not done a very good job of showing the value. Placing it under the chief financial officer brings two important influences: First, there is help with measurement in terms of showing the value of human capital. Second, there is emphasis on controlling the costs. The CFO philosophy is that if you cannot show the value, then focus on controlling the costs. Although this is a frightening scenario for many HR executives, it actually has very positive outcomes. Most CFOs go into this new responsibility with a very helpful spirit. They want to help the HR team show the value, improve efficiency, and save costs. This is sometimes the kind of support CHROs need as they struggle to get budgets approved and show the impact and ROI of human capital programs.

When organizing for results, the next issue is the actual structure of the HR organization. While there can be many different structures, four basic approaches are utilized. Most organizations will either follow these approaches or have a blend of the four. Figure 2.6 shows the approaches, ranging from functional to regional.

A functional approach structures HR into functional units, such as recruiting, selection, learning, and compensation. A structure based on programs builds on the specialties within human resources, such as analytics, design and development, delivery and implementation, and consulting and advice.

The business unit approach ensures that the learning organization is aligned with the business units and providing staffing support. A variation of this would be to have support for the different functional units for manufacturing, sales, finance, research and development, and so on.

The regional approach is to break the organization down into different regions and provide HR support to each particular geographic area. A broader version of this, the global approach, has the learning manager for each country reporting to the CHRO.

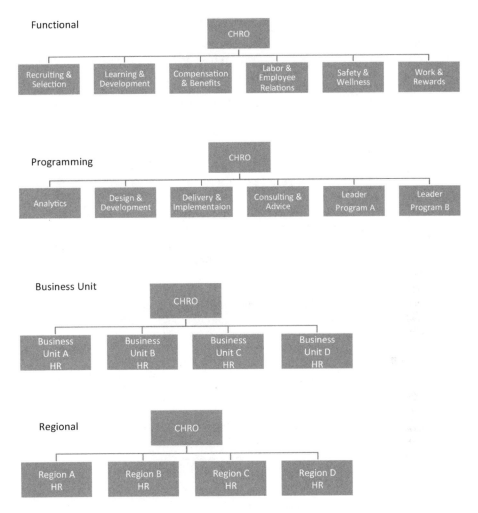

Figure 2.6. Potential structures.

Whatever the approach taken, the following recommendations must be considered when selecting the proper organizational structure:

1. Position the HR function as close as possible to where HR takes place.
2. Ensure that the HR function is as responsive as possible to changing business needs.
3. Avoid overlap and duplication across the organization.
4. Build the functional expertise within the HR organization so that its staff are expert providers of services.

These factors affect not only responsiveness and efficiency but the overall effectiveness and value added to the organization.

Human Capital Strategy

With the process model in place, a functional, flexible, and adjustable human capital strategy must be developed. It is helpful to examine the typical human capital strategy and then update that strategy to address the forces that are influencing organizations today.

Typical Human Capital Strategy

Figure 2.7 shows what most would consider a typical human capital strategy. This is arranged in a sequential format of how talent is cycled through an organization.

- Attract, recruit, and select talent that best fits the organization in the most efficient way.
- Align talent with the organization and integrate them into the organization. This focuses on issues such as on-boarding and socialization.
- Build capability within a team to perform and lead. For most operating employees, there is initial job-related learning and professional development. For managers and executives, management and leadership development must be provided.
- Provide competitive salaries and benefits. Salaries are often a critical element of attracting and retaining employees and can also be motivational. Benefits also lead to improved job satisfaction and can be an attraction and retention issue.
- Motivate individuals to perform and excel in their jobs. This often involves rewards systems, job design, motivational programs, and engagement programs.
- Create effective employee relations and communications, recognizing that great teamwork and communication in an organization are critical. Having an effective employee-relations climate keeps complaints, charges, and challenges to a minimum.
- Retain critical talent. Although most types of talent need to be retained, the particular focus is on those jobs or job groups that are considered to be critical to the organization's success.

This range of progressive steps is very typical and necessary in organizations.

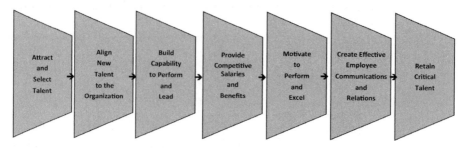

Figure 2.7. Typical human capital strategy.

Human Capital Strategy Reflecting Today's Climate

Figure 2.8 shows the updated version of the human capital strategy, where the twelve forces explained in this book have a significant impact on the organization. These forces must be addressed in the human capital strategy in specific statements as well as in policy, provisions, and actions taken:

1. *Investment*. This is critical for any function but particularly human resources. The organization must determine the optimum level of money to spend on human capital. This force is covered in Chapter 3.
2. *Business alignment*. It is essential that almost every program (particularly those representing major expenditures) and major effort be connected directly to the business. This force is covered in Chapter 4.
3. *Talent management*. In any part of the organization, there is a talent issue, but it is particularly important with human resources, as the HR function will affect talent decisions and processes throughout the organization. Consequently, this has tremendous impact on organizational performance. This force is covered in Chapter 5.
4. *Employee engagement*. Organizations must reexamine the nature of work in terms of not how and when but where it is actually performed, as employees have to be engaged to reach maximum productivity, quality, and efficiency goals. Engagement is also an important determinate of talent retention. This force is covered in Chapter 6.
5. *Performance and innovation*. An organization must develop a performance culture so that it can drive the success that is needed by the various stakeholders. At the same time, to thrive and grow, it must address innovation and constantly reinvent itself to be able to sustain outstanding performance for long periods of time. This force is covered in Chapter 7.
6. *Employee health*. The cost of healthcare has skyrocketed in most countries, especially the United States of America, to the point where it has become a critical issue for not only individuals and the government but employers as well. This is particularly important if employers are providing healthcare costs. However, the health of employees has an effect on the organization apart from the actual healthcare costs. This involves issues such as wellness programs, fitness programs, and a variety of health initiatives that try to keep employees healthy to maintain costs and reach optimum levels of productivity, quality, and efficiency while minimizing mistakes, accidents, and incidents. This force is covered in Chapter 8.
7. *Demographics and societal changes*. The demographics of the workforce are changing rapidly. Today, four generations may work together in the same organization. Women are steadily increasing their penetration into critical job groups, including leadership positions. The immigrant profile of companies is also rapidly changing. These demographic shifts can have a profound effect on the success of an organization. Chapter 9 discusses this force.
8. *Technology*. Technology has both a positive side and a negative side. On the one hand, it enhances communication, increases productivity, and makes organizations extremely profitable. On the other, it can leave an organization vulnerable

to employee distraction, cyberattacks, and lack of focus. This force is covered in Chapter 10.

9. *Globalization.* Whether employees know it or not, globalization radically affects their jobs, sometimes their pay, and even the future of their organizations. All organizations must take steps to minimize its negative effects and optimize its positive effects. This force is covered in Chapter 11.

10. *Environmentalism.* This is a critical issue throughout the globe. Employees are in the best position to make important changes in their habits that can have a profound effect on the environment. Human capital strategy must directly address this issue, maybe even driving the sustainability efforts in an organization. At the same time, the strategy must prepare employees for the problems that will occur because of the deterioration of the environment. This force is covered in Chapter 12.

11. *Global leadership.* Organizations are spending more on global leadership than ever before. Effective leaders are needed in all types of organizations, and the success of organizations rests on the quality of their future leaders. This force is covered in Chapter 13.

12. *Analytics and big data.* The last decade has brought changes in the way the human resources function analyzes and uses data to make improvements. The opportunities are far-reaching for human capital analytics teams, who must ensure that big data is driving the value that is needed. This force is covered in Chapter 14.

Together, the typical human capital strategy and these forces make an updated strategy. Figure 2.8 depicts the recommended strategy that is the basis of this book. The strategy is implemented through the process model described earlier in this chapter.

Top executives and CEOs of major organizations want this change in strategy. Ben Verwaayen, chief executive officer of British Telcom, made a speech in autumn 2014 for an audience of 350 HR professionals in the Netherlands. The key message he gave was very clear: HR leaders will have to leave their comfort zone and step up their efforts if they want to make a significant business contribution. Instead of accommodating current strategies, HR should play a proactive role when it comes to strategic changes and talent development.

When asked what CEOs do to provide the space to make HR an integrated part of the overall business strategy, he stated that CEOs do too little. They do not give these topics sufficient thought. They may find it scary to explore new approaches. HR does not challenge CEOs enough in this respect; they leave their bosses too much in the comfort zone.[4] In a study from the Economist Intelligence Unit involving more than 130 CEOs, the need for HR executives to be more involved in strategy was clear. When asked "How involved is the head of HR is strategic planning?" 55 percent said they were a key player. When asked "How involved should they be?" 70 percent wanted them to be a key player.[5] Ram Charon, trusted CEO advisor, weighed in on this issue: "I talk with CEOs across the globe who are disappointed in their HR people. They would like to be able to use their chief human resource officers (CHROs) the way they use their CFOs—as sounding boards and trusted partners—and rely on their skills in linking people and numbers

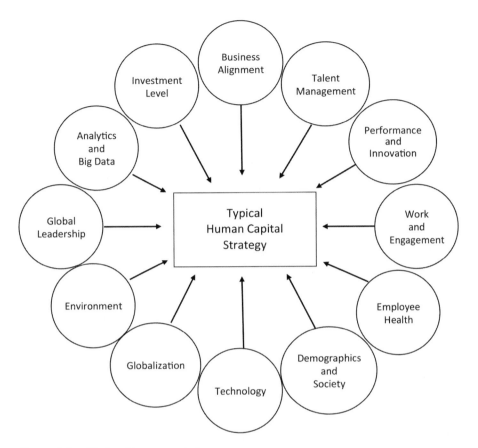

Figure 2.8. Updated human capital strategy.

to diagnose weaknesses and strengths in the organization, find the right fit between employees and jobs, and advise on the talent implications of the company's strategy. But it's a rare CHRO who can serve in such an active role."[6]

Final Thoughts

This chapter has explored the very beginning of the formal human resources process linking HR to strategy. Although all organizations have an ongoing HR function, it may be helpful to review the current approach to human capital and assess the degree to which HR is connected to strategy. A variety of issues and approaches were described, all focusing on how the CHRO can create value for the organization. This focus on accountability, results, and creating value is critical to the success of the HR function. A typical human capital model was presented along with an updated version that focuses on twelve of today's major forces that affect organizations. The remainder of the chapters are devoted to these twelve forces.

3

SET THE PROPER INVESTMENT LEVEL

Establishing the Appropriate Amount to Spend on Human Capital

> *Force 1: Investment.* This is an issue with any function, but it is particularly important for the human resources function. Deciding approximately how much to spend on employees is a very strategic issue that deserves much attention. Spending too little or too much can be disastrous. Five options are possible for the investment level.

One of the most critical strategic issues facing the CHRO is determining the appropriate investment level for human resources. How much you should spend on your employees is a fundamental issue, yet in practice, it doesn't receive enough attention. While some CHROs use benchmarking only—and maybe to a fault—other strategies may be appropriate. This chapter details five specific strategies for determining the investment level:

1. Let others do it. (Avoid the investment altogether.)
2. Invest the minimum. (Invest only what is absolutely necessary.)
3. Invest with the rest. (Use benchmarking to guide the appropriate investment.)
4. Invest until it hurts. (Spend too much on human resources either intentionally or unintentionally.)
5. Invest as long as there is a payoff. (Use a measurement system to understand the value of human capital compared with the investment.)

The majority, if not all, of organizations utilize one or more of these strategies. This chapter provides examples and information to help guide CHROs to determine which strategy will best fit their situation. Although the investment levels may be set initially, this is an issue that should be reviewed periodically.

Opening Stories

The retail industry, which represents one-fifth of American workers, struggles with the issue of how much to invest in employees. Typically, they invest the minimum:

retail businesses set wages low and provide few benefits. Executives feel that they have no choice, because most of them compete on low prices. The assumption is that if they invest more in employees, customers will have to pay more, and they will lose business. These same executives conclude that employee-friendly stores like Wegmans and The Container Store can offer more pay and benefits because customers are willing to pay higher prices. But this is not always the case. Recent research has shown that there is an alternative to low pay and few benefits. Here are three examples.[1]

Costco

Costco is a wholesale club with more than 663 stores and $110 billion in annual sales. Costco employees earn about 40 percent more than those of its largest competitor, Sam's Club. Annual turnover is 5.5 percent for employees who stay with Costco for more than a year. The average for the industry is more than 50 percent.

While dead-end jobs are the norm at most retailers, Costco provides advancement opportunities. About 98 percent of store managers started in the stores. The University of Michigan's American Customer Satisfaction Index ranks Costco as high as Nordstrom, a retail chain known for its outstanding service. Costco's rating is consistently above Sam's Club.

Costco is simplifying their operations. For example, Costco has only four thousand SKUs (stock-keeping units), compared to a supermarket average of thirty-nine thousand. Costco also works hard to eliminate waste in their supply chain, such as by purchasing directly from manufacturers and moving goods to retail stores through their own efficient distribution process. The bottom line on these processes is that sales per employee per square foot at Costco is $986, about twice that of Sam's Club at $588.

Trader Joe's

Trader Joe's is an American supermarket chain with 418 stores and $11.3 billion in annual sales. The starting wage for full-time employees is $40,000 to $60,000 per year, more than twice what competitors offer. All store managers are promoted from within, and many executives started in the stores. Turnover of full-time employees is less than 10 percent. Employees constantly engage customers in conversations and inform them about new products. They are known for suggesting products and recipes. Consumer Reports ranked Trader Joe's the second best supermarket chain in the United States after Wegmans, which is also known for employee-friendly practices and not very low prices. As with Costco, simplification is key.

Trader Joe's has only about four thousand SKUs and therefore offers fewer choices within categories than their rivals do. With fewer products, employees can be familiar with everything the store sells and make more knowledgeable recommendations to customers. Many perishable products are sold already packaged instead of loose, which speeds up checkout. Trader Joe's purchases most products directly from manufacturers, and employees decide how many units of each item to order for their stores, with support from IT. The bottom line is that sales per labor hour are more than 40 percent higher than those of an average U.S. supermarket. Sales per square foot are more than three times those at an average supermarket.

Quiktrip

Quiktrip, a U.S. convenience store chain, has more than 600 stores and $11.45 billion in annual sales. The wages and benefits at Quiktrip are so good that the chain has been named one of *Fortune*'s "100 Best Companies to Work For" every year since 2003, including the most recent list in 2015.[2] All store managers are promoted from within. Quiktrip's 13.9 percent turnover rate among full-time employees is substantially lower than the 59 percent average rate in the top quartile of the convenience store industry. Customers get in and out of Quiktrip quickly because merchandise is always where it is supposed to be, and employees have been trained to ring up three customers per minute (often by not having to scan merchandise and by calculating change in their heads). Quiktrip only offers high-demand products.

Part-time employees receive 40 hours of training, and full-time employees receive two weeks of training in all aspects of the job, including ordering merchandise and sweeping floors. When customer traffic is high, employees focus on customer-related tasks; when traffic is low, they focus on other tasks. Employees can move from one store to another. Employees have more predictable schedules and are more productive, and customers get faster service. World-class manufacturing practices are applied to store operations. Every in-store logistic process is timed and standardized. Employee feedback is incorporated into process design and improvement. Employees regularly discuss problems and opportunities. While most retailers operate with fewer employees, Quiktrip does the opposite and maintains a force of floaters who can fill in for employees who get sick, take vacations, or have an emergency. The bottom line is that Quiktrip sales per labor hour are 66 percent higher than the average convenience store chain. Sales per square foot is $804 compared to $522 for the average convenience store chain.

These three examples show that retailers can avoid the tradeoff between low prices and investing in employees by implementing a set of operating practices that focus on simplifying processes, eliminating waste, cross training, enhancing jobs, and empowering employees. They can move beyond investing the minimum to investing when there is a payoff.

Let Others Do It

Some executives prefer to take a passive role when investing in employees, attempting to minimize the investment altogether. While somewhat dysfunctional, this approach has proven effective for some organizations, depending on their strategic focus. This section explores the strategy of avoiding the investment in human resources in detail, the forces behind it, and the consequences—both positive and negative—of implementing it.

Basic Strategy

This strategy can be implemented using two different approaches. The first approach is to use contract and temporary employees in place of permanent employees. This arrangement allows the organization to add and remove employees with little or no commitment, thus reducing the expense connected to employee acquisition, training, development, and termination. The second approach is to outsource the job, often at lower cost. Taken to the extreme, employers can outsource most of the functions that would be performed by regular employees in the organization.

Several factors motivate executives to pursue one or both of these approaches:

- *The total cost of employees.* Some executives cannot—or will not—build the infrastructure to support human capital.
- *The need to bring stability to the organization.* Expansion and decline can be particularly challenging in cyclical or seasonal industries. Letting others make the investment in people enables businesses to balance employment levels, address particular needs, and control costs at the same time.
- *The unavailability of expertise in the organization.* It may not be practical to develop the experience needed, so executives will take advantage of external expertise.
- *Survival.* Some executives cannot afford to invest in human capital, at least not to the extent needed to build a successful team.

Employee acquisition and maintenance is expensive. Table 3.1 shows the processes in which HR staff are involved. Because of the magnitude of these accumulated expenses, executives avoid some costs by hiring contract employees. This avoids costs associated with payroll, benefits, and terminations, as well as some acquisition and training costs. Contract employees should be ready to make an immediate contribution. Executives also outsource major functions to lower the total cost of employees. Most outsourcing providers offer services at a lower cost; however, their cost premiums can sometimes outweigh the savings of outsourcing.

Employing Temporary and Contract Workers
Because of the high cost of attracting and retaining employees, particularly in cyclical industries, some firms resort to employing contract workers. This is based on the belief that the nature of the employment cycle can create unnecessary expense when employees are being acquired and removed, creating turnover. Table 3.2 shows all the cost categories related to turnover. In recent years, departing costs have become significant as employers spend large amounts on severance packages and services to enable employees to find other jobs. Some experts suggest that the

Table 3.1. Processes

- Recruiting
- Selection
- Indoctrination/orientation
- Socialization
- Initial job training
- Continuous development
- Career management
- Competitive pay and benefits
- Reward systems/motivation
- Maintenance/discipline
- Exit costs

Table 3.2. Turnover cost categories.

Pre-employment training	Exit costs
• Development • Delivery • Materials • Facilities • Travel (if applicable) • Overhead (administration)	• Administration time • Management time • Benefits termination/continuation • Pay continuation/severance • Unemployment tax • Legal expenses (if applicable) • Outplacement (if applicable)
Orientation/on-boarding program	**Replacement costs**
• Development • Delivery • Materials • Facilities • Travel (if applicable) • Overhead (administration)	• Recruitment/advertising • Recruitment expenses • Recruitment fees • Sign-up bonuses • Selection interviews • Testing/pre-employment examinations • Travel expenses • Moving expenses • Administrative time (not covered above) • Management time (not covered above)
Initial training	**Consequences of turnover**
• Development • Delivery • Materials • Facilities • Time off the job • Travel (if applicable) • Overhead (administration)	• Work disruption • Lost productivity (or replacement costs) • Quality problems • Customer dissatisfaction • Management time • Loss of expertise/knowledge
Formal on-the-job training	
• Development • Job aids • Delivery • Management time • Overhead (administration)	

cost of turnover for critical talent is up to three times a person's salary. Coupled with the high cost of attracting and developing employees, some organizations conclude that a highly capable contract employee is the best option, even for critical talent. For example, companies involved in exploration in the Alberta Oil Sands in Canada hire (and fire) contract workers as demand shifts, often driven by oil prices.

The alternative is to routinely reduce the number of employees, often through a "last-in-first-out" process, which is frequently used by unionized organizations. This leaves the most senior and highest paid, but not necessarily the most productive, employees on the payroll. Hiring temporary and contract workers avoids lowering regular employee morale by placing pay and jobs at risk.

Outsourcing

Recognizing the high cost of maintaining employees, particularly on a long-term basis, some organizations have resorted to outsourcing to keep their employee head count to a minimum. For some companies, this is a strategy that enables a highly flexible, adaptive organization. Outsourcing can benefit an organization that is using external providers to deliver leading-edge expertise. This approach essentially creates a small number of employees and a tremendous network of subcontractors who provide services that regular employees provide in other firms or that regular employees previously performed. Outsourcing usually costs less on a total basis and can bring in much-needed expertise and specialization. Additional information on outsourcing is presented in the chapter on globalization (Chapter 11).

Invest the Minimum

While the previous section examined organizations that let others do the investing in people, this one examines those organizations that invest only the minimum. A few organizations adopt this strategy by choice; others do it out of economic necessity. Either way, this is a viable option for some organizations. This section explores the issues involved in the strategy of minimum human capital investment and examines its challenges, consequences, and advantages. This strategy has several hidden land mines that can be detrimental in the long term if not recognized and addressed.

Basic Strategy

This strategy involves investing the very minimum in human resources, providing job training, salaries, benefits, and services only at the minimum level with almost no development and preparation for future jobs. Organizations adopting this philosophy operate in a culture that is sometimes reflective of the competitive forces in the industry. These organizations experience high turnover and usually adjust processes and systems to take into account the constant churning of employees.

Though efficiency is gained by keeping costs at a minimum, this strategy should not be confused with efficient resource allocation. The strategy presented here is a deliberate effort to dispense only the minimum investment. This strategy is about facing the inevitable in some situations or making a deliberate attempt to invest as little as possible in employees.

Forces Driving the Strategy

The primary forces driving this strategy can be put into three words—*cost, cost,* and *cost.* Some organizations work in such a low-cost, low-margin environment that a minimal human capital investment appears to be the only option. Low-cost businesses, such as Wal-Mart, operate on volume to make significant profits. Competition requires low wages and almost no benefits in many cases, and such conditions are inherent in some industries, such as retail or food service. However, the opening stories in this chapter illustrated that a low-cost pressure doesn't necessarily mean that investment in employees should be minimized.

Nevertheless, in some cases, the minimum investment strategy is adopted out of necessity—the organization must invest as little as possible to survive, particularly in the short term. These organizations are often managed by executives who see little value in their employees and view them only as a necessary cost to deliver the service. They consider employees to be dispensable, easily recruited and quickly discharged if they are not performing appropriately. For example, as part of Radio Shack's survival efforts, investment in employees went from low to even lower. But it didn't work out. Radio Shack filed for bankruptcy in February 2015, after years of struggling to survive.[3]

The Cost of Turnover

Organizations investing only the minimum amount in human resources will have high turnover, and they usually do not understand the true cost of turnover. They see the direct cost of recruiting, selection, and initial training, but they do not take the time to understand the other impacts. Both the direct and indirect cost of turnover must be taken into consideration. The total cost of turnover is rarely calculated in organizations investing minimally in their human capital. When the cost is estimated, it is often underestimated. More important, estimations of the total cost are not communicated throughout the organization, leaving the management team unaware of the potential costs. Earlier, Table 3.2 listed the costs in the sequence in which they occur. This table suggested that there are many different costs, some of which are never known with certainty but can be estimated if enough attention is directed to the issue.

Table 3.3 shows the cost of turnover expressed as a percent of annual pay for selected job groups. As shown in this table, these costs, arranged in a hierarchy of jobs, are significant. The data for this table were obtained from a variety of research studies, journals, academic publications, industry publications, private databases, and professional associations, all from a database labeled ERIC (http://eric.ed.gov). Collectively, these external studies provide a basis for understanding the total cost of this important issue, and understanding the impact of turnover is the first step toward tackling it.

Table 3.3. Turnover costs for selected job groups.

Job type/category	Turnover cost range (percentage of annual wage/salary)*
Entry-level hourly, unskilled (e.g., fast food worker)	30–50
Service/production hourly (e.g., courier)	40–70
Skilled hourly (e.g., machinist)	75–100
Clerical/administrative (e.g., scheduler)	50–80
Professional (e.g., sales representative, nurse, accountant)	75–125
Technical (e.g., computer technician)	100–150
Engineers (e.g., chemical engineer)	200–300
Specialists (e.g., computer software designer)	200–400
Supervisors/team leaders (e.g., section supervisor)	100–150
Middle managers (e.g., department manager)	125–200

*Percentages are rounded to reflect the general range of costs from studies. Costs are fully loaded to include all the costs of hiring a replacement employee and bringing him or her to the level of productivity and efficiency of the former employee.

When the phrase *fully loaded cost* is used, it is important to consider what goes into it. The turnover costs in Table 3.3 contain both direct and indirect cost components. A complete list of the cost components is included in Table 3.4. This table contains a list of cost items that can be derived directly from cost statements and others that have to be estimated. Essentially, those on the left side of the table can easily be derived, while those on the right side typically have to be estimated. When considered in total, excessive turnover is expensive and very disruptive.

Advantages and Disadvantages

There are many advantages to the minimum investment strategy. The first and most obvious is low labor costs. Executives taking this approach strive to be the lowest-cost provider of goods or services. In doing so, they must invest at minimum levels. Another advantage is that this strategy requires simplistic jobs, tasks, and processes. These job elements make recruiting, training, and compensation relatively easy. Finally, this may be the best strategy for survival, particularly on a short-term basis. Depending on the nature of the business, some organizations must operate with minimum commitment to employees.

These advantages aside, investing the minimum in human capital can result in negative consequences for organizations. First, a minimum investment strategy must be considered only in the context of simple, lower-level jobs. Automation is preferable if the jobs can be eliminated. If not, the jobs must be broken down into simple steps.

Second, organizations using this strategy must be able to cope with a high turnover rate. With little investment, employees will move on to another organization for just a slight increase in pay. Executives must ensure that hiring costs are minimal and initial training costs are extremely low. For example, McDonald's keeps its jobs simple and the training very efficient, resulting in a low cost to recruit and build capability. With these costs at a minimum, McDonald's executives expect high turnover and are willing to live with and adjust for it.

Third, this approach can have a long-term negative impact as the turnover costs cause inefficiencies in the organization, deterioration in the quality of service, and an increase in indirect costs. This is not a major issue in a fast food chain where jobs can be divided into small parts and administered efficiently. However, for a manufacturing or electric utility firm, it may be difficult to live with the high turnover

Table 3.4. Turnover cost components.

- Exit cost of previous employee
- Lost productivity
- Recruiting cost
- Quality problems
- Employee cost
- Customer dissatisfaction
- Orientation cost
- Loss of expertise/knowledge
- Training cost
- Supervisor's time for turnover
- Wages and salary while training
- Temporary replacement costs

inherent in this strategy on a long-term basis. CHROs in such companies usually seek to increase the investment in people. This is a difficult road, but with the right internal champions, changes can be made. Using benchmarks, demonstrating value-added contributions, and aligning to business goals will assist in increasing investment in human resources. For example, Wal-Mart and McDonalds are now investing beyond the minimum. They are investing in upward mobility, career development, and management development. These organizations are proud of their store managers who started in entry-level positions.

Invest with the Rest

Some organizations prefer to invest in human capital at the same level that others invest. Investing with the rest involves collecting data from a variety of comparable organizations, often perceived as implementing best practices, to determine the extent to which those organizations invest in human resources. The benchmarking data are used to drive changes, if necessary, to achieve the benchmark level. In essence, this strategy aligns the organization to a level of investment that the benchmarked organizations achieve.

There has been phenomenal growth in benchmarking in the last two decades. Virtually every function in an organization has been involved in some type of benchmarking to evaluate activities, practices, structure, and results. Because of its popularity and effectiveness, many CHROs use benchmarking to show the value of and ideal investment level for human capital. In many cases, the benchmarking process develops standards of excellence from "best practice" organizations. The cost of connecting to existing benchmarking projects is often very low, especially when the available data are considered. However, when a customized benchmarking project is needed, the costs are significant. Organizations such as the Society for Human Resource Management (SHRM) have benchmarking services that use standardized measures for human resources practices and compare them by industry, company size, and geographic location. Other helpful benchmarks come from *Workforce Magazine, Strategic HR Review, Human Resource Management, Talent Management,* and *People & Strategy.* These sources provide excellent opportunities to understand and validate investments in human capital.

An important force driving the invest-with-the-rest strategy is that it is a safe approach. Benchmarking has been accepted as a standard management tool, often required and suggested by top executives. It is a low-risk strategy. The decisions made as a result of benchmarking, when proven to be ineffective, can easily be blamed on faulty sources or processes, not the individuals who sought the data.

Benchmarking Basics

Benchmarking is a strategy that can be used in conjunction with other approaches. As a low-cost approach, benchmarking can provide an important view of the human resources function and the investment required for it. Several issues must be addressed.

Human Capital Benchmark Measures

The first issue is to identify key HR drivers and performance indicators so that meaningful measures can be developed. Internal client feedback about existing processes and practices should be gathered so that critical success factors within the HR function can be prioritized and the appropriate focus for benchmarking can be selected.

For human capital investment, an important issue is determining specifically what should be benchmarked and what data are available. Ideally, a complete profile of cost data should be monitored to understand the total investment in human capital. Table 3.5 shows the human capital benchmarks needed to determine the appropriate investment levels. The definition of a particular measure must be addressed and clarified in benchmarking along with the many options, combinations, and possibilities available.

The first measurement group represents the expenses of the traditional HR function. This is often referred to as the HR department costs included in the overall HR budget. This measure shows the efficiency of the HR staff to deliver services. Presenting these expenses as a percentage of operating costs or revenue or on a per-employee basis provides an easy comparison to other organizations in the same industry.

From the human capital perspective, the second grouping is more important. This represents the total investment in human capital, which is the total HR department expenses plus salaries and benefits of all other employees. In essence, this group includes every function that exists in the chain of HR acquisition and maintenance. Attracting, selecting, developing, motivating, compensating, and maintaining employees are accounted for in this total cost. Because the traditional HR department expenses do not include salaries of other functions, this measure has the effect of showing the total cost. It should be reported as a percent of operating costs or revenue or on a per-employee basis to show realistic comparisons with other organizations. All the direct employee-related costs are included in the human capital measure.

Human capital costs are sometimes associated with other functions that may not normally be captured in the HR budget. For example, finance and accounting may have transaction costs such as payroll; IT may be involved in the administrative issues of processing benefits claims or web-based activities; security may be involved in some of the safety-related issues; and property may be involved in providing facilities such as cafeterias and fitness centers. Identifying and capturing all the costs are important to show the total human capital investment and make realistic comparisons. It should be noted that the cost of maintaining office space and equipment for employees is not included. This cost is usually reported as tangible assets or operating expenses. Employee travel falls in the same category.

The third grouping is by function, which is important to compare the efficiency of the various parts of the HR organization. HR expenses are those normally found in the HR budget, and the grouping is organized by traditional functions:

- Recruiting and selection
- Talent development (including orientation and socialization)
- Compensation, which includes direct compensation, bonuses, and deferred compensation
- Benefits, which includes all benefits and the costs to the company as well as external providers
- Employee relations, which includes labor relations for organized groups

Table 3.5. Human capital investment benchmarks.

1. Human resources expenses (HR department costs/budget)
   a. As a percentage of operating costs
   b. As a percentage of revenue
   c. Per employee

2. Total investment in human capital (total HR expenses plus all salaries and benefits of non-HR staff)
   a. As a percentage of operating costs
   b. As a percentage of revenue
   c. Per employee

3. HR expenses by function
   a. Recruiting and selection cost as a percentage of total HR
   b. Recruiting and selection cost per new employee hired
   c. Training/learning/development costs as a percentage of total HR
   d. Training/learning/development costs per employee
   e. Training/learning/development costs as a percentage of compensation
   f. Compensation costs as a percentage of total HR
   g. Compensation costs as a percentage of operating expenses
   h. Compensation costs per employee
   i. Benefits costs as a percentage of total HR
   j. Benefits costs as a percentage of operating expenses
   k. Benefits costs as a percentage of compensation
   l. Benefits costs per employee
   m. Employee relations costs as a percentage of total HR
   n. Employee relations costs per employee
   o. Compliance and fair employment costs as a percentage of total HR
   p. Compliance and fair employment costs per employee

4. HR expenses by process/program
   a. Analysis and assessment costs as a percentage of total HR
   b. Design and development costs as a percentage of total HR
   c. Implementation and delivery costs as a percentage of total HR
   d. Operations and maintenance costs as a percentage of total HR
   e. Measurement and evaluation costs as a percentage of total HR

5. Selected HR costs
   a. Turnover costs per employee leaving
   b. Turnover costs as a percentage of compensation
   c. Accident costs per incident
   d. Safety costs per employee
   e. Absenteeism costs per absence
   f. Absenteeism costs as a percentage of average wage rate
   g. Healthcare costs per employee
   h. Healthcare costs as a percentage of total benefits
   i. Wellness and fitness costs per employee
   j. Sick leave costs per employee

- Compliance and fair employment, which cover legal issues including employee complaints, discrimination, and sexual harassment complaints, along with a variety of other compliance-related issues
- Safety, health, wellness, and fitness

The fourth group is not normally reported but is becoming an important issue: showing the costs of various HR processes. As HR programs are launched or modified, it is helpful to understand the relative costs of the different steps to develop and implement them. Beginning with analysis and assessment, these categories include the typical program development phases and end with measurement, evaluation, and analytics. Reporting these as a percentage of the total cost of HR provides insight into the relative investment in these processes in similar organizations. In recent years, there has been growth in costs as a percent of total HR in the initial analysis and assessment to ensure that a new program or project is needed and that it is aligned with the business. The same is true in measurement, evaluation, and analytics because of the need to show the contribution of the HR program.

The fifth group shows some selected HR costs that need to be reported and perhaps compared with other organizations. They represent employee-related cost variables and are measures that can be quite expensive and must be managed. Proactively, these costs also represent values of important measures that can be improved with new or modified HR initiatives. These are invaluable data items when an organization attempts to calculate the ROI in human capital programs. Perhaps the most expensive measure in this group is the cost of involuntary employee turnover as described in this chapter. Accident and safety costs are important for manufacturing and construction industries. Healthcare costs are becoming increasingly critical for organizations providing healthcare for employees. Preventive programs are often put in place to eliminate these costs whenever possible.

The Elusive Best Practice

Inherently, the benchmarking process is designed to show what others accomplish or experience. The concept of the best practice is often an elusive goal because, in reality, many benchmarking projects involve participants that just happen to be in the same industry, in the same setting, or willing to participate in the study. They may or may not represent a best practice. Even determining the best practice can prove elusive. How is "best practice" defined? What is the basis of determining best practice? Who decides what is or is not best practice? How credible are the data reflecting the best practices? These are important questions to consider when observing and using benchmark data.

Best practice is even more elusive when the concept of human capital cost or investment enters into the equation. Is a best practice the lowest investment? Not necessarily, because there is a perceived linkage between investing in human capital and subsequent organizational success: the larger the investment, the more successful the organization. In this case, the highest level of investment may be the appropriate choice to follow. But does a large investment in human capital infer best practice? Investment and cost must be explored from the perception of the outcomes and payoff. The investment in human capital should be examined in terms of its efficiency. For example, how has an organization been able to accomplish an impressive target at a cost lower than others? The concept of best practice must be clearly understood when benchmarking data are presented or when designing a custom process.

Benchmarking Sources

The sources for benchmarking involve two issues. The first challenge is to understand the sources that currently exist for benchmarking studies. Here, the principal organizations are needed for benchmarking studies involving credible data.

Table 3.6 shows some of the benchmarking sources that offer HR data across most of the United States as well as some international data. Although no one source provides all the data listed in Table 3.5, this list represents a cross-section of organizations developing some type of human capital data. When data are not available, it is important to find a suitable source with which to partner to develop a custom-designed benchmarking study. This issue is described in the next section.

For large organizations operating outside the local or regional area, it becomes more difficult to make comparisons—not all areas are the same, and there are huge geographic differences in the quality and quantity of the talent in the labor markets from which organizations must select employees. Certain areas have more effective systems and facilities for developing capable, top-quality employees.

Collecting national data presents a twofold dilemma. First, it is difficult to make comparisons because of geographic differences, unless the data are provided by region. (Consider, for example, the differences in human capital costs in New York City and Nashville, Tennessee.) The second issue is the limited sources available to provide credible data. It is even more difficult to benchmark at the international level. A replication process is necessary for benchmarking in each country. When there are differences in the practices of the countries, making comparisons to organizations located in another country becomes fruitless. If a particular employee benefit or HR program is implemented in one country, should it be included in other countries as well? These are dilemmas of operating globally, which make benchmarking data on a global basis unreliable. Still, attempts are made to benchmark each country through national surveys. A few of the organizations listed in Table 3.6 provide international data from the participating units in those countries.

Creating a Custom Benchmarking Project

Because of the concerns about the quality and availability of these data, some CHROs develop their own customized benchmarking for human capital measurement. Although this appears unnecessary and is expensive, it may be the only way to match the organization's interests and needs to comparable organizations. Incidentally, if more organizations developed their own benchmarking studies, there would be more available data from the various partners. Figure 3.1 shows a seven-phase benchmarking process that can be used to develop a custom-designed benchmarking project. Each phase is briefly described next.

Table 3.6.   Current benchmarking sources.

- Saratoga Institute/PWC: http://www.pwc.com
- Institute for Corporate Productivity (I4CP): http://www.i4cp.com
- American Productivity and Quality Center: http://www.apqc.org
- Society of Human Resource Management: http://www.shrm.org
- The Conference Board: http://www.conference-board.org
- Corporate Executive Board (Corporate Leadership Council): http://www.executiveboard.com
- American Management Association: http://www.amanet.org
- Mercer: http://www.mercer.com
- Towers Watson: http://www.towerswatson.com
- Aon Hewitt: http://www.aonhewitt.com
- ROI Institute: http://www.roiinstitute.net

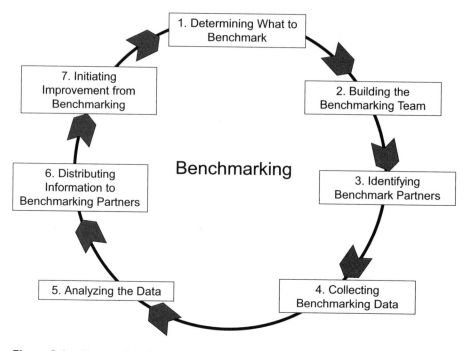

Figure 3.1. Phases of the benchmarking process.

Determining What to Benchmark

The first step is to identify precisely what type of information is needed from benchmarking. This step deserves much attention because of the tendency to explore more areas than are feasible or necessary. Because of the time involved in securing the information, the problem with information availability, and the difficulty in finding suitable partners, benchmarking initiatives must remain within prescribed boundaries. Attempts to collect data that are generally unavailable or difficult to obtain are usually unsuccessful. Also, a lengthy request can be overwhelming, making it difficult to obtain information from a benchmarking partner. The items included in Table 3.5 detail the human capital investment categories. In addition to these, other non-cost-related measures may be sought. These include information such as absenteeism and turnover rates, time to fill jobs, hours of training per year, and so on.

Building the Benchmarking Team

This phase is designed to ensure that an effective internal benchmarking team is in place. An effective team makes the difference between success and failure; it should be carefully selected and prepared to achieve the desired response. Ideally, the team should include the HR executive, several HR specialists representing the different HR functional areas, and a few non-HR managers and executives.

Although an individual could perform the tasks for the project, the team approach is recommended based on the volume of work alone. However, using a team approach also increases ownership of the process and enhances the credibility of the final product. Indeed, the team approach helps ensure that benchmarking results are understood throughout the organization.

Identifying Benchmarking Partners

Identifying benchmarking partners for the project is one of the most important parts of the process. Data can only be useful if collected from respected organizations. It is important to identify those organizations considered to follow best practices or be most successful according to some predetermined set of criteria. The targets may be competitors or noncompetitors in the same industry. Organizations in the same geographic area may be important because of concerns about local HR issues. Partnering with organizations sharing the same kind of structure (i.e., national, international, decentralized) may also be desirable. The best organization to benchmark against may actually be outside of the industry, and every attempt should be made to find partners who have an outstanding reputation in the area being benchmarked. It is important to think creatively.

A variety of sources can help categorize organizations and identify needed data. Table 3.7 shows some of the sources available for locating potential benchmarking partners. There are challenges: Some of the best organizations do not publish data about their successes, they are sometimes reluctant to make professional presentations, they may not apply for human capital awards, and they may not participate in an organization where the information is readily available. These limitations notwithstanding, it *is* possible to identify candidates that can make great benchmarking partners.

Collecting Benchmarking Data

The first issue in this phase is to collect internal data. The data-collection process, including the use of estimates, should be thoroughly tested within the organization to gain additional insight into the process. This provides a way to check the flow of data, quality of data collected, interpretation of data, and potential problem areas. If there are problems with internal information, other organizations will have problems delivering the data as well.

Table 3.7.   Finding the organizations.

- Previous award winners
- Governments
- Academic resources and databases
- Consultants
- Business information services
- Business newspapers and magazines
- Technical journals
- Vendors/suppliers
- Business school faculty
- Professional societies
- Trade associations
- Internal sources
- Directories and references
- Customers

Next, the data are collected from the partners. Data-collection arrangements should be negotiated in advance with organizations agreeing to participate. Typically, a detailed questionnaire is mailed and a telephone interview is conducted to explain all the questions, review the definitions, and address all concerns and issues. If feasible and appropriate, an on-site visit is conducted to capture high-quality data.

Analyzing the Data

After data are collected, they must be tabulated, organized, analyzed, and interpreted. Data are typically organized in a spreadsheet that lists the organizations and the various headings for capturing the data. Spreadsheet analysis is appropriate for tabulating much data, which can be formatted for presentation at a later date.

Distributing Information to Benchmarking Partners

If it is not perceived as adding value within the sponsoring organizations, developing and distributing a report for all benchmarking partners can easily be omitted. However, if the benchmarking partnership is to be a positive, long-term relationship, information distribution must be handled with utmost care. Benchmarking partners require a report containing useful information that can be used internally to improve their processes. The quality of the report promised often creates the eagerness to become involved in the project. The contents of a typical benchmarking report are as follows:

- An executive summary, which presents a brief conclusion from the survey data and provides a brief description of the overall process
- A statement of the purposes of the project with details on the objectives
- A listing of all participants
- A summary of benchmarked items
- A description of the methods for collecting and analyzing the data
- An outline of the overall results and conclusions that shows what the data may mean to the organization
- A description of the strengths within the group that attempts to determine best practices for each of the items benchmarked
- A request for this procedure to be a continuous process with potential future plans

Initiating Improvement from Benchmarking

The final, and probably most critical, phase in the benchmarking process is implementing the improvements the process has shown as necessary. Until the improvements are implemented, there is no return on the often extensive effort that goes into the benchmarking process. When implemented, the return can be great.

Initiating improvement involves three important issues: performance gaps, action plans, and an internal report.

1. Calculating the performance gap means looking at the difference between the desired (benchmarked) value and the current value. The difference translates into a gap that needs to be closed by improving a specific process.

2. Formulating the action plan involves selecting the appropriate actions to resolve the problem or improve the process and then detailing a series of steps that must be implemented over a predetermined period of time to complete these actions.

3. The final part of initiating improvement is writing a report for the internal customers in the sponsoring organization—the individual(s) for whom the process was initiated. This report shows the gaps found and the actions needed to close them. Updates of this report provide a view of the continued success being made.

Advantages and Disadvantages

The benchmarking process is not without its share of problems, consequences, and issues. Benchmarking must be approached as a learning process, not necessarily a process to duplicate or replicate accomplishments of others. Each organization is different. What is needed in one organization may not be the same in another. Also, benchmarking is time consuming when a custom-designed benchmarking project is developed. It requires discipline to keep the project on schedule, within budget, and on track to drive continuous process improvement.

Determining what the best practices are is an elusive goal; benchmarking can create a misunderstanding that average data taken from a group willing to participate in a study represents best practices. Gathering national and international data is a difficult issue that often limits benchmarking as a global tool. Finally, benchmarking is not a quick fix; it is a long-term improvement process. Table 3.8 shows some of the myths about benchmarking that cause the process to be misused or misunderstood.[4]

Benchmarking has many advantages, satisfies a variety of needs, and is used for several important purposes. It is extremely helpful in the strategic planning of the HR function and for determining the desired investment level. Information and measures derived from the process can enable HR executives to help the organization meet its strategic objectives. It is also useful in identifying trends and critical issues for human capital management. Measures from benchmarking can become

Table 3.8. Benchmarking myths.

- The only way to benchmark is against direct product competitors.
- Benchmarks are only quantitative, financially based statistics.
- Benchmarking investigations are focused solely on operations showing a performance gap.
- Benchmarking needs to be done occasionally and can be accomplished quickly.
- There is a single company somewhere, mostly like my firm only much better, which follows "the best practice."
- Staff organizations cannot be benchmarked.
- Benchmarking is a target-setting stretch exercise.
- Benchmarking can most effectively be accomplished through third-party consultants.
- It is not obvious what should be benchmarked for each business unit.
- Processes do not need to be benchmarked.
- Internal benchmarking between departments and divisions has only minimal benefits.
- There is no benefit in qualitative benchmarking.
- Benchmarking is comparing an organization to the dominant industry firm and emulating the firm six months later.

Source: Updated and adapted from R. C. Camp. *Benchmarking: The Search for Industry Best Practices that Leads to Superior Performance* Milwaukee, WI: ASQC Quality Press, 1989.

the standard of excellence for an activity, function, system, practice, program, or specific initiative. It has become an important measurement and evaluation tool, as well as a routine management tool. Benchmarking also allows the organization to compare certain product features and benefits with others. To be successful, several qualities must be fostered when developing a custom project.

- A strong commitment to benchmarking from management
- A clear HR understanding of present practices as a basis for comparison to best practices
- A willingness to change HR practices based on benchmark findings
- A realization that competition is constantly changing and there is a need to stay ahead of the trend
- A willingness to share information with benchmark partners
- The involvement of a small number of organizations that are recognized leaders in HR
- An adherence to the benchmarking phases
- A commitment to a continuous benchmarking effort for long-term improvement

With this approach, executives use benchmarking to determine the desired level of investment in human capital and the mix of human resources programs and activities to pursue or improve. Benchmarking has been used routinely for more than two decades and is a mainstream management tool, used by many HR executives to set the human capital investment level. It can be used as the primary way to determine the human capital investment, or it can supplement other strategies.

Invest Until It Hurts

While some organizations invest at the same level as other organizations, many operate under the premise that more is better. They overinvest in human resources. The results of such an approach can be both disappointing and disastrous. A few CHROs do this intentionally; others do it unknowingly. Either way, this is a strategy that deserves serious attention. With this strategy, CHROs invest in programs and services beyond what is needed to meet the goals and mission of the organization. Executives implement almost every human resources program they see and teach every new idea that comes over the horizon.

Some advocates suggest that overinvesting in employees is not an important issue—the more you invest, the more successful the organization. However, others will argue that overinvesting occurs regularly and is unnecessarily burdening organizations with excessive operating costs. Overinvesting puts pressure on others to follow suit, thus creating an artificial new benchmark. Investing until it hurts is not usually a deliberate strategy—executives are simply unaware that the increase in spending is not adding value.

Signs of Overinvesting

An example of overinvesting is an automotive company located in North America. This firm, with headquarters outside the United States, spent almost $4 million on a wellness and fitness center for its North American employees. The rationale for investing in this center was to increase the attraction and retention of employees. The executives wanted to maintain high job-satisfaction levels and thought that the wellness and fitness center would help accomplish this goal. In addition, they thought that a fitness center would be an excellent way to contain or lower healthcare costs. Some executives believed it would even reduce absenteeism and job-related accidents.

When these measures were examined after the center opened, the results were far from what one would expect:

- Job satisfaction levels were extremely high—beyond what was expected or perhaps could even be achieved in most organizations.
- Attraction was not an issue. Just a rumor that there might be additional jobs on the assembly line would create an overwhelming amount of applications in the HR department. (At one time, as many as ten thousand people applied after an announcement that two hundred jobs would be added in the plant.)
- Retention was not an issue. The company was experiencing less than 3 percent annual turnover—too low by some standards. Unless there is significant growth, a turnover level that low is unhealthy. Lower turnover probably could not be achieved, even if a variety of solutions were implemented. Low turnover was a product of satisfied employees, a superior benefits package, and wages that were double the average in the area. If attraction and retention improvement was the motive, the wellness and fitness center was a futile investment.
- Healthcare costs were below average for the manufacturing industry in the area. With the implementation of the wellness and fitness center, the costs were contained but not reduced; the cost differential was very small—only enough to cover a fraction of the cost of maintaining the wellness and fitness center.
- The manufacturing facility enjoyed one of the best safety records in manufacturing. Because there was not an accident problem to begin with, there was no reduction in accidents since the center was developed.
- Absenteeism was not an issue and did not change significantly with the implementation of the wellness and fitness center.

Thus, from the return on investment prospective, the wellness and fitness center failed to add value. This is a classic case of overinvesting—adding a benefit or service that does not add value to the organization yet adds significant costs.

A few years back, dot-coms littered the landscape with examples of overinvesting, as company after company lavished their employees with benefits, perks, programs, and opportunities to buy their loyalty, motivate them to high levels of achievement, and retain them at all costs. One interesting organization investing heavily in human capital is SAS Institute, based in Cary, North Carolina. In less than four decades, SAS has evolved into a world leader in intelligence software services, with more than thirteen thousand employees, offices in three countries, and annual revenues of more than $3 billion. Jim Goodnight, the cofounder and CEO, has a reputation for showering his employees with perks. For example, employees work only thirty-five hours per week. Sick days are unlimited and can be used for tending to ailing family members. Company specialists can arrange expert help for aging parents. Benefits are extended to domestic partners. Employees at headquarters can take their preschool children to one of four daycare centers (two on-site, two off-site). Each of the twenty-four buildings on this 250-acre campus has a break room on every floor stocked with refreshments and snacks. Employees can choose between four cafes and work off their meals in a 54,000-square-foot gym, complete with free personal trainers, an Olympic-size swimming pool, aerobics classes, and a dance studio. A soccer field, tennis courts, and a putting green round out the sports amenities.

Is all this necessary? Some would characterize this as going beyond what is needed to build a motivated, committed, and engaged workforce. Supporters suggest that this is the primary reason for their low turnover of less than 3 percent; however, according to internal executives including the HR executive, no analyses have been conducted to connect these perks to a specific retention amount.

SAS routinely appears in *Fortune* magazine as one of the "100 Best Companies to Work For." One publication characterized Goodnight as "extravagant."[5] In *Fortune*'s analysis, "This software maker is the closest thing to the worker's Utopia in America,"[6] highlighting the on-site childcare, health center with physicians and dentists, massage therapists, hair salon, roof-top garden, solar farm, and a profit-sharing program as well. Goodnight credits the success of the company to the gung ho, dedicated workforce. Through a variety of perks and benefits, he attempts to make the employees' lives easier and believes they will give their all to work. As a private organization, SAS is not subject to the scrutiny of Wall Street analysts. If that were the case, the employee benefit structure might be different.

Is investing in human capital to this extent a good thing? Some will argue that you cannot overinvest in human capital and that the more you provide employees, the better. Others would argue that each time a new program, project, or benefit is added—particularly one that becomes a permanent fixture—operating costs are added that will eventually place a burden on the company. At what point is there diminishing return on investing in human capital?

Forces Driving This Strategy

Several forces operate together to cause overinvesting. Some of these are realistic challenges; others are mythical. During the 1990s, retention became the main battle cry. The labor market was tight, skilled employees were scarce, and organizations would do almost anything to keep employees or attract new ones. This often led to investing excessively in signing bonuses, expensive benefits packages, and a variety of perks, well beyond what would be necessary or acceptable in many situations. Offering all types of benefits and opportunities was designed to keep turnover low and was considered necessary for business survival. However, many organizations—even industries—were able to maintain low turnover without having to resort to this strategy.

This placed a heavy burden on employers, which, at the time, seemed reasonable—they could afford it. When economic climate changed and they could no longer afford it, executives had to remove these perks. The result was a disgruntled workforce and increased turnover, the situation they were trying to avoid in the first place. This is a vicious cycle that can only be avoided by careful planning, with more focus on creating a workplace that is challenging and motivating, with exciting opportunities, instead of a place where employees are pampered and paid excessively. Part of the problem is that many executives believe that retention is primarily related to pay, when it is not.

Investing until it hurts is not always a deliberate strategy. Executives may be unaware that the increase in spending is not adding value, as the automotive case study illustrates. In many cases, companies add benefits, services, and perks without anticipating the full impact of these investments. The two most vulnerable areas are retirement plans and healthcare benefits. In the 1970s, some companies began to switch from defined benefit plans to defined contribution plans, shifting the investment risk to the employees. Many organizations still provide traditional defined benefit pension plans, however, which have proven to be extremely costly and difficult to change. Failure to make the switch has caused some firms to not only have excessive costs but even move into bankruptcy.

For the most part, executives did not anticipate the tremendous changes that lead to the burden of retirement. First, there is the investment risk of the pension plan. When you maintain defined benefit plans, it becomes more costly for employers than anticipated, particularly in a recession. Second, employees are living much longer, thus retirement costs are increasing. Third, employers are often much more generous because they think short-term rather than long-term as they provide benefits and negotiate lucrative labor contracts.

These organizations are unwilling or unable to conduct the proper initial analysis to see if benefits are needed. Analysis will indicate if the benefits are the right solution to a particular problem. Without the analysis, programs are conducted when they are not needed, wasting money.

Finally, some organizations overinvest because they can afford to do so. They are very profitable, enjoying high margins and ample growth, and want to share the wealth with employees through benefits, perks, and bonuses. During the 1990s, many high-tech companies made tremendous amounts of money. A number of them overinvested because they felt they could afford it. When the economy turned, the companies could not sustain some of these expenditures and benefits.

Concerns

Obviously, overinvesting is not a recommended strategy. There are many problems depicted in this section that are the byproducts of overinvesting, which can burden not only the company but also the industry. The most significant disadvantage of overinvestment is the less-than-optimal financial performance. By definition, overinvesting is investing more than necessary to meet the objectives of the organization. The relationship between investing in human capital and financial performance is depicted in Figure 3.2. As the figure shows, a certain level of investment yields additional financial results, but there is evidence of a point of diminishing return, where the added benefits peak and then drop as investments continue. As indicated, the "overinvesting" area reflects no increased financial performance for additional investments. Then there is a point reached where the actual performance goes down. This is excessive investing, which can eventually erode performance in the organization, particularly in industries where the human capital expense is an extraordinarily high percentage of the total operating cost. The knowledge industry

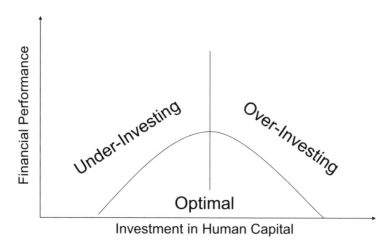

Figure 3.2. The relationship between human capital investment and financial performance.

is a good example, where the impact on the bottom line is severe when companies overinvest in human capital.

Invest as Long as There Is a Payoff

Some organizations prefer to invest in people when there is evidence that the investment is providing benefits. They often compare monetary benefits of learning programs with the costs of learning. This strategy is becoming more popular following the increased interest in accountability, particularly with the use of ROI as a business-evaluation tool. With this strategy, all HR programs are evaluated, and a few key programs are evaluated at the ROI level—that is, ROI is calculated the same way as it would be for an investment in buildings or equipment. The practices at Costco, Trader Joe's, and Quiktrip, detailed in the opening stories of this chapter, are excellent examples of investing more because of the payoff results.

The ROI Strategy

This ROI strategy focuses on implementing a comprehensive measurement and evaluation process for expenditures in an organization. This involves the possibility of capturing up to seven types of data in the value chain, as shown in Figure 3.3.[7] Using this philosophy, only a small number of programs are examined in terms of ROI, whereas every program is evaluated with reaction data. When business impact and ROI are determined for a program, one or more techniques are utilized to isolate the impact of the program on the business data. Chapter 14 provides more detail on this approach to accountability.

Organizations adopting this strategy will evaluate each HR program at some level, following the value chain. Table 3.9 shows the percentage of HR programs

The Chain of Impact of an HR Program

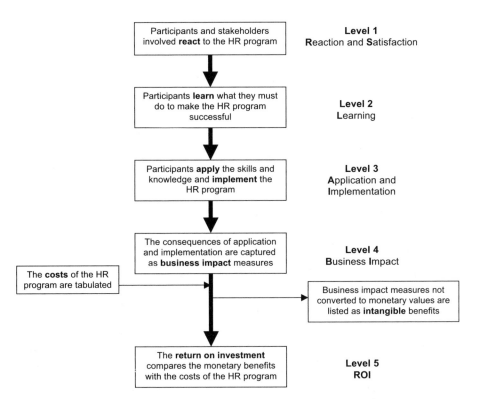

Figure 3.3. Business impact and ROI from an HR program.

Source: Adapted from Jack J. and Patricia P. Phillips. *Proving the Value of HR: How and Why to Measure ROI*, 2nd ed. Alexandria, VA: Society for Human Resource Management, 2012.

evaluated at each of the five levels of outcome each year for Scripps Health, a successful not-for-profit healthcare organization with 13,000 employees.

Forces Driving Change

Although the trend toward additional accountability has been increasing over the last decade, there are several reasons this strategy is critical at this time. In the last few years, CHROs have had to demonstrate the value their programs add to their organizations. They have also had to develop the skill to communicate with other managers—in the language of business—the human resources contribution to the financial bottom line. In a world in which financial results are carefully measured, a failure to measure HR policy and practice implementation dooms this function to second-class status, oversight, neglect, and potential failure. It has become apparent that CHROs need to be able to evaluate—in financial terms—the costs and benefits of different strategies and individual practices.

Table 3.9. Evaluation targets for Scripps.

Level of evaluation	Percent of HR programs evaluated at this level
Level 1—Reaction	100
Level 2—Learning	50
Level 3—Application	30
Level 4—Business Results	10
Level 5—ROI	5

The increasing cost of human resources is another driving force. As will be discussed throughout this book, investment in HR is quite large and growing. As budgets continue to grow—often outpacing other parts of the organization—the costs alone are requiring some executives to question the value. Consequently, these executives are often requesting or suggesting that the impact of human resources programs be determined or forecast. In some cases, the ROI is required at budget-review time. Production managers, for example, propose investments in new technology and incorporate into their proposals the projected increases in productivity and resultant decreases in unit-production cost. HR professionals must compete for scarce organizational resources in the same language as their colleagues and present credible information on the relative costs and benefits of interventions.

More CHROs are managing the human resources function as a business. These executives have operational experience and, in some cases, financial experience. They recognize that HR should add value to the organization, and consequently, these executives are implementing a variety of measurement tools, even in the hard-to-measure areas. These tools have gradually become more quantitative and less qualitative. ROI is now being applied in human resources just as it is in technology, quality, and product development. A decade ago, it was rare to use ROI in this area. Now, business-minded HR executives are attempting to show value in ways that top executives want to see. Top executives view human resources in a different way than they have in previous years and are no longer willing to accept HR programs, projects, and initiatives on faith. This is not to suggest that they do not have a commitment to human resources, but now they see that measurement is possible—and ROI is feasible—and they want to see more value.

Advantages and Disadvantages

The ROI methodology has several important advantages. With it, the human resources staff and the client will know the specific contribution of a program in a language the client understands. Measuring ROI is one of the most convincing ways to earn the respect and support of the senior management team—not only for a particular program but for the human resources function in general. The client who requests and authorizes a learning program or project will have a complete set of data to show the overall success of the process.

Because a variety of feedback data are collected during the program implementation, the comprehensive analysis provides data to drive changes in processes and make adjustments during implementation. Throughout the cycle of program design, development, and implementation, the entire team of stakeholders focuses on results. If a program is not effective, and the results are not materializing, the ROI methodology will prompt modifications. On rare occasions, the program may have to be halted if it is not adding the appropriate value.

This methodology is not suitable for every program. It has some very important barriers to success. The ROI methodology adds additional costs and time to the HR budget, but not a significant amount—probably no more than 3–5 percent of the total direct human resources budget. The additional investment in ROI should be offset by the results achieved from implementation. However, this barrier often stops many ROI implementations early in the process. Many staff members may not have the basic skills necessary to apply the ROI methodology within their scope of responsibilities. The typical human resources program does not focus on results but on qualitative feedback data. It is necessary to shift HR policy and practice from an activity-based approach to a results-based approach. Some staff members do not pursue ROI because they perceive the methodology as producing results that reflect on their individual performance. If it is negative, they fear that their program may be cancelled. They fail to see ROI as a process-improvement tool.

Human Capital Strategy Implications

This particular topic is rarely discussed in human capital strategy planning documents, yet as this chapter has detailed, without a clear-cut strategy for human capital investment, the investment levels can be influenced by all types of assumptions, philosophies, and processes, some of them dysfunctional and not adding value. There is a tendency for organizations to use benchmarking as a way to set their investment level. There is also growing interest in investing as long as there is a positive payoff. This requires a comprehensive measurement system to show the value of human capital and the results. Specifically, the human capital strategy should address these three requirements:

- Define the way in which the investment levels are set for major job groups.
- If benchmarking is used, outline the strategy for benchmarking in terms of comparison groups or customized projects.
- Invest as long as there is a payoff, defining the particular way in which human capital is valued.

4

ALIGN WITH BUSINESS NEEDS

Achieving Business Alignment with Human Resources Programs

> ***Force 2: Business Alignment.*** Every organization must ensure that projects and programs align with business needs. Too often, all types of programs are implemented in an organization that are not aligned to specific business needs in the beginning, during, or on follow-up evaluations. With human capital programs, it is critical to have this alignment. The only way to demonstrate business value is to have this alignment.

This chapter shows how to achieve business alignment by defining the need and the corresponding objectives for major programs. This step positions HR for success by aligning its intended outcome with the needs of the business. This alignment is essential if the investment in a project is to reap a return. The term *business* is used to reflect important outcome measures (e.g., output, quality, cost, time) that exist in any setting, including governments, nonprofits, and nongovernmental organizations (NGOs).

Opening Story: Bridgeport Hospital

Bridgeport Hospital decided to implement an employer-of-choice program. By doing so, the hospital would be listed among the community's preferred employers. The hospital would also be included in several national lists as an employer of choice.

In their analysis of the payoff of this proposed project, executives thought that if the project was successful, they would be able to sustain a positive work environment by recruiting, developing, and retaining a diverse, high-quality, engaged workforce. They needed to recruit and retain the best talent.

Next, the specific business needs were detailed. To achieve the designation of employer of choice, several specific measures had to be improved. The registered nurse (RN) turnover rate had to be less than 11 percent and the overall turnover rate less than 10 percent. The attrition rate among nursing students had to be less than

19 percent, and positive employee relations had to be maintained, as evidenced by the employee satisfaction and employee engagement scores.

To meet these business needs, the performance needs were defined. The first requirement was adequate professional and support staff to care for the patients and ensure that the staffing levels remained sufficient. Second, employees needed to be more engaged for organizational performance to improve. This engagement would come through increased employee participation, feedback, communication, and collaboration with the management team. Third, management development was needed to enhance customer service and employee retention.

Next, the executive team identified the learning needs in each of these categories, detailing specifically what must be learned by stakeholders to meet the performance needs. The team concluded that significant learning was necessary for each participant group.

Finally, the entire workforce, particularly the management team, had to see the value and need for this program. The management team had to be convinced that the program was critical to sustaining a competitive healthcare organization. All employees needed to see the program as motivational, satisfying, and important to their own success.

Addressing these multiple levels of needs and developing objectives ensured that the project was absolutely necessary, positioned for success, and included the proper solutions.[1]

The Importance of Business Alignment

Let's face it—not all programs are connected to the business. As mentioned in Chapter 1, the human resources function has a serious problem with showing the value of HR programs. New programs are implemented based on the assumption that they are needed and will probably drive value. This is essentially faith-based programming ("we have faith that this will work"). Unfortunately, many programs do not drive value, particularly those soft programs that are often initiated for the wrong reasons. The number-one cause of program failure is lack of business alignment at the outset.[2] New programs must begin with a clear focus on the desired outcomes. The end must be specified in terms of business measures so that the outcome—the actual improvement in the measures and the corresponding ROI—are clear. This establishes the expectations throughout the program analysis, design, development, delivery, and implementation stages.

Beginning with the end in mind requires pinning down all the details to ensure that the program is properly planned and executed according to schedule. This up-front analysis is not always simple, as it requires a disciplined approach, one that adds credibility and allows for consistent application so that the analysis can be replicated. A disciplined approach maintains process efficiency as various tools and templates are developed and used. This initial phase of analysis calls for focus and thoroughness, with little allowance for major shortcuts.

Not every program should be subjected to the type of comprehensive analysis described in this chapter. Some needs are obvious and require little analysis other than that necessary to develop the program. For example, the need for a safety program usually translates into specific safety measures that need to improve.

Additional analysis may be needed to confirm that the program addresses the perceived need and perhaps to fine-tune the program for future application. The amount of analysis required often depends on the expected opportunity to be gained if the program is appropriate or the negative consequences anticipated if the program is inappropriate.

When analysis is proposed, individuals may react with concern or resistance. Some are concerned about the potential for "paralysis by analysis," where requests and directives lead only to additional analyses. These reactions can pose a problem for an organization, because analysis is necessary to ensure that a program is appropriate. Unfortunately, analysis is often misunderstood—conjuring up images of complex problems, confusing models, and a deluge of data along with complicated statistical techniques to ensure that all bases are covered. In reality, analysis need not be so complicated. Simple techniques can uncover the cause of a problem or the need for a particular program. The remainder of this chapter delves into the components of analysis that are necessary for a solid alignment between a program and the business, presented here as Figure 4.1.

Determining the Payoff Needs

The first step in up-front analysis is to determine the potential payoff of solving a problem or seizing an opportunity. This step begins with answers to a few crucial questions: Is this program worth doing? Is it feasible? What is the likelihood of a positive ROI?

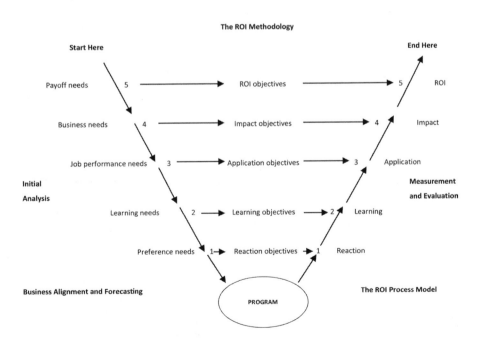

Figure 4.1. Business alignment model.

For programs addressing significant problems or opportunities with high potential rewards, the answers are obvious. The questions may take longer to answer for lower-profile programs or those for which the expected payoff is less apparent. In any case, these are legitimate questions, and the analysis can be as simple or as comprehensive as required.

Essentially, a program will pay off in profit increases or in cost savings. Profit increases are generated by programs that drive revenue—for example, those that improve sales, drive market share, introduce new products, open new markets, enhance customer service, or increase customer loyalty. Other revenue-generating measures include increasing membership, increasing donations, obtaining grants, and generating tuition from new and returning students—all of which, after subtracting the cost of doing business, should leave a profit.

However, most programs drive cost savings. Cost savings can come through cost reduction or cost avoidance. Improved quality, reduced cycle time, lowered downtime, reduced employee complaints, lower employee turnover, and minimized delays are all examples of cost savings.

Cost-avoidance programs are implemented to reduce risks, avoid problems, or prevent unwanted events. Some professionals may view cost avoidance as an inappropriate measure to use to determine monetary benefits and calculate ROI. However, if the assumptions prove correct, an avoided cost (e.g., noncompliance fines) can be more rewarding than reducing an actual cost. Preventing a problem is more cost-effective than waiting for the problem to occur and then having to focus on solving it.

Although determining the potential payoff is the first step in the needs-analysis process, it is closely related to the next step, determining the business need, since the potential payoff is often based on a consideration of the business. The payoff depends on two factors: (1) the monetary value derived from the business measure's improvement and (2) the approximate cost of the program. Identifying these monetary values in detail usually yields a more credible forecast of what can be expected from the chosen solution. However, this step may be omitted in situations where the business need must be met regardless of the cost or if it becomes obvious that the proposed program has a high payoff.

The target level of detail may also hinge on the need to secure program funding. If the potential funding source does not recognize the value of the program compared with the potential costs, more detail may be needed to provide a convincing case for funding.

Knowledge of the actual payoff is not necessary if widespread agreement exists that the payoff from the program will be high or if the problem in question must be resolved regardless of cost. For example, if the proposed program involves a safety concern, a regulatory compliance issue, or a competitive matter, a detailed analysis is not needed.

Obvious Versus Not-So-Obvious Payoffs

The potential payoff is obvious for some programs and not so obvious for others. Here are examples of opportunities for improvement with obvious payoffs:

- Operating costs 47 percent higher than industry average
- Customer satisfaction rating of 3.89 on a 10-point scale
- A cost to the city of $75,000 annually for each homeless person

- Noncompliance fines totaling $1.2 million, up 82 percent from last year
- Turnover of critical talent 35 percent above benchmark figure
- System downtime twice the average of last year's results
- Very low market share in a market with few players
- A safety record among the worst in the industry
- Excessive product returns, 30 percent higher than previous year
- Excessive absenteeism in call centers, 12.3 percent, compared to 5.4 percent industry average
- Sexual harassment complaints per thousand employees the highest in the industry

Each of these statements appears to reflect a serious problem that needs to be addressed by executives, administrators, or politicians. The business issue is clear. Action is needed.

For most other programs, the issues are unclear and may arise from political motives, bias, or misguided assumptions. The payoffs of these potential opportunities are not so obvious, as in these examples:

- Becoming a "green" company
- Improving leadership competencies for all managers
- Improving branding for all products
- Creating a great place to work
- Implementing a physician engagement program
- Organizing a business development conference
- Establishing a program management office
- Providing job training for unemployed workers
- Implementing lean Six Sigma
- Training all team leaders on crucial conversations
- Providing training on sexual harassment awareness for all associates
- Developing an "open book" company
- Implementing the same workout process that GE has used
- Changing the culture
- Implementing a change management program
- Implementing a transformation program involving all employees
- Implementing a career advancement program
- Creating a wellness and fitness center
- Implementing a team-building program

With each of these "opportunities," there is a need for more specific detail regarding the business measure in question. For example, if the opportunity is to become a "green" company, we should ask these questions: What is a green company? How will we know when we're green? How is green defined? Programs with not-so-obvious payoffs require greater analysis than those with clearly defined outcomes.

The potential payoff establishes the fundamental reason for pursuing new or enhanced programs. But the payoff—whether obvious or not—is not the only reason for moving forward with a program. The cost of a problem is another factor. If the cost is excessive, it should be addressed. If not, then a decision must be made whether the problem is worth solving.

The Cost of a Problem

Sometimes programs are undertaken to solve a problem. Problems are expensive, and their solution can result in high returns, especially when the solution is inexpensive. To determine the cost of a problem, examine its potential consequences and convert those to monetary values. Problems may encompass time, quality, productivity, and team or customer issues. To calculate the cost of a problem, all these factors must be converted to monetary values. Inventory shortages are often directly associated with the cost of the inventory as well as with the cost of carrying the inventory. Time can easily be translated into money by calculating the fully loaded cost of an individual's time spent on unproductive tasks. Calculating the time for completing a program, task, or cycle involves measures that can be converted to money. Errors, mistakes, waste, delays, and bottlenecks can often be converted to money because of their consequences. Productivity problems and inefficiencies, equipment damage, and equipment underuse are other items whose conversion to monetary value is straightforward.

When examining costs, consider all the costs and their implications. For example, the full cost of an accident includes not only the cost of lost workdays and medical expenses but its effects on insurance premiums, the time required for investigations, damage to equipment, and the time spent by all involved employees addressing the accident. The cost of a customer complaint includes not only the cost of the time spent resolving the complaint but also the value of the item or service that has to be adjusted because of the complaint. The costliest consequence of a customer complaint is the price to the company of lost future business and goodwill from the complaining customer and from potential customers who learn of the complaint. Placing a monetary value on a problem helps in determining if the problem's resolutions are economically feasible. The same applies to opportunities.

The Value of an Opportunity

Sometimes programs are undertaken to pursue an opportunity. Just as the cost of a problem can be easily tabulated in most situations, the value of an opportunity can also be calculated. Examples of opportunities include implementing a new process, exploring new technology, increasing research and development efforts, and upgrading the workforce to create a more competitive environment. In these situations, a problem may not exist, but an opportunity to get ahead of the competition or to prevent a problem's occurrence by taking immediate action does. Assigning a proper value to this opportunity requires considering what may happen if the program is not pursued or acknowledging the windfall that might be realized if the opportunity is seized. The value is determined by following the different possible scenarios to convert specific business impact measures to money. The difficulty in this process is conducting a credible analysis. Forecasting the value of an opportunity entails many assumptions compared with calculating the value of a known outcome.

To Forecast or Not to Forecast?

The need to seek and assign value to opportunities leads to an important decision: to forecast or not to forecast ROI. If the stakes are high and support for the program is not in place, a detailed forecast may be the only way to gain the needed support and funding for the program or to inform the choice between multiple potential programs. When developing the forecast, the rigor of the analysis is an issue. In some cases, an informal forecast is sufficient, given certain assumptions about alternative outcome scenarios. In other cases, a detailed forecast is needed that uses data collected from a variety of experts, previous studies from another program, or perhaps more sophisticated analysis. When the potential payoff, including its financial value, has been determined, the next step is to clarify the business needs.

Determining Business Needs

Determining the business needs requires the identification of specific measures so that the business situation can be clearly assessed. The concept of business needs refers to gains in productivity, quality, efficiency, time, and cost savings, in the private sector as well as in government, nonprofit, and academic organizations.

A business need is represented by a business measure. Any process, item, or perception can be measured, and such measurement is critical to this level of analysis. If the program focuses on solving a problem, preventing a problem, or seizing an opportunity, the measures are usually identifiable. The important point is that the measures are present in the system, ready to be captured for this level of analysis. The challenge is to define the measures and to find them economically and swiftly.

Hard Data Measures

To focus on the desired measures, distinguishing between hard data and soft data may be helpful. Hard data are primary measures of improvement presented in the form of rational, undisputed facts that are usually gathered within functional areas throughout an organization. These are the most desirable data because they are easy to quantify and are easily converted to monetary values. The fundamental criteria for gauging the effectiveness of an organization are hard data items such as revenue, productivity, and profitability, as well as measures that quantify such processes as cost control and quality assurance.

Hard data are objective and credible measures of an organization's performance. Hard data can usually be grouped into four categories, as shown in Table 4.1. These categories—output, quality, costs, and time—are typical performance measures in any organization.

Hard data from a particular program involve improvements in the output of the work unit, section, department, division, or entire organization. Every organization, regardless of the type, must have basic measures of output, such as number of patients treated, students graduated, tons produced, or packages shipped. Since these values are monitored, changes can easily be measured by comparing "before" and "after" outputs.

Quality is a very important hard data category. If quality is a major priority for the organization, processes are likely in place to measure and monitor quality. The rising prominence of quality-improvement processes (such as Total Quality Management, Continuous Quality Improvement, and Six Sigma) has contributed to the tremendous recent successes in pinpointing proper quality measures—and assigning monetary values to them.

Table 4.1. Examples of hard data.

Output	Quality	Costs	Time
Units produced	Failure rates	Shelter costs	Cycle time
Tons manufactured	Dropout rates	Treatment costs	Equipment downtime
Items assembled	Product returns	Budget variances	Overtime
Money collected	Scrap	Unit costs	On-time shipments
Items sold	Waste	Costs by account	Time to project
New accounts	Rejects	Variable costs	completion
generated	Error rates	Fixed costs	Processing time
Forms processed	Accidents	Overhead costs	Supervisory time
Loans approved	Rework	Operating costs	Time to proficiency
Inventory turnover	Shortages	Accident costs	Learning time
Patients served	Product defects	Program costs	Adherence to schedules
Applications processed	Deviation from standard	Sales expenses	Repair time
Students graduated	Product failures		Efficiency
Tasks completed	Inventory adjustments		Work stoppages
Output per hour	Incidents		Order response
Productivity	Compliance		Late reporting
Work backlog	discrepancies		Lost-time days
Shipments	Agency fines		
Project completions			

Cost is another important hard data category. Many programs are designed to lower, control, or eliminate the cost of a specific process or activity. Achieving cost targets has an immediate effect on the bottom line. Some organizations focus narrowly on cost reduction. For example, consider Wal-Mart, whose tagline is "Always low prices. Always." All levels of the organization are dedicated to lowering costs on processes and products and passing the savings along to customers.

Time is a critical measure in any organization. Some organizations gauge their performance almost exclusively in relation to time. When asked what business FedEx is in, company executives say, "We engineer time."

Soft Data Measures

Soft data are probably the most familiar measures of an organization's effectiveness, yet their collection can present a challenge. Values representing attitude, motivation, and satisfaction are examples of soft data. Soft data are more difficult to gather and analyze, and therefore they are used when hard data are not available or to supplement hard data. Soft data are also more difficult to convert to monetary values, a process requiring subjective methods. They are less objective as performance measurements and are usually behavior related, yet organizations place great emphasis on them. Improvements in these measures represent important business needs, but many organizations omit them from the ROI equation because they are soft data. However, they can contribute to economic value to the same extent as hard data measures. The key is not to focus too much on the hard-versus-soft data distinction. A better approach is to consider data as tangible or intangible. Table 4.2 shows common examples of soft data by category.

Table 4.2. Examples of soft data.

Work habits	Customer service
• Excessive breaks	• Customer complaints
• Tardiness	• Customer satisfaction
• Visits to the dispensary	• Customer dissatisfaction
• Violations of safety rules	• Customer impressions
• Communication breakdowns	• Customer loyalty
	• Customer retention
	• Lost customers

Work climate/satisfaction	Employee development/advancement
• Grievances	• Promotions
• Discrimination charges	• Capability
• Employee complaints	• Intellectual capital
• Job satisfaction	• Requests for transfer
• Organization commitment	• Performance appraisal ratings
• Employee engagement	• Readiness
• Employee loyalty	• Networking
• Intent to leave	
• Stress	

Initiative/innovation	Image
• Creativity	• Brand awareness
• Innovation	• Reputation
• New ideas	• Leadership
• Suggestions	• Social responsibility
• New products and services	• Environmental friendliness
• Trademarks	• Social consciousness
• Copyrights and patents	• Diversity
• Process improvements	• External awards
• Partnerships/alliances	

Tangible Versus Intangible Benefits: A Better Approach

A challenge with regard to soft versus hard data is converting soft measures to monetary values. The key to this problem is to remember that, ultimately, all roads lead to hard data. Although creativity may be categorized as a form of soft data, a creative workplace can develop new products or new patents, which lead to greater revenue—clearly a hard data measure. Although it is possible to convert the measures listed in Table 4.2 to monetary amounts, it is often more realistic and practical to leave them in nonmonetary form. This decision is based on considerations of credibility and the cost of the conversion. According to the standards of the ROI methodology, an intangible measure is defined as a measure that is intentionally not converted to money. If a soft data measure can be converted to a monetary amount credibly using minimal resources, it is considered tangible, reported as a monetary value, and incorporated in the ROI calculation. If a data item cannot be converted to money credibly with minimal resources, it is listed as an intangible measure. Therefore, in defining business needs, the key difference between measures is not whether they represent hard or soft data but whether they are tangible or intangible. In either case, they are important contributions toward the desired payoff and important business-impact data.

Business Data Sources

The sources of business data, whether tangible or intangible, are diverse. The data come from routine reporting systems in the organization. In many situations, these items have led to the need for the program. A vast array of documents, systems, databases, and reports can be used to select the specific measure or measures to be monitored throughout the program. Impact-data sources include quality reports, service records, suggestion systems, and employee-engagement data.

Some HR program planners and program team members assume that corporate data sources are scarce because the data are not readily available to them. However, data can usually be located by investing a small amount of time. Rarely do new data collection systems or processes need to be developed in order to identify data representing the business needs of an organization.

In searching for the proper measures to connect to the program and to identify business needs, it is helpful to consider all possible measures that could be influenced. Sometimes, collateral measures move in harmony with the program. For example, efforts to improve safety may also improve productivity and increase job satisfaction. Weighing adverse impacts on certain measures may also help. For example, when cycle times are reduced, quality may suffer; when sales increase, customer satisfaction may deteriorate. Finally, program team members must anticipate unintended consequences and capture them as other data items that might be connected to or influenced by the program.

In the process of settling on the precise business measures for the program, it is useful to examine various "what if" scenarios. If the organization does nothing, the potential consequences of inaction should be made clear. The following questions may help in understanding the consequences of inaction:

- Will the situation deteriorate?
- Will operational problems surface?
- Will budgets be affected?
- Will we lose influence or support?

Answers to these questions can help the organization settle on a precise set of measures and can provide a hint of the extent to which the measures may change as a result of the program.

Determining Performance Needs

The next step in the needs analysis is to understand what led to the business need. If the proposed program addresses a problem, this step focuses on the cause of the problem. If the program makes use of an opportunity, this step focuses on what is inhibiting the organization from taking advantage of that opportunity. This step determines the performance needs.

Uncovering the causes of the problem or the inhibitors to success requires a variety of analytical techniques. These techniques—such as problem analysis, nominal group technique, force-field analysis, and just plain brainstorming—are used to clarify job performance needs. Table 4.3 lists a few of the analysis techniques. The technique that is used will depend on the organizational setting, the apparent depth of the problem, and the budget allocated to such analysis. Multiple techniques can be used, since performance may be lacking for a number of reasons.

Analysis takes time and adds to a program's cost. Examining records, researching databases, and observing individuals can provide important data, but a more cost-effective approach might include employing internal and/or external experts to help analyze the problem. Performance needs can vary considerably and may include ineffective behavior, a dysfunctional work climate, inadequate systems, a disconnected process flow, improper procedures, a nonsupportive culture, outdated technology, and a nonaccommodating environment, to name a few. When needs vary and there are many techniques to choose from, the potential exists for overanalysis and excessive costs. Consequently, a sensible approach is needed.

Determining Learning Needs

The solution to the performance needs uncovered in the previous step often requires a learning component—such as participants and team members learning how to perform a task differently or how to use a process or system. In some cases, learning is the principal solution, as in competency or capability development, major technology change, and system installations. For other programs, learning is a minor aspect of the solution and may involve simply understanding the process, procedure, or policy. For example, in the implementation of a new ethics policy for an organization, the learning component requires understanding how the policy works as well as the participants' role in the policy. In short, a learning solution is not always needed, but all solutions have a learning component.

Table 4.3. Analysis techniques.

- Statistical process control
- Brainstorming
- Problem analysis
- Cause-and-effect diagram
- Force-field analysis
- Mind mapping
- Affinity diagrams
- Simulations
- Diagnostic instruments
- Focus groups
- Probing interviews
- Job satisfaction surveys
- Engagement surveys
- Exit interviews
- Exit surveys
- Nominal group technique

Various approaches are available for measuring specific learning needs. Often, multiple tasks and jobs are involved in a program and should be addressed separately. Sometimes the least effective way to identify the skills and knowledge that are needed is to ask the participants involved in implementing the program. They may not be clear on what is needed and may not know enough to provide adequate input. One of the most useful ways to determine learning needs is to ask the individuals who understand the process. They can best determine what skills and knowledge are necessary to address the performance issues that have been identified. This may be the appropriate time to find out the extent to which the knowledge and skills already exist.

Job and task analysis is effective when a new job is created or when an existing job description changes significantly. As jobs are redesigned and the new tasks must be identified, this type of analysis offers a systematic way of detailing the job and task. Essentially, a job analysis is the collection and evaluation of work-related information. A task analysis identifies the specific knowledge, skills, tools, and conditions necessary for the performance of a particular job.

Observation of current practices and procedures in an organization may be necessary as the program is implemented. This can often indicate the level of capability and help identify the correct procedures. Observations can be used to examine work flow and interpersonal interactions, including those between management and team members. Observers may be previous employees, third-party participant observers, or mystery shoppers.

Sometimes, the demonstration of knowledge surrounding a certain task, process, or procedure provides evidence of what capabilities exist and what are lacking. This demonstration can be as simple as a skill practice or role play or as complex as an extensive mechanical or electronic simulation. The point is to use this as a way of determining if employees know how to perform a particular process. Through demonstration, specific learning needs can evolve.

Testing as a learning needs assessment process is not used as frequently as other methods, but it can be very useful. Employees are tested to reveal what they know about a particular situation. This information helps guide learning issues.

In implementing programs in organizations where there is an existing manager or team leader, input from the management team may be used to assess the current situation and to indicate the knowledge and skills required by the new situation. This input can be elicited through surveys, interviews, or focus groups. It can be a rich source of information about what the users of the program, if it is implemented, will need to know to make it successful.

Where learning is a minor component, learning needs are simple. Determining learning needs can be very time-consuming for major programs in which new procedures, technologies, and processes must be developed. As in developing job performance needs, it is important not to spend excessive time analyzing learning needs but rather to collect as much data as possible with minimal resources.

Determining Preference Needs

The final level of needs analysis determines the preferences that drive the program requirements. Essentially, individuals prefer certain processes, schedules, or activities for the structure of the program. These preferences define how the particular program will be implemented. If the program is a solution to a problem, this step defines how the solution will be executed. If the program makes use of an opportunity, this step outlines how the opportunity will be addressed, taking into consideration the preferences of those involved in the program.

Preference needs typically define the parameters of the program in terms of scope, timing, budget, staffing, location, technology, deliverables, and the degree of disruption allowed. Preference needs are developed from the input of several stakeholders rather than from one individual. For example, participants in the program (those who must make it work) may have a particular preference, but the preference could exhaust resources, time, and budgets. The immediate manager's input may help minimize the amount of disruption and maximize resources. The funds that can be allocated are also a constraining resource.

The urgency of program implementation may introduce a constraint on the preferences. Those who support or own the program often impose preferences on the program in terms of timing, budget, and the use of technology. Because preferences correspond to a Level 1 need, the program structure and solution will relate directly to the reaction objectives and to the initial reaction to the program.

In determining the preference needs, there can never be too much detail. Programs often go astray and fail to reach their full potential because of misunderstandings and differences in expectations surrounding the program. Preference needs should be addressed before the program begins. Pertinent issues are often outlined in the program proposal or planning documentation.

Case Study: Southeast Corridor Bank

At this point, following a case study through the different levels of needs may be helpful. The following discussion explores the analysis at Level 5, determining payoff needs. Southeast Corridor Bank (SCB) operated branches in six states. (SCB has since been acquired by Regions Bank, one of the nation's top ten banks.) Like many other fast-growing organizations, SCB faced merger and integration problems, including excessive employee turnover. An HR manager was assigned the task of reducing the voluntary turnover.[3]

The Analysis
SCB's annual employee turnover was 57 percent, compared with an industry average of 26 percent. The first step in addressing the problem was answering these questions:

- Is this a problem worth solving?
- Is there a potential payoff to solving the problem?

To the senior vice president of human resources, the answers were clear. After reviewing several published studies about the cost of turnover—including one from a financial institution—he concluded that the cost of employee turnover ranged between 110 and 225 percent of annual pay. At the current rate, employee turnover was costing the bank more than $6 million per year. Lowering the rate to the industry average would save the bank at least $3 million annually. Although the structure and cost of the solution had not been determined at this point, it became clear that this problem was worth solving. Unless the solution appeared to be very expensive, solving the problem would have a tremendous impact. This was the only analysis that was needed at this level.

The specific measure in question was voluntary turnover: the number of employees leaving voluntarily divided by the average number of employees, expressed as a percentage. Clearly defining the measure was important. Still, with improvement in any one measure, other measures should also improve, depending on the specific solution. For example, staffing levels, job satisfaction, customer service, sales revenue, and other measures could change. These considerations are detailed in the context of determining the solution.

To identify the job performance needs, the cause of the problem had to be determined. When the cause was determined, a solution could be developed.

The nominal group technique was selected as the analysis method because it allowed unbiased input to be collected efficiently and accurately across the organization. Focus groups were planned consisting of twelve employees from each region, for a total of six groups representing all the regions. In addition, two focus groups were planned for the clerical staff in the corporate headquarters. This approach provided approximately a 10 percent sample, which was considered sufficient to pinpoint the problem.

The focus group participants who represented areas in which turnover was highest described why their colleagues were leaving, not why they themselves would leave. Data were collected from individuals using a carefully structured format—during two-hour meetings at each location, with third-party facilitators—and were integrated and weighted so that the most important reasons were clearly identified. This process had the advantages of low cost and high reliability, as well as a low degree of bias. Only two days of external facilitator time were needed to collect and summarize the data for review.

The following are the ten major reasons given for turnover in the bank branches:

1. Lack of opportunity for advancement
2. Lack of opportunity to learn new skills and gain new product knowledge
3. Pay level not adequate
4. Not enough responsibility and empowerment
5. Lack of recognition and appreciation of work
6. Lack of teamwork
7. Lack of preparation for customer service problems
8. Unfair and nonsupportive supervisors
9. Too much stress at peak times
10. Not enough flexibility in work schedules

A similar list was developed for the administrative staff. However, the remainder of this case study will focus on the efforts to reduce turnover in the branch network. Branch turnover was the most critical issue, because of its high rate and the large number of employees involved, and the focus group results provided a clear pattern of specific needs. Recognizing that not all causes of the turnover could be addressed immediately, the bank's management concentrated on the top five reasons and considered a variety of options.

The Solution

The program manager determined that a skill-based pay system would address the top five reasons for employee turnover. The program was designed to expand the scope of the jobs, with increases in pay awarded for the acquisition of skills and a clear path provided for advancement and improvement. Jobs were redesigned from narrowly focused duties to an expanded role with a new title: Every teller became a banking representative I, II, or III.

A branch employee would be designated a banking representative I if he or she could perform one or two simple tasks, such as processing deposits and cashing checks. As an employee at this level took on additional responsibilities and learned to perform different functions, he or she would be eligible for a promotion to banking representative II. A representative who could perform all the basic functions of the branch, including processing consumer loan applications, would be promoted to banking representative III.

Training opportunities were made available to help employees develop the needed skills, and structured on-the-job training was provided by the branch managers, assistant managers, and supervisors. Self-study information was also available. The performance of multiple tasks was introduced to broaden responsibilities and enable employees to provide excellent customer service. Pay increases were used to recognize skill acquisition, demonstrated accomplishment, and increased responsibility.

Although the skill-based system had obvious advantages from the employee's perspective, the bank also benefited. Not only was turnover expected to decline, but required staffing levels were expected to decrease in the larger branches. In theory, if all employees in a branch could perform all the necessary duties, fewer employees would be needed. Previously, certain critical jobs required minimum staffing levels, and employees in those positions were not always available for other duties.

In addition, the bank anticipated improved customer service. The new approach would prevent customers from having to wait in long lines for specialized services. For example, in the typical bank branch, long lines for special functions—such as opening a checking account, closing out a certificate of deposit, or accepting a consumer loan application—were not unusual under the old setup, whereas routine activities such as paying bills and receiving deposits often required little or no waiting. With each employee now performing all the tasks, shorter waiting lines could be expected.

To support this new arrangement, the marketing department featured the concept in its publicity about products and services. Included with checking account statements was a promotional piece stating, "In our branches, there are no tellers." This document described the new process and announced that every employee could now perform all branch functions and consequently provide faster service.

More Analysis

At Level 2, learning needs fell into two categories. First, for each learning program, both skill acquisition and knowledge development needs were identified. Learning measurements included self-assessment, testing, and demonstrations, among others, and were connected to each specific program.

Second, it was necessary for employees to learn how the new program worked. As the program was introduced in meetings with employees, a simple measurement of learning was necessary to capture employee understanding of the following issues:

- How the program is being pursued
- What employees must do to succeed in the program
- How promotion decisions are made
- The timing of various stages of the program

These major learning needs were identified and connected specifically with the solution being implemented.

As the program was rolled out and the solution was developed, the preference needs were defined. The program had to be rolled out as soon as possible so that its effects could be translated into lower employee turnover. All the training programs had to be in place and available to employees. The amount of time employees must spend away from their jobs for training was an issue, as was the managers' control over the timing of promotions. This process had to move swiftly, or it would result in disappointment to employees who were eager to be trained and promoted. At the same time, the staffing and workload concerns had to be balanced so that the appropriate amount of time was devoted to training and skill building. More specifically, with the program's announcement, the desired employee reaction was defined. Program leaders wanted employees to view the program as very challenging, motivational, rewarding, and fair and as a solid investment in their futures. These needs were easily translated into the solution design.

Developing Objectives for HR Programs

Programs are driven by objectives. These objectives will position the program for success if they represent the needs of the business and include clearly defined measures of achievement. A program may be aimed at implementing a solution that addresses a particular dilemma, problem, or opportunity. In other situations, the initial program is designed to develop a range of feasible solutions, with one specific solution selected prior to implementation. Regardless of the program, multiple levels of objectives are necessary. These levels follow the five-level data categorization scheme and define precisely what will occur as a program is implemented. They correspond to the levels of evaluation and the levels of needs presented in Figure 4.1.

Reaction Objectives

For a program to be successful, the stakeholders immediately involved in the process must react favorably—or at least not negatively—to the program. Ideally, those directly involved should be satisfied with the program and see the value in it. This feedback must be obtained routinely during the program in order to make adjustments, keep the program on track, and redesign certain aspects as necessary.

Unfortunately, for many programs, specific objectives at this level are not developed, nor are data collection mechanisms put in place to allow channels for feedback.

Developing reaction objectives should be straightforward and relatively easy. The objectives reflect the degree of immediate as well as long-term satisfaction and explore issues important to the success of the program. They also form the basis for evaluating the chain of impact, and they emphasize planned action, when this is feasible and needed. Typical issues addressed in the development of reaction objectives are relevance, usefulness, importance, appropriateness, rewards, and motivation.

Learning Objectives

Every program involves at least one learning objective, and most involve more. With programs entailing major change, the learning component is quite important. In situations narrower in scope, such as the implementation of a new policy, the learning component is minor but still necessary. To ensure that the various stakeholders have learned what they need to know to make the program successful, learning objectives are developed. The following are examples of learning objectives.

After the launch of the program, participants should be able to do the following:

- Identify the six features of the new ethics policy.
- Demonstrate the use of each software routine within the standard time.
- Score 75 or better on the new-product quiz.
- Explain the value of diversity in a work group.
- Successfully complete the leadership simulation.
- Know how to apply for housing assistance.

Objectives are critical to the measurement of learning because they communicate the expected outcomes from the learning component and define the competency or level of performance necessary to make the program successful. They provide a focus to allow participants to clearly identify what it is they must learn and do—sometimes with precision.

Application Objectives

The application and implementation objectives clearly define what is expected of the program and often the target level of performance. Application objectives are similar to learning objectives but relate to actual performance. They provide specific milestones indicating when one part or all of the process has been implemented. Examples of typical application objectives are as follows:

- Within one year, 10 percent of employees will submit documented suggestions for cutting costs.
- Ninety-five percent of high-potential employees will complete individual development plans within two years.
- Forty percent of the city's homeless population will apply for special housing within one year of program launch.
- Eighty percent of employees will use one or more of the three cost containment features of the healthcare plan.

- Fifty percent of conference attendees will follow up with at least one contact from the conference.
- The average 360-degree leadership assessment score will improve from 3.4 to 4.1 on a 5-point scale.
- Employees will routinely use problem-solving skills when faced with a quality problem.
- Sexual harassment activity will cease within three months after the zero-tolerance policy is implemented.
- At least 99.1 percent of software users will be following the correct sequences after three weeks of use.
- By November, pharmaceutical sales reps will communicate adverse effects of a specific prescription drug to all physicians in their territories.
- Managers will initiate three workout programs within fifteen days.
- Sales and customer service representatives will use all five interaction skills with at least half the customers within the next month.

Application objectives are critical because they describe the expected outcomes in the intermediate area—between the learning of new tasks and procedures and the delivery of the impact of this learning. Application and implementation objectives describe how things should be or the desired state of the workplace once the program solution has been implemented. They provide a basis for evaluating on-the-job changes and performance.

Impact Objectives

Every program should drive improvement in one or more business-impact measures. Impact objectives indicate key business measures that should improve as the application and implementation objectives are achieved. The following are typical impact objectives:

- System downtime should be reduced from three hours per month to no more than two hours per month in six months.
- Incidents should decrease by 20 percent within the next calendar year.
- The average number of product defects should decrease from 214 to 153 per month in the Midwest region.
- The customer satisfaction index should rise by 2 percent during the next calendar year.
- Sales expenses for all titles at Proof Publishing Company should decrease by 10 percent in the fourth quarter.
- The average number of new accounts opened at Great Western Bank should increase from 300 to 350 per month in six months.
- The shelter costs per homeless person should be below $70,000 in two years.
- There should be an across-the-board reduction in overtime for front-of-house managers at Tasty Time restaurants in the third quarter of this year.
- Employee complaints should be reduced from an average of three per month to an average of one per month at Guarantee Insurance headquarters.
- The company-wide employee engagement index should rise by one point during the next calendar year.

- There should be a 10 percent increase in Pharmaceuticals Inc. brand awareness among physicians during the next two years.
- The dropout rate for high school students in the Barett County system should decrease by 5 percent within three years.

Impact objectives are critical to measuring business performance because they define the ultimate expected outcome from the program. They describe the business unit performance that should result from the program. Above all, impact objectives emphasize achievement of the bottom-line results that key client groups expect and demand.

ROI Objectives

The fifth level of objectives for programs represents the acceptable return on investment—the monetary impact. Objectives at this level define the expected payoff from investing in the program. An ROI objective is typically expressed as an acceptable ROI percentage: annual monetary benefits minus cost, divided by the actual cost, and multiplied by one hundred. A zero percent ROI indicates a breakeven program. A 50 percent ROI indicates recapture of the program cost and an additional 50 percent "earnings" (50 cents for every dollar invested).

For some programs, such as the purchase of a new company, a new building, or major equipment, the ROI objective is large relative to the ROI of other expenditures. However, the calculation is the same for both. For many organizations, the ROI objective for a program is set slightly higher than the ROI expected from other "routine investments" because of the relative newness of applying the ROI concept to the types of programs described in this book. For example, if the expected ROI from the purchase of a new company is 20 percent, the ROI from a new recruiting program might be around 25 percent. The important point is that the ROI objective should be established up front and in discussions with the program sponsor. Excluding the ROI objective leaves stakeholders questioning the economic success of a program. If a program reaps a 25 percent ROI, is that successful? Not if the objective was a 50 percent ROI.

Human Capital Strategy Implications

Because of the importance of business alignment, it should be included as part of human capital strategy. The following items should be addressed in the strategic plan:

- The method or process used to connect projects to business needs
- The percentage of programs that will be aligned through this method
- The specific criteria for deciding which programs to align to business needs (if not all of them)
- How and when business alignment is validated in follow-up

MANAGE TALENT FOR VALUE

Optimizing the Most Important Asset

> *Force 3: Talent Management.* A very critical part of the human capital strategy must focus on managing talent for value. Every organization is faced with the serious issue of attracting, selecting, motivating, maintaining, and retaining critical staff. The human resources function, particularly the chief human resources officer, is responsible for managing talent. In today's competitive market, managing talent must be accomplished with value in mind, delivering value to and enabling the success of the organization.

Talent management is one of the most important strategic objectives of companies today, many CHROs have the primary responsibility for the talent management system. The CHRO's role represents a great opportunity to add value to the organization by acquiring, developing, and retaining critical talent. This chapter explores the importance of talent in the organization. From every viewpoint, talent is essential, and it is often regarded as a key strategy for maintaining a competitive advantage. A systems approach to talent management is needed for success, efficiency, and consistency. The systems approach follows a step-by-step process, beginning with attracting talent and ending with removing unwanted talent.

Opening Story: Tata Group

Tata is India's largest enterprise group, with businesses in seven sectors, representing 100 companies, operations in some 80 countries, more than 500,000 employees, and annual revenue in excess of $100 billion. In recent years, it has grown through a series of strategic acquisitions and joint ventures. Global growth and diversity have brought a complex mix of talent management challenges. Tata receives more than 58 percent of its revenue from outside of India.[1]

Tata's HR and talent organization has become skilled at determining the value (real and potential) of the people in the companies it acquires, as well as risk management and talent capture. Risk management involves assessing the culture of an acquired company. HR works alongside finance and strategy to ascertain "where the target company has come from" and how it has dealt with challenges in the past, says Satish Pradhan, who recently retired as executive vice president of group human resources. "You need to understand their fears, their drama, and their anxieties." By providing insight into the acquired company's readiness for change and the distance between its culture and Tata's, the talent team helps mitigate risk. This process, which stretches through postmerger integrations, can take one to two years.

Talent capture is all about unlocking the ambition and potential of a leadership team that may be dispirited by a history of challenging performance or subordination to short-term goals. Pradhan grew accustomed to stories of resignation and even despair: "They'd say things like, 'Why don't you guys just tell us what you want us to do.'" When Tata sees opportunity in an acquisition candidate, it seeks to unlock potential at the outset by creating a shared vision: What does the company aspire to be, and how can Tata enable that aspiration? "Initially there is cynicism and disbelief and 'What are they not telling us? What's the game here?'" Pradhan says. "Then, over time, they realize that we are actually serious about what we're saying. We actually want the acquired company to have aspirations."[2]

Talent Management Issues

Let's review the basic issues of talent management. These fundamentals begin to define the scope and importance of talent.

Critical Roles and Succession Management

The CHRO should create a process for evaluating critical roles within the organization. Sometimes, people who are in critical jobs are not the best performers, and the best performers are not in critical jobs. A successful talent management system identifies critical jobs in the organization and finds ways to ensure that current and back-up incumbents are top performers. Figure 5.1 provides an example of the type of data collected for talent management.

An executive talent management system also plans for organizational transitions. Some companies have extensive succession plans for several layers of management;

Figure 5.1. Critical talent chart.

First name	Current title	Department head	Capability score	Contribution index	Flight risk score	Top leader?	Critical role?	Short-term successor
Kris	VP Engineering	Rick Satterfield	5	4	5	Yes	Yes	Beryl Oldham
Michelle	Director of Advertising	Lars Rhinstone	3	3	6	No	No	Madison Smithfield
Emma	VP Logistics	Stacey Hatch	5	5	5	Yes	Yes	Frasier Wilson

others only create plans for the top leaders in the company. To avoid disruption in business performance, it is critical that the company plan for departures of talent. Evaluating ready-now talent, growing internal leaders, and sourcing external talent are all responsibilities of CHROs who manage talent in their companies. Essentially, organizations have shifted from success planning to succession management.

Another key element of a successful talent management system is a clear process for identifying and developing high potentials—people in the organization who are identified as the next leaders in the company. Many organizations carefully review and manage a small segment of their talent as high potentials. Others do not clearly segment out this group or provide preferential development or treatment. Either way, understanding who top performers are and fostering their development provides greater chances for business and leadership success.

Talent Movement

Companies inherently struggle with movement of talent because of the gaps it can leave in an organization. Talent mobility occurs when movement of talent happens regularly and has minimal impact on the business. If an employee's skills can be better used in another function, business leaders should support moving that individual. Unfortunately, many managers become territorial and fear gaps in their departments. Planning for these gaps and creating a culture that believes talent belongs to the company—not a specific department—takes time and effort. When managed appropriately, there should be no gaps, because the talent management system is so robust that it can fill the openings quite quickly.

Before the Securities and Exchange Commission's (SEC's) rules on segment reporting, many companies had centralized talent pools that could be used across the company transparently. For example, a centralized engineering function would enable engineering leads in the businesses to pull on resources with specific skill sets. Today, companies have typically aligned functional employees in a business, which limits movement or rotations. Formal rotation programs have flourished to simulate the concept of a centralized pool of talent. These programs enable new graduates or existing employees to work for different functions during their rotation assignments. Finance departments, for example, use this model quite frequently with new MBA graduates. A rotation program that exposes the grad to financial accounting, financing strategy, financial analysis, and, sometimes, tax/treasury issues provides robust experiences and develops talent effectively for future career mobility. At the end of the formal program, the employee can select a function, manager, or group for his or her work assignment. This provides the employee with exposure to different functions and develops his or her skills, which enables more growth and talent readiness as needs arise.

Talent Management Outcomes

Many CHROs share information about company-wide organizational talent with the executive team and sometimes the board of directors. Providing exposure to management about the number of employees with international experience, the number of leaders with marketing education, or the percentage of employees with advanced degrees can provide critical information for business planning. Boards have an increasing interest in understanding the talent within a company as well as strategies for acquisition, development, and retention. CHROs are in a critical position as keepers of the talent profile of a company.

Table 5.1 shows how the talent management measurement systems are changing. The traditional group of measures of talent management focused on activity; the emerging group is focused on results, using the methods described in Chapters 4 and 14. The Institute for Corporate Productivity and AMA Enterprise (Talent Transformation Section) recently conducted a study that compared high-performing and low-performing organizations on issues affecting talent. They found that high-performing organizations, challenged by the uncertainty of continuous change, turned to workforce analytics and workforce planning to gain visibility of gaps pertaining to critical roles and skills needed to support sustainable business success. Transparency was identified as a common thread that correlates with effectiveness in virtually all talent processes and programs. This applies to everything from ensuring employees know where they stand with regards to their work expectations, progress, and development opportunities, to establishing accurate visibility into specific talent pools within the workforce, as well as building and communicating organizational strategy. In the future, transparency must be purposely incorporated into organizations to ensure high performance.[3]

Talent Analytics

Human capital analytics practices have been developed throughout major organizations, and these practices are tackling all kinds of issues. In a recent study of more than one hundred organizations with dedicated human capital analytics practices, the number-one area the practices were serving was in the recruiting and selection

Table 5.1. Measuring success of talent management.

Traditional examples	Emerging examples
• Three job groups defined as critical talent • Six recruiting channels utilized • 2,439 new employees recruited • Cost per hire reduced by 10 percent over the last year • Time to fill jobs reduced by 30 percent in two years • Individual development plans (IDPs) developed for 95 percent of high potentials • Ninety-two percent of managers and executives involved in 360-degree feedback process • Seven formal talent-development programs in place • Five informal talent-development programs in place • 1,479 individuals involved in talent-development programs	• Recruiting effectiveness increased by 30 percent • Eighty-five percent of individual development plans (IDPs) completed within one year • Turnover rate 30 percent below industry average • Promotion readiness rating increased by 42 percent • External hire ratio reduced by 35 percent • Performance rating of newly promoted managers increased 36 percent • Manager/executive failure rate sliced in half • Regrettable turnover rate for three critical talent groups at half of the industry average • In sales and marketing, a revised talent management system adding $15 million in sales • In IT, a new talent management system saving $2.3 million in costs • Three ROI studies in talent management completed with an average of 139 percent

process.[4] In this scenario, the analytics are used to understand the effectiveness of different recruiting sources and selection processes. Not only do the analytics track effectiveness in terms of correlation and causation; they are also developed into models that can be used in the processes to predict which individuals will be more successful. This is a great development that holds much promise for the future, particularly for the high-performance organization.[5]

Talent Mismanagement

The unfortunate reality is that most organizations have not addressed critical talent management issues. There have been some mismanagement practices. Another report showed that the majority of organizations are ineffectively employing important talent capabilities. Consequently, the workforce is not performing to its potential, and gaps in leadership and critical roles exist due to failure to develop adequate bench strength and ineffective development of leadership competencies throughout the organization. This is particularly true for performance management, succession planning, and leadership development. The high-performing organizations reviewed in the study were much better at this, but still there is much room for improvement.[6] This chapter focuses on many of the issues that need to be addressed to avoid talent mismanagement.

Why Talent Is Critical to Success

Talent is considered the most critical source of success in an organization, and no executive will argue this point. How did it get this way? How critical is it now? How critical will it be in the future? There are several major reasons talent is so important and will be even more critical in the future. While these reasons were presented in Chapter 1, a few others are briefly described in the following pages.

Talent Adds to Market Value

When considering the value and importance of talent, you need look no further than the stock market. Investors place a tremendous value on talent in organizations. The balance sheets of very progressive knowledge industries reveal the dramatic difference talent makes. When you compare the market capitalization to the assets listed on the balance sheet, there is a big difference. Investors see something that has a value much greater than the assets listed on the balance sheet. This "hidden value," as it is sometimes called, comes from intangible assets, which now represent major portions of the value of organizations, particularly those in knowledge industries. Talent makes up a big part of intangible assets.

The Best Idea Will Fail Without Proper Talent and Execution

Talent management is fundamentally about ensuring that the right people are positioned in the right places and utilized to the fullest potential for optimal success of the organization. Business leaders clearly understand their talent pool. They work hard to identify the key players who have critical relationships with customers and suppliers, and then they work even harder to nurture and keep those key resources.

A number of business leaders have asserted that acquiring and developing the best talent for their companies is the most important task they have to perform.

These leaders put a premium on keeping the talent they need for growth. They do what is necessary to ensure that key people are secure and do not leave because of low morale, thus preventing a defection domino effect.

Talent Is a Major Source of Competitive Advantage

Today's organizations have access to most of the key success factors. Financial resources are available to almost any organization with a viable business model. One company no longer has an advantage over another to access the financial capital needed to run a business. Access to technology is equal; a company can readily adapt technology to a given situation or business model. It is difficult to have a technology advantage in an information technology society.

Businesses also have relatively equal access to customers, even if there is a dominant player in the market. Newspapers are laced with stories of small organizations taking on larger ones and succeeding. Having entry and access to a customer database is not necessarily a competitive advantage. What makes the difference, clearly, is the talent of the organization.

Companies Want to Be Talent Magnets

Probably no document about the importance of talent is more visible than the list of organizations selected as the "100 Best Companies to Work For" in America. This list is published each year in *Fortune* magazine and has become the bellwether for focusing on the importance of talent. Although other publications have spin-offs, this is the premier list that organizations strive to make. The most important factor in selecting companies for this list is what the employees themselves have to say about their workplaces. For a typical list, at least 350 randomly selected employees from each candidate company fill out a survey created by The Great Place to Work Institute based in San Francisco.[7] For more methodology on these criteria for this list, please see www.Fortune.com.

These lists are alive with tales of how employers focus on building a great place to work and building employee respect, dignity, capability, and talent. These firms are successful in the market. A typical list includes well-known and successful companies such as American Express, Cisco Systems, FedEx, Eli Lilly, Marriott International, General Mills, Merck, Microsoft, Proctor & Gamble, QUALCOMM, and others. Inclusion in the list has become so sought after by organizations that they change many of their practices and philosophies in an attempt to make this list. This list underscores the importance of talent and how much emphasis companies place on it. It shows how diversity, job growth, turnover, and learning make a significant difference in an organization. For the most part, these organizations are investing heavily in human capital—far exceeding those on any other list. Investment, in their minds, translates into payoff.

Talent Is a Game Changer

A group of Harvard professors studied three very successful organizations to try to understand what made them so effective. One organization was BlackRock, the world's largest asset management firm, with a tremendous track record. Another was Envision Energy, a very successful Chinese company, and the third was Tata Group, a very successful conglomerate in India with more than 500,000 employees.

These very successful companies had one important common thread: they each had a very effective talent management strategy.[8] Collectively, their work developed very precise actions that an organization should take to have a game-changing talent strategy. Table 5.2 lists the statements that an employee can make in a company with highly successful talent policies and practices.

Talent Is a Major Expense

Successful talent acquisition and management is expensive. The total investment in competent talent is the total HR department expenses for talent management plus the salaries and benefits of the talent. HR expenses include every function that exists in the chain of talent acquisition and management. Attracting, selecting, developing, motivating, compensating, and managing talent are accounted for in this total cost. Because the traditional HR department expenses do not include salaries of other functions, this broader measure has the effect of showing the total cost of talent. It should be reported as a percentage of operating costs or revenue or on a per-employee basis to show realistic comparisons with other organizations. All direct employee-related costs are included in the human capital measure.

Executives in some organizations realize the magnitude of these expenses and have a desire to manage them efficiently. Although the costs do not include office space and support expenses, they are still very significant, often two to three times an employee's annual pay. In many—if not most—industries, the cost of talent is the largest operating expense category. Because talent is so expensive, it must be managed carefully and systematically.

Talent Departures Are Extremely Costly

When talent leaves, the costs are high. Executives see the direct cost of recruiting, selection, and initial training, but they may not understand other impacts. The total cost of turnover is not calculated routinely in organizations. When the

Table 5.2. Talent strategies for game changers.

1. My company places "purpose" at the heart of its business model.
2. My company has a high-performance culture.
3. Leaders in my company follow well-understood guiding principles.
4. Our people policies help drive our business strategy.
5. Our leaders are completely committed to excellence in talent management.
6. Our talent management practices are highly effective.
7. Our leaders are deeply engaged in and accountable for spotting, tracking, coaching, and developing the next generation of leaders.
8. Our talent practices are strategically oriented, but they also put a premium on operational efficiency.
9. Our talent practices engender a strong sense of collective purpose and pride yet work very well for my career as an individual.
10. Our talent practices strike the right balance between global scale and local responsiveness.
11. My company has a long-standing commitment to people development, but we are very open to changing our policies when circumstances dictate.

Source: Adapted from Douglas A. Ready, Linda A. Hill, and Robert J. Thomas. "Building a Game-Changing Talent Strategy." *Harvard Business Review*, January–February 2014.

cost is estimated, it is often underestimated. Estimations of the total cost are also not communicated throughout the organization, leaving the management team unaware of the potential costs. If turnover is a problem, the costs are always significant. In some cases, the actual impact can be devastating and can result in the organization's demise.

The total cost of turnover involves both the direct and indirect costs. Figure 5.2 lists the costs in the sequence in which they occur. This figure suggests that there are many different costs, some of which are never known with certainty but can be estimated if enough attention is directed to the issue.

As Table 3.3 showed, these costs are significant. There is healthy turnover in any organization—people who retire, leave to work in nonprofit organizations, or go back to school. The area of most concern in managing talent is when top performers or critical employees depart their jobs unexpectedly. The CHRO's role is emerging to manage this turnover successfully and on-board new employees quickly. In an ideal scenario, the CHRO is prepared with talent sources, so there are no gaps in organizational performance or product road maps. Managing talent in an organization is a critical responsibility. CHROs must be aware of talent needs, know the sourcing strategies for aligning great talent, be prepared to build capable talent internally, and manage the employment brand.

Summary: Why Talent Is Critical

It may be helpful to summarize this information, which clearly details the critical role of talent in the organization. Table 5.3 provides a quick summary, showing many of the reasons talent is critical to success. The remainder of this chapter describes a system to provide the focus, attention, and care needed for this strategic issue.

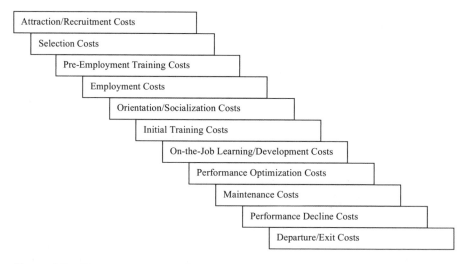

Figure 5.2. Turnover cost categories.

Table 5.3. Why talent is critical.

1. Talent adds to market value.
2. Companies cannot be successful without talent, as talent executes ideas.
3. Talent is the last source of competitive advantage.
4. Great workplaces attract and retain talent.
5. The most successful and admired companies have great talent.
6. The cost of competent talent is high.
7. The cost of turnover of talent is high.

Needed: A System for Talent Management

The most effective way to tackle talent management is to use a systems approach, ensuring that the different elements and pieces of the process are working in concert to acquire and integrate talent into the system. Several issues support the need for this system.

Disconnected Efforts

The traditional way to deal with this issue is to have the responsibility assigned to various groups that cut across functional HR lines. Recruiting, learning and development, reward systems, and employee relations are traditional functional groups. Several problems may surface with this approach. First, in this traditional HR model, talent management is in a reactive mode, reacting to critical issues, problems, and talent shortages. There are few early signs—other than the lack of communication between groups—to signal an impending problem. Also, because individuals involved are not tightly integrated with open communication, inefficiencies abound in the processes, often creating duplications and delays throughout the system. Consequently, this is a very expensive approach to the problem—one that fails to generate the success needed and leaves voids, omissions, and delays. The results can be disastrous for an organization in need of talent and attempting to grow. Most of all, the traditional approach creates confusion—not only in roles and responsibilities but in the process of designating who is in charge. This confusion can be minimized by a systems approach.

A Systems Approach

Figure 5.3 shows the traditional model for a talent management process, where the focus is on acquiring and retaining talent.[9] Today, more issues must be addressed and integrated.

Figure 5.3. The traditional talent management process.

Source: Deloitte Research. *It's 2008: Do You Know Where Your Talent Is? Why Acquisition and Retention Strategies Don't Work.* Deloitte Development LLC, 2004.

A systems approach to talent management is presented in Figure 5.4. It includes the major issues of planning, acquiring, developing, managing, and retaining employees. These are often subdivided into responsibility areas, as outlined in the figure. Traditionally, many of these have been under different sections apart from the typical learning and development area of responsibility. However, this is a system that must work together in close coordination and integration, ideally under the direction of a central person whose key responsibility is talent management—the CHRO. When this is in place, the benefits are tremendous from the client's perspective. First, this approach presents consistent attention throughout the process. Problems can be spotted quickly and adjustments can be made. Second, talent acquisition can be more effective, ensuring that adequate talent is recruited and integrated into the system and the appropriate quality and quantities are secured. Finally, value is added as costs are reduced when the process is more efficient and duplications are avoided. The systems approach is rational and logical; it is the economic way to address talent management.

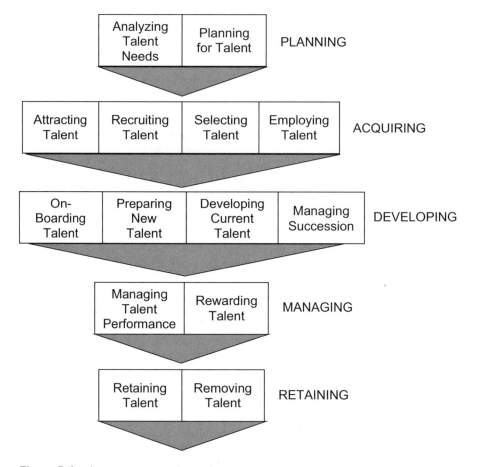

Figure 5.4. A systems approach to talent management.

In the traditional model, when a company needs to quickly hire thirty multimedia engineers for a new technology deployment, the staffing lead receives notification, opens thirty position requisitions, creates an advertisement, posts the job on a website, and begins the candidate-screening process.

In an ideal model, the HR staff would be working closely with the executive team and know the business strategy is moving toward multimedia. The HR team could scan a database of talent profiles that would identify twenty internal candidates that either have multimedia skills or need a few courses/development opportunities to acquire the skills. In this case, the request for external talent drops to ten people, and the ramp-up time for the other twenty employees is much shorter. Time to fill productivity is reduced. The HR team then works to backfill the jobs that were filled by employees who are now in the multimedia jobs. This is a true talent management model—HR deploys resources where they are needed most and develops internal talent for optimum performance and long-term value to the company.

Defining the Critical Talent

Before describing the mechanics of talent management, it is helpful to define the critical talent in an organization. Critical talent refers to the employees who drive a major part of the company's business performance and who generate above-average value for customers and shareholders. Typically, the critical talent possess highly developed skills and deep knowledge. They don't just "do their job" but go above and beyond to contribute to the organization's success. Surprisingly, these are not always the high-tech or highest-paid employees; often, they are the valuable employees that are seldom mentioned in the annual report. Take FedEx, for example—the world's largest overnight package delivery firm. One report suggested that the couriers might be more critical to the operation than the pilots who fly the packages through the night. The couriers have direct contact with the customers and must make continual decisions that impact efficiency and the effectiveness of the supply chain, such as how to reconfigure a route and how long to wait for a customer's packages.[10]

Critical talent can vary considerably by industry and organization. At Merck, critical talent may include the scientists and clinicians who discover and develop pharmaceuticals that fuel the company's growth. At ExxonMobil, it may include the geologists and petroleum engineers who find and extract oil. At YRC Trucking, the critical talent may be the long-haul truck drivers. At Toyota, the critical talent may be the machinists who perform precision operations to develop parts for automobiles using Six Sigma standards. At Amazon, the critical talent may be the IT staff who develop and support the innovative online marketing. At Wal-Mart, they may be the inventory managers who ensure that the right goods are in the right store at the right time.

Recruiting wars often erupt when there is a shortage of critical talent, leading to much inefficiency, cost, and many disruptions along the talent management system.

Competencies: A Starting Point

In recent years, there has been a tremendous focus on the use of competency characteristics and traits of individuals. Some experts indicate that attracting talent can only be achieved if it is focused on identifying competencies and using them throughout the talent management system. Competency models are fundamental to talent management systems. Many organizational units use a unique language when describing recruiting standards, training requirements, and promotional criterion. The problem is exacerbated when organizations span cultures and countries. By using an agreed-upon competency model, the organization can communicate via a common language that describes performance from one unit to the next.[11]

As shown in Figure 5.5, competencies ideally drive the entire talent management system. A competency is a reliably measureable, relatively enduring characteristic of a person, community, or organization that causes or statistically predicts a criterion or level of performance. Competency characteristics are knowledge, behavioral skills, competency processing (IQ), personality traits, values, motives, and occasionally other perceptional capabilities.[12] Competencies are a critical part of planning, recruiting, and selecting talent at the beginning of the process. The processes of preparing and developing talent should focus on the same competencies as the processes of managing, rewarding, and motivating employees. The competencies for a particular job—even among similar jobs—can vary.

The key challenge is to determine, to the extent possible, the competencies needed for talent in specific divisions, groups, functions, or even job categories and use them to drive the talent management system. Some companies use behavior dimensions, leadership characteristics, or behavioral quotients instead of competencies. Whatever the language, it is important that the basis for the talent management system fit the organization.

Planning for Talent

Planning is perhaps the area that has been most neglected in many talent management systems. The objective of planning is to have an orderly process for acquiring

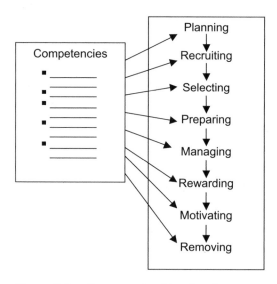

Figure 5.5. Competencies drive the talent management system.

the appropriate types of employees to meet the needs of the organization, given the constraints of market forces and the available labor supply. The three areas that are often addressed, sometimes by separate individuals or units within the talent management system, are discussed in the following sections.

Analyzing Talent Needs

Several factors will determine the need for talent, as defined earlier. First, the growth of the organization often translates into the largest component of talent requirements. The CHRO must be aware of the organization's strategy, both short- and long-term. Needs are sometimes driven by shifts in products and services, acquisitions, mergers, and routine growth through expansion. Whatever the reason, growth translates into the need for a specific number of individuals in different job categories.

Second, replacement needs are created by employees leaving the organization. If turnover is excessive, replacement needs become significant. If there is low turnover, replacement needs are minimal. In the context of managing retention, only the avoidable turnover is considered. However, when replacements are needed, all types of turnover must be considered—including those individuals who retire, leave due to disability, or transfer to other regions. The retirement issue alone is a critical problem for many organizations. NASA, for example, faces a tremendous loss of talent as much of its science and engineering capability will be retiring in the next few years.[13] This situation will have a tremendous impact on their talent management system, which will have to ensure that the proper replacement talent is recruited and prepared for their assignments.

Third, changes in skills and competencies translate directly into human capital needs. As technology advances, markets change, and products shift, a different set of skills and competencies are sometimes needed, either in addition to or beyond those currently in the organization. These three issues generate needs that must be translated into specific numbers forecasted in both short- and long-term scenarios.

Market Analysis

Since the majority of needs must be filled from the available labor market, a market analysis is critical. When examining the labor market, several issues must be taken into consideration. First is the supply of labor in the recruiting area—this is a critical issue for some organizations because of labor shortages. This may require the relocation of facilities to ensure a better source of labor. For example, many automobile companies based outside the United States are developing plants in record numbers in the southern part of the United States. For example, Toyota, Honda, Mercedes Benz, and Hyundai have all developed major plants in the state of Alabama, making this state the automobile capital of the South. A major part of the attraction is the available labor supply—in both quality and quantity—as well as a strong work ethic.

Developing Plans

After the needs are determined and the market is analyzed, the plans are developed, generating a schedule of the number of employees that will be acquired at what times from what sources, sometimes by job group. If it becomes apparent that the market will not be able to supply the required resources, the shortages must be addressed and alternatives developed. For example, due to the difficulty of recruiting fully trained nurses, hospitals have created their own nursing schools, sometimes in conjunction with a university. This is a classic case of attempting to regulate supply and demand—taking control of the situation and creating the supply. This situation illustrates an important issue that must be part of talent planning—scenario planning. Because all forecasts contain error and there are many events that can have a significant effect on the sources of talent, different scenarios should be developed, including worst-case conditions. This process provides insight into what can, should, and perhaps must be done to ensure that available talent is onboard when needed.

Acquiring Talent

Acquiring talent involves four key issues: attracting, recruiting, selecting, and employing. Each of these is an important step, often performed by different individuals.

Attracting Talent

Attracting talent is a long-term issue. The attraction of a workplace comes from many factors, but two very important ones relate to the issue of developing the company into a talent magnet. One factor is being an employer of choice, representing a great place to work. The second is the overall reputation, or employment brand, of the organization. Employers of choice have several things in common. They organize a work–life balance program that meets needs across the business; they give professional and personal development opportunities to all; they enable employees to make contributions to the firm tied to personal responsibility; they foster a friendly and culturally rich environment; and they operate a business that is responsible to the community as a whole.[14] In the United States, employer-of-choice lists are developed by a variety of organizations and publications. The most common is *Fortune*'s "100 Best Companies to Work For" in America, described earlier in the chapter.

Organizations are working harder to polish their image in the eyes of prospective talent. Some have staff who do little but keep the firm's name in front of both faculty and students, promoting their "employer brand."

Organizational reputation is based on several factors. Harris Interactive and the Reputation Institute published a corporate reputation poll based on the views of almost thirty thousand respondents.[15] They developed six categories to rank reputation:

- Emotional appeal
- Products and services
- Workplace environment
- Social responsibility
- Vision and leadership
- Financial performance

Reputations, particularly of workplaces, often evolve and develop over time and have to be driven by senior leadership. A few scandals, ethical concerns, or ineffective leadership can spoil an otherwise superb reputation. Many companies work very hard to ensure that their image, from a talent-attraction perspective, is superb. In essence, they are attempting to brand their organization as a great place to work as well as a great place to invest. Sears perfected this sentiment in their overall strategy to create a compelling place to shop, a compelling place to invest, and a compelling place to work, putting the customers, shareholders, and employees on equal footing.

Recruiting Talent

Recruiting has changed significantly in the last decade, not only the methods, but the overall approach. Table 5.4 shows how the recruiting strategies have shifted.[16] The newer approaches involve constant recruiting, using many sources, branding, and involving many individuals. Recruiting strategies are reflecting a comprehensive process with long-term focus.

Table 5.5 shows the shift in the actual methods of recruiting. Although the traditional methods are still being used, newer methods are being adopted, particularly those involving web resources and networking. Monitoring current events in specific areas to understand where the talent may be located or what may be driving available talent is an effective tactic. Using employees as talent scouts is another useful approach. Because of the scarcity and competition for quality talent, a talent war is being waged in certain industries. Nontraditional recruiting methods are often needed to capture the interest of the passive prospect. Recruiting has become so subtle that some organizations—such as Cisco Systems—have a philosophy of not hiring candidates that are actually looking for a job.

An important development in the recent years is being able to predict success with assessments. Sometimes these assessments are used in the selection process as candidates are being considered for employment. Others are used internally to see who may be high potentials in the organization. The applications are varied and almost limitless. Table 5.6 shows some examples of predicting success, taken from SHL Talent Measurement, a part of CEB. This organization had tremendous success

Table 5.4. The shifts in strategies of recruiting.

Old recruiting strategies	New recruiting strategies
Grow all your own talent.	Recruit talent at all levels.
Recruit only for vacant positions.	Search for talent all the time.
Go to a few traditional sources.	Tap many diverse sources of talent.
Recruiting is limited to a few individuals.	Every employee is a recruiter.
Advertise to job hunters.	Find ways to reach passive candidates.
Specify a compensation range and stay within it.	Break the compensation rules to get the candidates you want.
Recruiting is about screening.	Recruiting is about selling as well as screening.
Hire as needed with no overall plan.	Develop a recruiting strategy for each type of talent.
Keep a low profile except during employment growth.	Brand your company as an employer of choice.

Source: Adapted and updated from Ed Michaels, Helen Handfield-Jones, and Beth Axelrod. *The War for Talent.* Boston: Harvard Business School Press, 2001.

Table 5.5. The shifts in recruiting methods.

Traditional recruiting methods	Nontraditional recruiting methods
Job service agencies	Web resources
Recruiting ads	Open houses
Professional recruiters	Receptions at conferences
Campus recruiting	Information seminars
Internships	Diverse profile candidates
Employment support groups	Military recruiting
Community recruiting	Employee talent scouts
Job fairs	Networking
Walk-in applicants	Employee referrals
Trade and professional associations	Monitoring current events
Employment hotlines	Pre-employment programs

Table 5.6. Predicting success.

- Predicting which account managers will boost revenues 24 percent per quarter
- Predicting which bank employees are more than twice as likely to handle money accurately
- Finding out which sales reps will sell $2.5 million more per year
- Understanding which collection agents are twice as likely to be top performers
- Uncovering customer service reps who are five times as likely to deliver to schedule
- Discovering salespeople who will sell 14 percent more per hour
- Finding out which general managers will grow sales more than three times faster
- Predicting which care staff will be more than seven times more effective in dealing with complex patient issues
- Identifying financial services staff who are twice as likely to achieve goals
- Identifying warehouse workers who are four times more likely to turn up for work
- Predicting which technicians are 52 percent more likely to meet customer expectations
- Identifying agents who achieve 11 percent more collections revenue per hour
- Identifying customer service reps who will resolve calls 13 percent faster
- Discovering telesales agents who will sign up 24 percent more new customers per month

Source: Adapted from CEB/SHL Talent Measurement.[17]

with this process, and these examples show a wide variety of evolving possibilities for predicting the success of talent in an organization.

Selecting and Employing Talent

Recruiting brings the prospects for consideration. Next comes one of the most critical talent decisions—the employment decision. How it is made, who makes it, when it is made, or whether or not it is accepted are important issues. Although selection is only one component in the talent management system, it must be consistent. It is at this stage that there is the most scrutiny in terms of being fair and equitable. An inconsistent selection process is doomed to be challenged and may be difficult to defend. A systematic process should be followed for each selection so that no one is subject to disparate treatment and the selection does not represent an adverse impact. Figure 5.6 shows the selection system for a commercial banking officer for a large banking firm in the United States. The figure shows steps in the

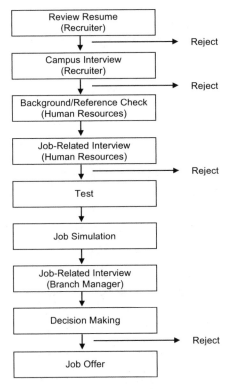

Figure 5.6. Selection system for commercial banking officer.

process and where the applicant can be rejected. Because there are so many components in a typical selection process, it has to be organized very carefully so that the selection time is minimized.

Just as recruiting methods have changed, so have selection methods. Table 5.7 shows the nontraditional selection methods now being utilized to make better employment decisions. Executives are anxious to ensure a good fit for an employee

Table 5.7. The shifts in selection methods.

Traditional selection methods	Nontraditional selection methods
Resumes	Behavioral interviews
Background checks	Job simulations
Reference checks	Pre-employment training
Testing	Assessment centers
Physical exams	Work samples
Drug testing	Referral profiles
Interviews	Internships

before the ultimate selection is made. After it is made, it becomes expensive, time consuming, and disruptive to make adjustments or changes.

Employing talent comprises the processing and administrative steps. Timing and convenience are the concerns as new talent joins the organization. All payroll tax forms and employee benefits forms need to be completed. An organized system is the key to handling these steps efficiently, effectively, and with as little frustration as possible. Two important problem areas must be avoided: administrative delays in the processing and unpleasant surprises, particularly those that can create a negative first impression.

Developing Talent

After the new talent is hired, the learning and development process begins with on-boarding, initial training and learning for the job, and development to refine processes and improve capability as well as prepare individuals for other job positions.

Initial indoctrination and orientation (or on-boarding, as it is sometimes called) creates early impressions that are lasting. It is important for new talent to have a positive first day on the job and an outstanding first week. In some job situations, where employees have an opportunity to move quickly to another job with little investment, an unpleasant experience in the first week of work may result in an early turnover. The early turnover measure is the number of departures in the first month of employment. When this number is excessive, 10 percent for example, this is an indication that either the selections are improper or something is happening in the early days of employment to change their opinion.

On-boarding helps individuals align with the organization and its values, mission, philosophy, policies, and practices. Employees must understand the rules, practices, and policies—even the unwritten ones—so that initial success can be ensured. It is important to avoid frustrating experiences, missteps, miscues, and unpleasant surprises. At the same time, this is the best opportunity to secure employee commitment to the organization. Both the motivation and the potential for engagement is extremely high. The efficiency and effectiveness of handling the orientation are important.

Regardless of the level of talent, a certain amount of preparation for the job is necessary. For some, it may be significant, as in preparing for skills or applications unique to the job. For most, it will be a matter of adjusting to the situation and learning specific practices, technology, and procedures. If the competencies are already in place, significant skill building will not be needed. If these competencies do not exist, significant training may be required.

A variety of learning and development programs must be available to continue to improve performance, refine skills, learn new techniques, and adjust to changing technology. A variety of development methods should be used, with specific emphasis on the nontraditional ones.

Succession management is preparation for the next job. Because today's employees are interested in all types of career movement and development opportunities, several approaches are utilized and explored. Succession planning is part of this, as well as other types of replacement planning.

Managing Talent

With talent in place and performing, the next challenge is to ensure that performance improves and employees are highly motivated and thoroughly utilized. Managing talent involves two new responsibilities of the CHRO: managing performance and rewarding talent appropriately.

To ensure that performance is discussed, recognized, rewarded, and understood appropriately, many organizations are focusing renewed efforts on performance management systems. The old approach was the traditional performance review conducted quarterly, semiannually, or annually, which was usually a one-way conversation from a manager to an employee. All parties typically disliked the process. Managers did not like it because there was the potential for conflict and they did not have the skills or the confidence to do it properly; employees did not like it because it did not meet their needs and often left them confused, frustrated, and sometimes angry. The human resources staff did not like it either, because it was not conducted properly, effectively, or consistently.

CHROs are attempting to make this process less painful by automating the system. For example, a typical approach to performance management is to develop briefing sessions and maybe even e-learning modules that show how the process should work and the benefits of conducting these types of discussions. Discussions are often more frequent, and there are meetings between the employee and the manager to discuss performance improvement and set goals that align with organizational goals. These goals are entered into an online system, posted for constant review, follow-up, and adjustment. As progress is made, the status is updated. Performance data are available to others who need to keep track of key issues and see how well the system is working overall. Progress is monitored and the feedback is obtained in a variety of follow-up discussions. This approach brings constant overview, feasible goals, challenging assignments, and alternative delivery, and it saves time and provides excellent documentation. Figure 5.7 shows the performance

Figure 5.7. Performance management system example.

management system at a large financial services firm. An important challenge for the CHRO is to track and manage this type of process so that it becomes a motivational tool to drive performance instead of a headache that creates confusion.

Rewarding performance, accomplishments, and milestones is very important. If used appropriately, recognition is one of the most effective motivators, and another one of the best ways to motivate is to tie bonuses and incentives directly to performance. Nonmonetary rewards can often be just as motivational. The development of these programs is beyond the scope of this book and can be found in many other references.

When providing recognition, both the substance and the style must be considered. Substance is the value of the reward or recognition from the perspective of the person receiving it. If that person places no value on the reward, it will have very little motivational effect. The style is the manner in which the recognition is provided, including how, when, and where. The style relates foremost to the sincerity of the communication and is just as important as the substance.

Retaining Talent

Keeping talent on board, the retention process, is perhaps one of the most critical challenges for the CHRO, representing one of the newest responsibilities. A strategic accountability approach, outlined in Figure 5.8, is needed to tackle the retention issue.[18] This approach has five important advantages:

1. *It considers the retention process to be an important part of strategy.* The executive team is very involved in the retention issues.
2. *The retention issues are measured with bottom-line results.* Accountability is built in throughout the process so that those involved can fully understand the cost of the problem, the cost of the solutions, the potential impact of the solutions, and the actual impact of the solutions—all in monetary terms.
3. *The approach moves logically from one issue to another.* A series of steps are followed with this approach.
4. *The approach is a discipline and a methodology.* With this approach, it is easy to stay on track, because each of the different issues has to be addressed before moving onto another issue.
5. *It is a continuous cycle of improvement.* Starting with a problem ultimately leads to a reduction in turnover. The process continues until turnover is at the desired level.

Ultimately, the approach positions the organization in a preventative stance, working to maintain the appropriate level of staffing and reduce the risk of turnover. Each segment of the strategic accountability approach is briefly discussed in the remainder of the chapter.

Measure and Monitor Turnover

For many organizations, turnover is defined solely as voluntary. For others, resignations and terminations based on unsatisfactory performance are included in the definition. The cleanest definition to use is *avoidable* turnover—employees leaving

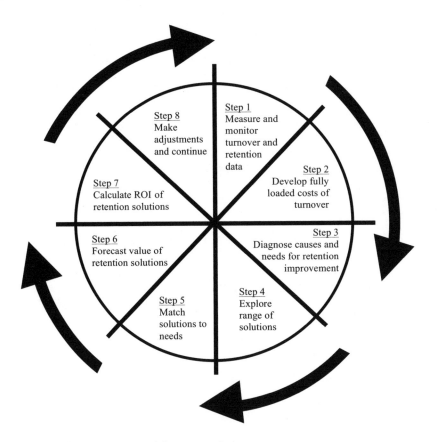

Figure 5.8.   Strategic accountability approach.

(voluntarily) or being forced to leave (involuntarily) when such departures could have been prevented. It is important for the classification to match the definition in benchmarking studies, industry reports, or trade publications. Turnover by demographics should be reported, showing the regions, divisions, and branches as well as the sex, age, and personal characteristics of the individual employees. Job groups are also important.

When using benchmark data and other comparisons, trigger points for action must be developed. When should an alarm sound? Is it a rising trend or a sudden spurt? Is the measure going up when it should go down? Each of these could signal that it is necessary to begin exploring causes and creating solutions.

Develop the Fully Loaded Cost of Turnover
The impact cost of turnover is one of the most underestimated and undervalued costs in organizations. It is often misunderstood because it does not reflect the stated costs in turnover statistics, and it is not regularly reported to management teams, who are left unaware of the actual cost. Although turnover rates are reported routinely, additional reporting of actual costs can be more effective. The fully

loaded cost of turnover, detailed in Table 5.3, should be reported even if it is only an estimate. The total cost will attract the attention of the senior management team, revealing the true impact that turnover is having in the organization.

Identify Causes of Turnover and Needs for Retention Improvement

The causes of turnover must be determined. Some causes appear obvious, whereas others can be deceptive. Collecting appropriate data is often a challenge because of the potential for bias and inaccuracies that surface during the data collection process. Several diagnostic processes are available. A variety of tools are available for use with turnover analysis, beginning with analyzing trends and patterns in particular groups and demographic categories to pinpoint the problem area. As Table 5.8 lists, the tools range from conducting a survey to coordinating a focus group to uncover the causes of turnover.

Explore a Range of Solutions and Match Solutions to Needs

Creative approaches to the turnover problem have resulted in hundreds of excellent solutions. In fact, because there are so many potential solutions to the problem, confusion often results. The solution must be appropriate and feasible for the organization. When matching solutions to needs, five key recommendations should be considered:

1. Avoid mismatches.
2. Discourage multiple solutions.
3. Select a solution for maximum return.
4. Verify the match early.
5. Check the progress of each solution.

Forecast the Value of Solutions

Forecasting is an expert estimation of what a solution should contribute, and the process can be difficult, challenging, and risky. When a forecast for the value of a solution is developed, this allows the team to establish priorities, work with a

Table 5.8. Tools to diagnose turnover problems.

- Demographic analysis
- Diagnostic instruments
- Focus groups
- Probing interviews
- Job satisfaction surveys
- Organizational commitment surveys
- Exit interviews
- Exit surveys
- Nominal group technique
- Brainstorming
- Cause-and-effect diagram
- Force-field analysis
- Mind mapping
- Affinity diagram

minimum number of solutions, and focus on solutions with the greatest ROI. When as much data as possible is accumulated, the estimate is supported and credibility is built around the process. The payoff value can be developed if the percentage of expected turnover reduction can be related to it.

Ideally, the forecast should contain an expected ROI value, particularly if the solution is expensive. However, a more realistic approach is to offer a range of possible ROI values, given certain assumptions, which removes some of the risk of making a precise estimation. This step is perhaps one of the most difficult parts of the process.

Calculate ROI for Turnover Reduction Solutions

Another commonly neglected step is the calculation of the impact of a turnover reduction strategy. This step is often omitted because it appears to be an unnecessary add-on process. If accumulating solutions is the measure of success of turnover reduction or prevention, the impact to those solutions may appear to have no value. However, from a senior executive's point of view, accountability is not complete until impact and ROI data have been collected, at least for major solutions.

Make Adjustments and Continue

The extensive set of data collected from the ROI process will provide information that can be used to make adjustments in turnover reduction strategies. The information reveals success of the turnover reduction solution at all levels, from reaction to ROI. It also examines barriers to success, identifying specifically what kept the solution from being effective or prevented it from becoming more effective. This information also identifies the processes in place that enable or support a turnover reduction solution. All the information provides a framework for adjusting the solution so that it can be revised, discontinued, or amplified. The next step in the process goes back to the beginning—monitoring the data to ensure that turnover continues to meet expectations—and then the cycle continues.

Implications for Human Capital Strategy

Talent management is a critical force for any type of organization. It makes a difference in the success or failure of most organizations. In the current economic climate, critical talent is in demand. We are in a war for talent, and an organization must find ways to acquire the best talent and develop critical talent internally as well. This is an important part of the human capital strategy, which must address the following issues:

- Developing a talent management system
- Defining critical talent
- Assigning responsibilities for talent management
- Implementing measurement systems to understand how the system is working
- Adjusting the system as needed

6

ENGAGE EMPLOYEES AT WORK

Changing the Nature of
Work to Maximize Performance

> *Force 4: Employee Engagement.* Employee engagement is an issue that attracts a tremendous amount of management attention and many resources. The challenge is to make sure employees are actively engaged in their work so that productivity is enhanced, quality is increased, and they stay with the organization. This involves not only the nature of the work itself but the why of the work and the how of the work. This focuses on the different projects and processes designed to improve job engagement. It also involves where and when the work is accomplished. There is a trend toward more alternative work solutions, including allowing employees to work at home in many settings. There is also a push to allow employees to adjust their hours, so they determine when to complete their work. Finally, the design of the workspace makes a difference in employee performance. All these issues need to be addressed in the human capital strategy so that employee performance is maximized.

There is probably no other topic more frequently discussed in the human resources area than employee engagement. Articles, conferences, and books are filled with issues about employee engagement, usually for good reason. Fully engaged employees will remain with their organization, produce more, have better quality, and be more efficient. In addition, they will satisfy customers and increase sales. This is achieved by examining not only the *why*, *what*, and *how* of the work but also *where* and *when* the work is done, addressing alternative and flexible work systems and workspace design. When these issues are addressed properly, they can foster a long-lasting, high-performing work team. This chapter explores a variety of issues about employee engagement, how to make it successful, and how to know when it is successful. It also discusses different arrangements for alternative and flexible work systems and how to make them work—all leading toward a particular set of strategies for these issues.

Opening Story: Quicken Loans

Quicken Loans is a banking and credit services company with $3.6 billion in annual revenue. Founded in 1985 in Detroit, Quicken Loans has nearly twelve thousand employees. At Quicken Loans, employee engagement is not a process, a department, or survey. Engagement is part of the business strategy and culture of this intentionally flat organization. Every employee (called a "team member"), from new hires to CEO Bill Emerson, is responsible for identifying problems and creating and implementing solutions, and team member engagement is evident from its twelfth-place ranking in *Fortune*'s 2015 list of the "100 Best Companies to Work For."[1]

The Quicken Loans "ISMs" book is a physical embodiment of team member engagement at the company. ISMs are simple, easy-to-digest principles that form every business decision at Quicken Loans. The book has a pop-art look and details what is and is not accepted at Quicken Loans, a reminder of the lessons learned from day one: the expectations for empowered team members to not wait for a form or a process, to do what needs doing, fix what needs fixing, and call every customer back, every time, no excuses.

ISMs are written in simple and accessible language, and the ISMs book is updated continually. The spring 2015 edition includes this list:

- Always raising our level of awareness.
- The inches we need are everywhere around us.
- Responding with a sense of urgency is the ante to play.
- Every client. Every time. No exception. No excuses.
- Obsessed with finding a better way.
- Ignore the noise.
- It's not about WHO is right, but WHAT is right.
- We are the "they."
- You have to take the roast out of the oven.
- You will see it when you believe it.
- We will figure it out.
- Numbers and money follow, they do not lead.
- A penny saved is a penny.
- We eat our own dog food.
- Simplicity is genius.
- Innovation is rewarded. Execution is worshipped.
- Do the right thing.
- Every second counts.
- Yes before no.[2]

Employee onboarding is a cornerstone of the culture. Programs host 100 to 400 new team members at a time for an eight-hour session with CEO Bill Emerson and Chairman Dan Gilbert on the ISMs. The ISMs book is distributed, along with Emerson's email address and phone number, to new team members.

All other talent management practices are based directly or indirectly on the ISMs, including career development, performance management, training and development, leadership development, and succession management.

There are no formal engagement surveys. Instead, leaders have regular sessions with their teams to ask what can be done to help them work more productively and be more satisfied with their work and the company.

The workspaces look deceptively whimsical. At first glance, for instance, the customer service area looks like colorful chaos. But the ceilings and dividers are functional, diluting background noise so each customer feels as if he or she is talking to a person, not a call center. The basement copy room, in which the main job is the logistics of shifting paper—a high-volume product for a mortgage company—is light and airy. The ceiling fixtures are playful representations of paper, and natural light is funneled from the street. Team members know that they are key parts of the "mortgage machine" that drives company profits, not just workers in the mundane world of paper supplies.

Elements of fun and functionality are integrated, promoting collaboration and teamwork and ensuring that safety and physical comfort are met so that team members can focus on clients. Venues for relaxation and leisure help team members regain focus. The company also offers team members free snacks, benefits such as pet insurance, and at the Detroit headquarters, on-site amenities from child care to Zumba classes. The philosophy is that while the company's purpose is not popcorn and slushy frozen treat machines in the break room, those things help the company achieve its purpose, because giving team members both concierge service and a sense of fun quickly transfers to customer service. Team members know what customer service is because they receive it themselves.[3]

The Shifting Nature of Work

When you look into any kind of organization, you can see that the nature of work has changed. In some organizations, it has changed dramatically, particularly for knowledge workers in office spaces. This change in work involves the work itself, the meaning of work, and how it is accomplished, including the place, time, and environment in which it is accomplished. This shift is illustrated in Figure 6.1 as the drastic differences between employee behaviors of the past the future. Many of these changes focus on engagement, having an employee who is more connected to the organization, and that feeling of belonging and ownership translates into more effort, more productivity, and more success for both the individual and the organization. Many of the issues in this figure are described in this chapter, and some are captured in later chapters, such as the changes in technology.[4] They all represent important opportunities for change and improvement, and they reflect excellent topics to be addressed in the human capital strategy.

Employee Engagement Is *the* Critical Difference

We've seen the headlines from newspapers in the developed economies of the United States and Europe about anemic economic growth, massive layoffs, scarce job openings, and worker disillusionment due to the demise of the "employee contract." For those still working, they often find a working environment characterized by company instability, frequent management turnover, reductions in health benefits, reduction or elimination of pension contributions, and high levels of stress that

Past	Future
Disengaged with work	Engaged
Keeps busy	Gets results
Finds satisfaction away from work	Finds satisfaction at work
Hoards information	Shares information
No ownership of work	High levels of ownership
Focuses on knowledge	Focuses on adaptive learning
Minimal collaboration	High levels of collaboration
Predefined work	Customized work
No voice	Can be a leader
Focuses on inputs	Focuses on outcomes
Works in a cube	Works in a variety of open space formats
Relies on email	Relies on collaboration technologies
Uses company equipment	Uses many devices
Works 8–5	Works anytime
Works in the office	Works anywhere

Figure 6.1.   The shifting nature of employees at work.

Source: Adapted from Jacob Morgan. *The Future of Work: Attract New Talent, Build Better Leaders, and Create a Competitive Organization*. Hoboken, NJ: Wiley, 2014.

result from either the fear of losing a job or having to shoulder the burden of additional work left by departed coworkers. For those who do find a new job after long-term unemployment, they are often overqualified, underutilized, or hired at lower compensation levels because it is a buyer's market. In rapidly growing, emerging markets, the abundance of low-skilled workers often means a booming economy built on the backs of laborers in modern-day sweatshops and factories, sometimes with disastrous workplace tragedies. Over the past few years in the hotter job markets (and tighter talent pools) in parts of Asia, many employees jump from one job to another in order to move quickly up their personal title and salary ladder with little commitment to a company, its customers, or its mission.

Against that backdrop, it's hard to believe that any company, anywhere, has the kind of employee population that can make it successful, given the challenging economies, increasing pressures from new competitors, rising pace of technological change, increasing government regulation, and heightened geopolitical risk. Yet there are companies who outperform their industry peers even when so many of the products, services, structures, and challenges are surprisingly similar. These companies excel at a variety of business metrics from shareholder value, to operating margin, to workplace safety. They are more likely to be innovative. They have stronger employee value propositions to retain key employees and a compelling brand to attract new talent.

What makes this critical difference? Many would argue, as would we, that the difference is an engaged workforce, which consistently delivers superior performance, creates innovative products and solutions, and serves as brand ambassadors to both drive customer loyalty as well as attract great candidates. But how can companies stem the tide of worker malaise and distrust? What can companies do to drive high levels of employee engagement? How can organizations build a culture of engagement that fosters the kind of employee performance that can make the difference between survival and success? And even more important, how do they measure the impact so that they know whether they are successful?

The focus of this chapter is on employee engagement programs and initiatives at the organizational or business unit level. This begins with an examination of the macro level of employee engagement: what employee engagement is, the factors the drive (or hinder) engaged workforces, the evolution of the concept of engagement, the state of engagement and engagement practices today, and thoughts on building a culture of engagement.

The Drivers of Engagement

There is a great deal of alignment in numerous studies about the drivers (factors that have significant influence) of engagement, which usually reflect aspects of the business culture, relationships with supervisors, and workload. Among the more well-known assessments of engagement drivers are the following:

Towers Watson's 2012 Global Workforce Study lists these five priority areas of focus and the behaviors and actions that matter to employees:

- *Leadership* (is effective at growing the business; shows sincere interest in employees' well-being; behaves consistently with the organization's core values; earns employees' trust and confidence)
- *Stress, balance, and workload* (manageable stress levels at work; a healthy balance between work and personal life; enough employees in the group to do the job right; flexible work arrangements)
- *Goals and objectives* (employees understand the organization's business goals, steps they need to take to reach those goals, and how their job contributes to achieving goals)
- *Supervisors* (assign tasks suitable to employees' skills; act in ways consistent with their words; coach employees to improve performance; treat employees with respect)
- *Organization's image* (highly regarded by the general public; displays honesty and integrity in business activities)[5]

The Merit Principles Survey, which is administered to more than thirty-six thousand workers by the U.S. Merit Systems Protection Board, asks questions to elicit information about these drivers:

- Pride in one's work or workplace
- Satisfaction with leadership
- Opportunity to perform well at work

- Satisfaction with recognition received
- Prospect for future personal and professional growth
- A positive work environment with some focus on teamwork[6]

Research from The Conference Board revealed these eight drivers of engagement to be key:

- Trust and integrity
- Nature of the job
- Line of sight between individual performance and company performance
- Career growth opportunities
- Pride about the company
- Coworkers/team members
- Employee development
- Personal relationship with one's manager[7]

Drivers of engagement have been relatively consistent over time; however, there are now more frequent mentions of both recognition and the desire to do meaningful work (aligning with the mission of the organization).

Stages of Engagement

Engagement science has been evolving for some time, and it has already had a major impact in organizations in terms of what they do and their success. But there is a lot more potential for the future. It is through human capital strategy that additional efforts will be made in this important area. It is helpful to review the status of engagement through the stages of its development—first, with research pinpointing how it arrived and morphed into a powerful topic in almost every human resources function. Next, the status of engagement as a process and a practice is underscored. Finally, its impact, the value of engagement in terms of what is being reported now, is covered.

Research

From its humble origins as research about "employee motivation" in the mid-1950s, predominantly among companies in the United States, to "job satisfaction," to "employee commitment," and finally to the current concept of "employee engagement," these attempts have sought to link worker attitudes to productivity with the belief (even in the absence of definitive proof) that engaged workers are more productive and valuable than those who are not.

Management theory, including the early work of Mary Parker Follett in the 1920s, has long sought to understand the ways in which organizational structure and management practice can impact employee behavior, resulting in improved business performance. In the 1950s and 1960s, researchers like Frederick Herzberg studied employee motivation and the elements of the workplace that drove either satisfaction or dissatisfaction, concluding that these elements are often very different things.[8] Perhaps the most important pioneer in terms of engagement is Scott Myers, who integrated the research of many people, including Rensis Likert,

Douglas McGregor, David McClelland, Abraham Maslow, Chris Argyris, and Fredrick Hertzberg. Combining all this research and making sense of it in terms of its implications for employees and their work, Myers published a book in 1970 to name and explain the concept he developed: *Every Employee a Manager*.[9] In his work, Myers showed how each employee can and should manage their work to a certain extent, with some obvious limitations. For the most part, jobs can be managed by individuals so they feel ownership and responsibility for their work, the ultimate form of engagement. Myers was able to make it understandable and put it into practice as he worked with many executives, bringing this concept to job design and supervisory practices as well as human resources programs.

Job satisfaction surveys elicit information about the way employees feel about their work environment, compensation, company benefits, and management, among other aspects of their workplace. Examinations of the concept of job satisfaction began to appear in the academic literature in the mid-1960s, notably *The Measure of Satisfaction in Work and Retirement: A Strategy for the Study of Attitudes*.[10]

Rates of job satisfaction in the United States have suffered for a variety of reasons, including the erosion of employee loyalty in the 1980s when pension plans changed and off-shoring, layoffs, and plant closures shattered what had become an employee expectation of stable, long-term employment. As part of one of the longest-running examinations of job satisfaction in the United States, The Conference Board's latest annual study reveals that less than half (47.3 percent) of U.S. workers say that they are satisfied with their jobs, compared to the 61.1 percent in 1987, the first year of analysis. This reflects a steady decline in job satisfaction over the decades, which only recently returned to pre–Great Recession levels after hitting its lowest point in 2010 at 42.6 percent.[11] However, while these concepts are related, job satisfaction is not the same as engagement.

Academic research specifically regarding employee engagement began to appear in the early 1990s. Even then, research posited that engaged and disengaged workers offer varying degrees of "effort" and are, at various times, more or less committed to the work and the workplace, as explained in "Psychological Conditions of Personal Engagement and Disengagement at Work."[12] This more esoteric academic work continued to explore the ways in which employees feel (or fail to feel) connected to the workplace.

The 2002 *Journal of Applied Psychology* article "Business-Unit-Level Relationship between Employee Satisfaction, Employee Engagement, and Business Outcomes: A Meta-Analysis"[13] was among the very first attempts to quantify engagement in terms of business results, and business leaders finally took notice, causing a dramatic shift in the level of attention paid to, and investments in, employee engagement.

Practice

Despite all the energy, effort, and resources (financial and otherwise) devoted to the issue of employee engagement for decades, the overall level of engagement in the workforce remains low and largely unchanged even in the face of the ongoing global recession. A research report called *The State of the Global Workplace* reveals that only 13 percent of workers are engaged, 63 percent are not engaged, and 24 percent are actively disengaged. There are, of course, regional differences, ranging from workers in East Asia (largely China) being among the least engaged, at 6 percent, to workers in New Zealand and Australia, where 24 percent of workers are engaged and only 16 percent are actively disengaged. The highest levels of active disengagement in the world can be found in the Middle East and North Africa.[14] In the United States, among its nearly one hundred million full-time employees, 30 percent are engaged, 50 percent are not engaged, and 20 percent are actively disengaged.[15]

Engagement rates, of course, differ by region, country, and state; by occupation; by gender; by seniority level; by remote versus on-site location; by educational level; and by age. When organizations can determine levels of engagement on a granular level (by business unit or division, by employee population or team leader) then a clearer picture emerges from the data as to the relative performance of the groups against their peers. It is only when that data becomes actionable for the short term or even predictive for the long term that employee engagement data has any real value.

Among the most common issues that surface in employee engagement surveys are poor management/leadership, a lack of career opportunities or limited professional growth, a disconnect from the mission or strategy of the organization, a negative perception of the organization's future, and an unmanageable workload.[16]

In 2012, The Conference Board surveyed engagement leaders at 209 companies in twenty-one countries to determine, among other things, what engagement practices, programs, and initiatives are most prevalent. *Employee Engagement—What Works Now?* reported these findings:

- The engagement function reports to the CHRO 52 percent of the time and to another senior HR executive 27 percent of the time, making this clearly a process still owned by human resources.
- Eighty-nine percent of surveyed human capital practitioners said that they have an engagement strategy in place.
- Fifty-two percent report that their organizations have been focused on engagement for more than five years.
- Sixty percent work with an external vendor and 16 percent work with a consulting firm to develop survey questions.
- Forty-one percent administer an annual survey and 27 percent administer one biannually, while 25 percent survey more frequently, leaving 7 percent who do not survey at all.
- Eighty-four percent indicated that their company's approach to employee engagement strategy has changed in the last six to twenty-four months, either greatly (26 percent) or somewhat (58 percent), with many indicating that the change was a matter of "more focus" on engagement or increased accountability.
- Companies are using surveys to measure not only engagement but also leadership behaviors (66 percent), job satisfaction (63 percent), and organizational culture (60 percent).
- Only 49 percent of organizations link employee performance and results to engagement.
- Despite the importance of engagement, 48 percent said that they had no one dedicated full-time to engagement activities, and another 29 percent indicated that they had only one to three full-time employees dedicated to administering, monitoring, and analyzing these programs.[17]

Value

Employee engagement is critical to business performance and a success factor on many levels, from executing business strategy, to financial performance, to worker productivity, to the ability to create innovative products and services. In a recent annual study in which more than one thousand CEOs, presidents, and chairmen listed their most critical areas of concern for the coming year as well as the strategies they plan to use to address these challenges, it was revealed that, on a global basis, human capital issues are the top challenge, first- or second-ranked in every region, including China and India.[18]

Continuing its steady rise in the ranking of strategies to address the human capital challenge, "raise employee engagement" ranked second in 2014, up from third in the 2013 survey and eighth in the 2012 survey. In addition, respondents indicated the critical linkage between "Human Capital" and their next four challenges: "Customer Relationships," "Innovation," "Operational Excellence," and "Corporate Brand and Reputation." In fact, engagement is also a top-five strategy to address the challenges of Innovation and Operational Excellence. Respondents in this survey have clearly put employees at the center of everything.

One of the most comprehensive studies showing the business impact of employee engagement, *The Relationship Between Engagement at Work and Organizational Outcomes*, reveals that engagement is indeed related to the nine performance outcomes selected for the study, with consistent correlations across organizations. Among the other findings are the following:

- Business/work units scoring in the top half on employee engagement nearly double their odds of success compared with those in the bottom half.
- Those at the ninety-ninth percentile have four times the success rate as those at the first percentile.
- Median differences between top-quartile and bottom-quartile units were 10 percent in customer ratings, 22 percent in profitability, 21 percent in productivity, 25 percent in turnover (for high-turnover organizations), 65 percent in turnover (for low-turnover organizations), 48 percent in safety incidents, 28 percent in shrinkage (theft), 37 percent in absenteeism, 41 percent in patient safety incidents, and 41 percent in quality (defects).[19]

A longitudinal study of market performance, *Employee Engagement and Earnings per Share: A Longitudinal Study of Organizational Performance During the Recession*, reveals a correlation between earnings per share and employee engagement levels, finding that those organizations with the most engaged workers exceeded the earnings per share of their competition (even widening their lead during the recession) by 72 percent.[20]

These findings regarding superior earnings per share (EPS) are underscored in Gallup's latest *State of the Global Workplace*, which states that engaged employees worldwide are almost more than twice as likely to report that their organizations are hiring (versus disengaged employees) and that "organizations with an average of 9.3 engaged workers for every actively disengaged employee in 2010–2011 experienced 147 percent higher EPS compared with their competition in 2011–2012. In contrast, those with an average of 2.6 engaged employees for every actively disengaged employee experienced 2 percent lower EPS compared with their competition during the same period."[21]

The linkage between employee engagement and business metrics can also be found in Towers Watson's *Global Workforce Study*:

- Higher levels of engagement can translate into higher operating margins, from just below 10 percent for companies with low "traditional" engagement levels, to just over 14 percent for those with high "traditional" engagement, to more than 27 percent for those with high "sustainable" engagement (defined by the "intensity" of employees' connection to their organization based on three core elements: being engaged, feeling enabled, and feeling energized).
- Highly engaged workers have lower rates of "presenteeism" (lost productivity at work at only 7.6 days/year versus 14.1 days/year) and "absenteeism" than disengaged workers (at 3.2 days/year versus 4.2 days/year).
- Highly engaged workers are less likely to report an intention to leave their employers within the next two years (18 percent) versus the highly disengaged (40 percent), and 72 percent of the highly engaged also indicated that they would prefer to remain with their employer even if offered a comparable position elsewhere.[22]

A Watson Wyatt study, *Using Continual Engagement to Drive Business Results*, found "striking" differences in the performance of high-engagement workers and low-engagement workers: the highly engaged are 79 percent more likely to be top performers.[23]

Great Place to Work, a consulting and research firm, has studied engagement in the workplace for decades and includes trust as part of its model. Companies selected for inclusion on the "Great Places to Work" list, in partnership with *Fortune* magazine, exhibit a higher degree of trust and engagement in the workplace than other companies. Great Place to Work articulates these benefits of trust and engagement in the workplace:

- Committed and engaged employees who trust their management perform 20 percent better and are 87 percent less likely to leave an organization, resulting in easier employee and management recruitment, decreased training costs, and incalculable value in retained tenure equity.
- Analysts indicate that publicly traded companies on the "100 Best Companies to Work For" list consistently outperform major stock indices by 300 percent and have half the voluntary turnover rates of their competitors.[24]

We live in an age where maintaining an organization's reputation and brand is a constant challenge, especially as organizations seek to retain current customers and attract new ones. Frontline employees are the key to success with customers. Numerous studies point to the importance of employee engagement on customer satisfaction, as listed in the *Employee Engagement in a VUCA World* report from The Conference Board. For example, research indicates that the customers of engaged employees use their products more, which leads to higher levels of customer satisfaction, and that these employees influence the behavior and attitudes of their customers, which drives profitability.[25]

The subject of a Harvard Business School case study and later author of a best-selling business book, *Employees First, Customers Second*, Vineet Nayar, had a then radical philosophy when he was vice chairman and CEO of India-based HCL Technologies: focus first on employees and make management accountable to them, as that will result in higher levels of engagement and effectiveness, making for stronger customer relationships.[26]

Engagement (or lack thereof) can also be measured in terms of economic impact with wide-ranging implications for countries and regions. While few employees are engaged and many more are not engaged, companies would do well to take action to mitigate the impact of the actively disengaged. Gallup estimates that economic loss from active disengagement costs the United States between $450 and $550 billion per year. In Germany, that figure ranges from €112 to €138 billion per year (US$151 to $186 billion). In the United Kingdom, actively disengaged employees cost the country between £52 and £70 billion (US$83 billion and $112 billion) per year.[27]

In addition to determining the impact on business performance, human capital programs and initiatives also rely on employee engagement data. According to a report by Bersin, 57 percent of HR practitioners indicated that the employee engagement metric was their most important in terms of determining talent management success.[28]

A Model for Implementation

It is helpful to understand engagement from the perspective of how it is introduced and implemented in an organization. The implementation usually follows several prescribed steps, and there are many different approaches offered in terms of how engagement is delivered. Using the focus on delivering value, we have adopted a model that brings engagement into the organization with a constant focus on the business contribution of the engagement process.

Figure 6.2 shows the nine-step engagement model covered in this chapter. As with most important processes, engagement starts with alignment to the business in the beginning and ends with measuring the impact on the business in a very logical, rational way. It is also presented in a cyclical fashion to show that this is a never-ending adjustment process, always collecting data to see how things are working and making adjustments when they are not. The next nine sections provide more detail on this model.

Align Employee Engagement to the Business

The beginning point with any process is alignment to the business, and engagement should be no different. Business needs and business value is the beginning point that executives want to see. This is expressed through classic measures in the system, usually reflecting output, quality, cost, and time. These critical data are reported throughout the system in scorecards, dashboards, key performance indicators, operating reports, and many other vehicles. A new HR program or human capital initiative should begin with the end in mind, focusing on one of those business measures, such as productivity, sales, customer satisfaction, employee retention, quality, cycle times, and so forth.

Figure 6.2. Engagement model.

The challenge is to identify those measures that should change if employees are more actively engaged. The literature is full of hypotheses on these issues, all claiming a variety of results. This quick review can help management understand what might come out of this. The important point is that if a measure is identified, it is more likely that the engagement process will actually achieve its goal. Beginning with the end in mind is the best driver for the outcomes of the process.

Employee engagement scores, taken either annually or biannually, are impact data, because they indicate the collective impact of all the engagement processes in the organization. These data only describe perceptions, but they are still very important. Engagement, on its own, is an intangible measure in the scheme of impact measures. Unfortunately, many organizations early in the process stop there, merely reporting improvements in engagement scores. This leads many executives to respond, "So what?" So we have to do more, and doing more means that the results of engagement must be identified at the macro and micro levels.

The business impact is the linkage of engagement with certain outcome measures in the business category. The efforts of the HR team should be to illustrate the significant correlation and causation between improvements in engagement scores and outcome measures, which can typically be expressed in statements such as the following:

- Engagement drives productivity.
- Engagement drives quality.
- Engagement drives sales.
- Engagement drives retention.
- Engagement drives safety.

Others have developed more specific measures to link to engagement, such as processing times for loans to be underwritten, purchase cost for the procurement function, or security breaches in the IT function. The point is that engagement scores can be linked to many outcomes, and the HR function's challenge is to show that.

Another way to show the business value of engagement is to connect it to individual projects. In this case, it is not just the overall engagement score that is linked to the business measures from a macro prospective but also an individual project involving individual participants. For example, a leadership development program for IAMGOLD, a large gold mining organization, was developed as a result of low engagement scores. After the program was implemented, which involved almost one thousand managers and cost the company $6 million, not only was the engagement score monitored for improvement, but individual measures that were selected by the participants were also linked directly to the leadership program.[29] The leadership program actually challenged the first level of management to get employees more engaged and to focus their efforts on improving two measures that each participant supervisor in the program selected. As these measures changed, the effects of the program were isolated from other influences, converted to monetary value, and compared to the cost of the program. This yielded a 46 percent ROI in this important job group. In another example, a manufacturing plant used job engagement to improve quality of work, and the study tracking the success of the program examined improvements in quality, converted them to a monetary value, and then compared it to the cost of the program to yield a ROI of 399 percent.[30]

Define and Explain Employee Engagement

While there are many definitions of employee engagement, they are remarkably similar in their emphasis on several common elements. The following come from a review of engagement definitions found in *Employee Engagement in a VUCA World*:

- According to The Conference Board, "Employee engagement is a heightened emotional and intellectual connection that an employee has for his/her job, organization, manager, or co-workers that, in turn, influences him/her to apply additional discretionary effort to his/her work."
- Towers Watson delineated employee engagement along three dimensions:
  o *Rational.* How well employees understand their roles and responsibilities.
  o *Emotional.* How much passion they bring to the work and their organizations.

o *Motivational.* How willing they are to invest discretionary effort to perform roles well.
- The independent, quasi-judicial agency in the executive branch of the U.S. government, the U.S. Merit Systems Protection Board, states, "Employee engagement is a heightened connection between employees and their work, their organization, or the people they work for or with."
- According to management consultancy and executive search firm Korn Ferry, "Employee engagement is a mindset in which employees take personal stakeholder responsibility for the success of the organization and apply discretionary efforts aligned with its goals."[31]

These definitions suggest both alignment with the organization as well as the willingness to expend discretionary effort as critical components of employee engagement. Further, the Gallup Organization delineates three types of employees as follows:

- *Engaged* employees work with passion and feel a profound connection to their company. They drive innovation and move the organization forward.
- *Not-engaged* employees are essentially "checked out." They're sleepwalking through their workday, putting time—but not energy or passion—into their work.
- *Actively disengaged* employees aren't just unhappy at work; they're busy acting out their unhappiness. Every day, these workers undermine what their engaged coworkers accomplish.[32]

Of note, one of the more recent developments in this space has been a focus on "well-being," which links engagement to health issues as part of a movement toward holistic work environments. Another development is a focus on "happiness," which seeks a holistic approach to worker contentment by weighing two components: overall life satisfaction and affect balance. (For an overview of this concept as well as profiles of examinations of happiness at Zappos, Google, HCL, Best Buy, and Southwest Airlines, please see *The Happiness Premium: What Companies Should Know About Leveraging Happiness in the Workplace.*)[33]

Executives must communicate not only what engagement means but how it affects them and how their role will change. This part of this step in the model is very critical, because it connects the executives to the process and fully explains what is involved. Some of this may involve stories that are told about what it means to be engaged. For example, there is the classic story of the janitor at NASA who was asked, "What is your job?" while he was sweeping the floors. He answered that he was helping put a man on the moon. Although this may appear to be an odd example, this is the kind of thinking and attitude that is sought through the engagement process. Stories, memos, meetings, speeches, and even formal documents can help define and explain the goal of the process.

Implement Policies and Programs to Drive Engagement

The next part of the process is to enact the different formal processes that will address the engagement issue.

The starting point is to show the mission, vision, and values of the organization. These are well-documented in most organizations, but the key is to integrate some language around engagement. For example, here is what Tony Hsieh, CEO of Zappos.com, says about engagement:

> We have 10 core values, and when we hire people, we make sure they have similar values. For example, one of our values is to be humble. If someone comes in and is really egotistical, even if they are the greatest, most talented person technically and we know they could do a lot for our top or bottom line, we won't hire them, because they are not a culture fit.[34]

After engagement is clearly defined and the dimensions of work that connect with the definition are clearly described, a survey is usually developed that secures the perception from employees. This is an initial survey to reveal the current status of engagement, and the survey data are used to make improvements. This is a classic survey-feedback-action loop that many organizations use as they survey employees, provide feedback to the survey respondents, and plan actions during the year to improve engagement. This is not only a routine, formal practice; it becomes the principal process improvement tool as changes and adjustments are made each year based on the engagement survey results.

Engagement is usually a principle component or determinate of a "Great Place to Work." There are many Great Place to Work programs, ranging from the most well-known, *Fortune*'s "100 Best Companies to Work For," to those of a particular professional field, locale, or specialty (such as diversity). For example, in *Fortune*'s "100 Best Companies to Work For," two-thirds of the determinate for being on the list is the score of an engagement survey given to a randomly selected sample of employees. This is very powerful data, and a positive score is desired by the executive team as they build a great place to work. Being included on such a list helps attract and retain employees, and although the award itself is an intangible, it is obviously connected to tangible measures, as discussed earlier.

Among HR functions, specific adjustments can be made to improve various components of engagement. For example, recruiting and selection processes can include letting potential audiences know about the organization's efforts to have employees fully engaged. Selection may be based on the desire of employees to be engaged in the organization, and more emphasis may be given to on-boarding as a process of aligning people with the philosophy of the organization.

The training and learning programs can be developed to reinforce the principles of engagement; even the method of learning is sometimes adjusted to be more adaptive to the individuals in organizations. Ideally, training is perceived as just in time, just enough, and just for me. That means it is customized for individuals and provided at the time they need it.

Compensation can be adjusted to reward individuals for being more engaged. Since engagement often leads to improved financial outcomes, sometimes this means paying for bonuses, as is particularly true for sales people. It also can be expanded into general recognition programs where individuals are rewarded for displaying proper engagement behaviors or managers and supervisors are rewarded for reinforcing them. In essence, any HR function that involves employees and influences employee behavior can have an important impact on engagement.

Design Work to Focus on Engagement

A huge part of this process is to make sure that the work inherently allows for engagement—for thinking and being empowered. It can be very frustrating for employees when they are asked to be more engaged but then they are still constrained by old job descriptions and structures.

Sometimes it is helpful to think about "where the work comes from." Before work can be done, there are management functions that must be fulfilled:

- Planning—objectives, goals, strategies, programs, systems, policies, forecasts
- Organizing—staffing, budgets, equipment, materials, methods
- Leading—communicating, motivating, facilitating, delegating, mediating, counseling
- Controlling—auditing, measuring, evaluating, correcting

Traditionally, these functions are all centralized in a manager, supervisor, or designated leader, and work is prescribed for employees exactly, sometimes allowing no deviation from their job descriptions. But with an engagement perspective, employees are expected to get more involved in planning what work to do, when to do it, how goals and standards can be met, and maybe even how to source the information or materials needed. They may be involved in not only doing the job but controlling it, verifying the quality of the product, checking to see how procedures are working, making adjustments, and so forth.

This concept of empowerment is a vital part of engagement. Empowered employees take initiative and are held responsible for the things they do. They have ownership in the process, and thus they become fully engaged. Empowerment programs have been implemented for some time and have become an important part of driving the engagement process.

Design Workspaces to Enable Engagement

The workspaces of organizations have changed dramatically from private offices and cubicles to rotating desk assignments, couches, standing desks, treadmill desks, and even to no desks. One constant thing in the process is that offices have become more open. In fact, this openness has been evolving for many years. According to the International Facility Management Association, today more than 70 percent of employees work in an open-space environment, and the size of the workplace has shrunk from 225 square feet per employee in 2010 to 190 square feet in 2013. Work places are smaller and more open, and this leads to some concerns.

The first concern is the actual size of the office. Since it's shrinking, does it provide enough space? This is a concern for individuals who often need space for all their accessories, devices, files, and work. This has led to some alternative configurations that provide this kind of space apart from the actual workspace.

Another concern is privacy. Privacy issues have changed over the years as workplace design has evolved. As shown in Figure 6.3, there has been a shifting need for privacy according to Steelcase, one of the largest makers of office systems. According to their research, in the 1980s there was a call for more privacy and less interaction,

1980s	1990s	Now
More privacy	Less privacy	More privacy
Less interaction	More interaction	More interactive devices

Figure 6.3. Shifting needs of privacy and interaction.

but by the 1990s there was a need for less privacy and more interaction. Now there has been another swing in the pendulum, and there is a call for more privacy and more interaction, but through interactive devices.[35]

This leads to a concern for transparency in that now everyone has access to everything that everyone else is doing. In an open office, employees can see computer screens, hear conversations, read documents, and access all kinds of messages from different devices, making it perhaps too transparent for some. Because of this, there is a need to be less transparent.

Another concern is interruptions. Open offices invite people to interrupt frequently, as sometimes there is simply no way to shut the door in an open office. Managing interruptions can become a very difficult process. A similar concern is distraction within open offices. Hearing noises and seeing what is going on with other employees is a huge distraction to many people.

There are several major trends that have been occurring in workspace design. The first trend is to recognize the power of the open space environment, despite the concerns that arise from it. Figure 6.4 shows the relationship of space and performance.[36] Assigned cubicles and private offices are certainly good for individual performance, but they are not helpful for group productivity where there is a need

	Private Offices	Open Offices
Flexible Seating	Individual and Small Group Creativity • Brainstorming • Small Group Creativity • Refinement	Group Innovation • No Silos • Increased Collaboration • More Innovation
Assigned Seating	Individual Performance • Focused Work	Group Performance • Project Management • Group Work

Figure 6.4. Relationship of space and performance.

Source: Adapted from Ben Waber, Jennifer Magnolfi, and Greg Lindsey. "Work Spaces That Move People." *Harvard Business Review*, October 2014.

for collaboration that leads to innovation. An innovative organization is in the upper right-hand corner of the diagram, where offices are open and flexible and movement is possible between different offices, rooms, and activity areas. Collaboration is an important part of engagement, and it is also an important value for organizations trying to encourage high performance and innovation at the same time.[37]

Another important trend is that the space assigned to individuals depends on the time that they spend in the office. When people are using offices only a small part of the time, they will have a much smaller office. This is a departure from the traditional way in which office space has been allocated according to the title and rank of the employee. Executives who travel a lot may in some cases have a small office because they are not there very often. On the other hand, workers involved in major projects may need the extra space. Big, private offices are disappearing. They are too expensive and not necessarily functional, and problems are created when a person is unwilling to be a part of the social experiment of an open-space environment.

Common areas are developed, like conference rooms or meeting spaces at different places in an open environment, to give people ample opportunities to have discussions. Even little nooks can be set aside for people to meet quickly, reflect, communicate with a small team, or otherwise pull people together. Workspaces are also being designed to get people to interact. For example, Samsung recently unveiled plans for a new U.S. headquarters designed in stark contrast to its traditional buildings.[38] Vast outdoor public spaces are sandwiched between floors, a configuration that executives hope will lure engineers and sales people into mingling. Likewise, Facebook will soon put several thousand of its employees into a single mile-long room. These companies know that a chance meeting with someone else in an office environment is a very important activity for collaboration.

A final trend is that workplaces are becoming more agile. They are not just for sitting anymore but also standing, walking, and moving. Research has shown that sitting at the computer all day is a very unhealthy practice, and many organizations are now trying to give employees the opportunity to get up often, move around, and in some cases even use a treadmill desk.[39]

Design Alternative Work Systems to Maintain Engagement

In the last decade, much progress has been made with alternative work systems, particularly in allowing employees to do their work at home. In this arrangement, actual employees (not contractors) perform work for their organization at home every day of the week. This enables a huge savings in real estate for the office, but there are many other benefits as well.

Several arrangements are available. The one that has perhaps the most impact is *working completely at home*. Under this arrangement, employees essentially do all their work in the home environment and make very infrequent trips to the office, if any at all. To accomplish this, the home office has to be configured as an efficient, safe, and healthy work place. This requires effort on the part of the organization to ensure, from a technology perspective, that the employee functions the same way he or she would in the office.

A second type of arrangement is *office sharing*, where one or more employees share an office. They predominantly work at home, additionally spending short periods of time in the office. In an ideal situation, two people share one office, but the schedule is arranged so that the two employees are not there at the same time.

A third option is *hoteling*, where several employees work at home but come into the office occasionally to do work as well. A suite of offices is available for them to use, and they have to make a reservation to use an office. This office space functions, essentially, as a hotel where employees check in and out of workspaces.

A fourth type of work arrangement is *flex-time*, where employees work sometimes at home, sometimes in the office, and set their own working hours as long as they work the prescribed number of hours. This often takes the form of a compressed work week, where employees may work three days with longer hours and then have an extra two days off. It could also mean working slightly longer hours each day to have a half-day off or coming to work early in the morning and leaving early in the afternoon.

Another option is *job sharing*, where two people are charged with doing one specific job. Each person works about half of the hours, and they coordinate their schedules so that they are not both there at the same time. Essentially, they are teaming up to get the job done but still working individually (each on a part-time basis).

Finally, there is *part-time* work, where individuals work reduced hours, receive limited benefits, and free up office space for others when they are not there. This allows employees the flexibility of having more time off while still remaining employed with the organization.

Whatever the arrangement, it has to be fully prescribed and have specific conditions and rules. The following box details the work-at-home program for a life and health insurance company called Family Mutual Insurance (FMI).

Working at Home at FMI

Family Mutual Insurance implemented a work-at-home program for two job groups: claims examiners and claims processors. The details of the solution were developed with proper input, as the design had to be acceptable and the execution flawless for this program to be successful.

Design

The design of the program followed the traditional work-at-home model, in which employees work a full forty-hour week in a home office designated for this work. Each office was equipped with the appropriate interconnectivity to the company, databases, and functions, much like an office in one of FMI's buildings. The pertinent ground rules for this arrangement included the following:

1. The office had to be free of distractions. For example, not locating a television in the room was recommended.
2. Employees had to work on a set schedule if they were required to have direct contact with customers, which most did. Employees had to log on at the time they began their work and log off when they had completed their work for the day.

---

continued

3. The workflow system contained mechanisms for monitoring the work being accomplished. Each activity could be easily tracked to provide a user performance profile. In essence, the system determined if a person was working and recorded the results.
4. The home office had to be designed for efficiency, good health, and safety.
5. Employees were urged to take short breaks and reenergize as necessary and to always take a lunch break. The total amount of expected actual work time was forty hours per week.
6. Employees were required to negotiate expectations and agreements with their families and significant others.
7. When employees took time off for personal errands, visits to the doctor, or other breaks, this time was subtracted from their time worked. Employees were required to make up that time during the week.
8. Employees had to stay in touch with the office and periodically make contact with their immediate manager.
9. Employees had to sign a work-at-home pledge and attend a training session on working at home.
10. Because there was an initial investment in equipment, computers, and connections, employees were required to sign a two-year commitment to continue to work for FMI, with certain conditions. If they were to leave the company before the end of two years, they would be required to pay back the setup charges, estimated to be about $5,000.

The principal stakeholders agreed on the design. It was reviewed by a group of employees in focus groups and then modified to produce the final set of regulations.

Execution

With the design finalized, the program was launched via communications to the target group of 950 employees. Employees received memos explaining the program and were asked to attend briefing sessions during formal working hours to discuss the work-at-home arrangement. In all, twenty-one employee meetings were held for the 950 employees, and managers held meetings with their respective teams to discuss the advantages and disadvantages of the process. Employees were given three weeks to decide whether to enroll in the program.[40]

For a complete copy of the case study, please see *Measuring ROI in Employee Relations and Compliance: Case Studies in Diversity and Inclusion, Engagement, Compliance and Flexible Working Arrangements* by Jack Phillips and Patti P. Phillips.

Benefits of Working at Home

There are many benefits derived from this type of program. First and foremost, this often leads to high levels of job satisfaction, as employees have the convenience of working at home and the personal savings of time and money from the elimination of their commute. This is particularly important for employees who have to drive long distances to go to work. These employees often come to work stressed, and their lengthy commutes may take many hours out of their day.

Job satisfaction often leads to retention. Some employees want to work in organizations where they have an opportunity to work at home, so this is a good way to attract employees and keep them. Most studies point to this flexibility leading to increased tenure.

Absenteeism is usually reduced with these arrangements. Sometimes employees need time to take care of personal errands and unexpected situations. With flexible arrangements, they can work those situations into their schedule. Of course, part of the rules are for them to ensure that they are completing all their work and working the numbers of hours required. Having a work-at-home situation may give them the flexibility they need to take care of emergencies or critical appointments so they do not have to take time off. Additionally, there is less sick time, because employees are not exposed to contagious illnesses that may come through an office or spread through public contact.

In offices where there is a high risk of accidents, these arrangements will eliminate those accidents. This is not a payoff for all organizations, but it is significant if there are hazards in the office where employees work.

Most studies show that employees are actually more productive when working at home. There are several explanations for this. The first is that they are less stressed and are more energized to do the work. Second, they often give a little more, because they are saving so much time from not commuting that they do not mind a little extra effort to make sure their performance is where it needs to be. Third, employees are sometimes concerned that their immediate manager may think they are not working a full eight hours a day, so they give more just to ensure that it does not become an issue. Fourth, there are often distractions at work that are avoided at home, such as frequent interruptions by coworkers, longer lunch periods, and unnecessary breaks. These productivity payoffs are observed in both businesses and governments. For example, one case study for the Internal Revenue Service showed improvements in productivity for examiners. Essentially, they could handle more cases working at home than they did in the office.

Eliminating the commute alone means there is much less stress with this arrangement. Due to stressful commutes, employees are often frazzled when they get to work, frazzled when they get home, or both. Working at home eliminates that kind of high-stress activity and often leads to a better work–life balance. Many people credit their work-at-home program for making their work–life balance acceptable.

However, the principle payoff for the organization is the savings in office space—but only if the office space is given up. Sometimes an organization will let an employee work at home but still keep an office for them. This is very inefficient, as the principle benefit is not realized. When an office space is given up, there is often a tremendous savings for an organization, even taking into account the costs of the modifications necessary to make the home office acceptable.

This arrangement also brings much applause from politicians and government agencies who are trying to ease traffic congestion in cities. Some major cities around the world have such congested streets that it takes employees three to four hours to make it to work and back each day. Thus some governments provide incentives for employers to let employees work at home. In the Netherlands, a proposed law gives the employee the right to work at home. The employer must prove that it will not work. Additionally, because automobiles are taken off the streets, there are fewer accidents and traffic incidents. Although it is not a dramatic reduction, it is certainly enough to add more monetary benefits to the ROI of working at home.

Finally, the most important benefit is the effect on the planet. Although this is not an immediate benefit for a company in terms of monetary savings, it is an intangible asset, and it is certainly a very tangible benefit for the environment, because for each automobile that is removed from the traffic flow, the actual tonnage of carbon emissions that are prevented from going into the atmosphere can be calculated. This is why so many environmental groups uphold working at home as a way of the future. Some environmental groups suggest that this is the single greatest action employers can take to help the environment. These benefits are huge, and when compared to the cost of the program, a very high ROI is delivered.

The FMI example represents a project that was measured all the way through to the financial ROI. In this case, 350 claims processors and claims examiners transitioned to working at home. Although their offices at home had to be equipped with the latest technology, including security software, so that they could effectively do at home what they were doing at the office, there was still a huge ROI. The payoffs included a reduction in office expenses by giving up the office space, reduced turnover, and increased productivity as more claims were processed at home than at the office. When this improvement was spread over one year and compared to the cost of the program, the savings generated a 299 percent ROI, with significant intangible benefits as well.[41]

Making It Work

Obviously, the use of home-office arrangements, although still growing, represents only a fraction of the total workforce. It is not always appropriate, and there are some rules that must be followed to make it work:

1. It should be voluntary. Forcing individuals to work at home usually will not be successful. Individuals must also be eligible. They must understand the terms and conditions, must want to pursue it, and must follow the rules.
2. The office must be designed properly for efficiency, effectiveness, and well-being.
3. There cannot be any distractions, including parental care for children or other types of concerns. For example, there can be no television in the room where the work is being done.
4. There must be certain transparency procedures (like logging in and logging out each day), guidelines regarding how to make up time when hours are missed, communication requirements, and so forth. Work rules must fit the specific organization and what is comfortable for the executives and management team.
5. Along with work rules comes the training that is needed to ensure compliance. Not all employees know how to work remotely, although they may be convinced that they do. There must be some assurance that they understand the ground rules and that they are willing to make them work in their situation.
6. Parallel with the training of the employees, the managers have to have training as well. They need to know how to work with employees remotely and how to adjust to not having a person always available there at the office.

7. There must be effective two-way communication so that there is regular reporting from the employee and regular follow-up with the manager. Good, clear communications are very critical.

8. Engagement must be maintained otherwise it could actually dip with a work-at-home arrangement. If employees are not around their support team, receiving constant feedback from their manager and coworkers, they might not feel as actively engaged.

9. Career aspects should be considered in the process. Remote employees cannot be left out of career development and career enhancement planning. They are often concerned that their career may suffer because they are not considered an integral part of the group.

10. Finally, all legal and compliance requirements must be followed. There must be no discrimination for this offering that would violate any of the regulations for equal employment opportunities and any other contractual or legal requirements.

Barriers

The reason that working at home has not become a widespread and common practice is that there are many barriers to these types of work arrangements. Perhaps the number-one barrier is resistance from the management group. Most managers follow the typical command-and-control model, and they want to see their employees regularly so that they can control their work. A lack of trust between managers and employees will also keep these arrangements from being effective. Managers have to trust employees to act in good faith and make it work.

Having remote employees makes some managers feel that they are less valuable to the organization. After all, if managers don't have to be with the employees, see the employees, or meet with the employees, it might be assumed that the managers are not needed. This concern will have to be addressed so that managers fully understand the purpose of the arrangement and how they can manage employees remotely.

Another barrier is that it doesn't work for every job, of course. Most jobs require a presence—in a factory, hotel, retail store, and restaurant. When a job requires employees to be at a particular place at a particular time, they will not be able to work at home.

This arrangement also doesn't work for every employee. Almost everyone may want to take advantage of this arrangement, as it is a nice-sounding opportunity, but there are certain personalities that cannot function alone in an office setting. To work at home, a person has to be disciplined and work well without social interaction on a routine basis.

Furthermore, this working arrangement can be abused, and this keeps many organizations from making this move. Managers may worry that employees will say that they are working when they are actually not. Unless employee output can be easily measured and monitored, a working-at-home arrangement may not work. Although its potential has been proven in even creative jobs like those of graphic designers and editors, it is certainly more effective when managers can count standardized items such as processed claims or completed transactions.

Another barrier is that employees may worry about being out of sight and out of mind—that they may be forgotten and that their career advancement prospects will suffer because of it. There is also a fear that engagement may be reduced without the social interaction that comes from being in the same space as coworkers.

Finally, the biggest barrier is that it represents a significant change. Some executives like to measure the magnitude of their organization by the number of employees that they can actually see, the big buildings they occupy, and the large meetings that they can conduct. A remote workforce, no matter how vast, is not quite so visible.

Along with the barriers come the enablers, and there are many of them, as this section has already detailed. As evidenced by studies, there are many benefits of working at home for employees and for the organization. It is a good financial investment for an organization to pursue. Perhaps the most important benefit is the reduction in traffic congestion and environmental pollution. This is why this kind of arrangement is pushed by government agencies, environmental groups, and technology companies who indicate that they can now duplicate the work at the office in the home office. The technology is there, the reasons are there, and this should be an important consideration going forward.

Involve Top Executives in the Engagement Process

The role of top executives is very critical in any process, but particularly with engagement. With so much evidence that engagement adds value and so much potential for it to add more, most executives are willing to step up and commit resources, time, and effort to make sure that engagement works. This involves several areas:

1. *Commitment.* The first executive action is committing resources, staff, and other processes to make sure that engagement is properly developed, implemented, and supported in the organization.
2. *Communication.* Employees carefully weigh messages from the senior executive team, and what the team says about the engagement process sets the tone for others. It also shows the position of executives. Top executives should be involved in major announcements, the roll out of programs, and even progress assessments. When major actions are taken as a result of engagement input, top executives should be involved as well.
3. *Involvement.* Top executives must be involved in these programs. They should kick off programs and moderate town-hall meetings about engagement. They should participate in learning programs on preparing leaders and managers to build engagement in the organization.
4. *Recognition.* Top executives have to recognize those who are doing the best job. The best way to recognize exemplars of engagement is to promote them, reward them, and publicly recognize them. Engagement data should be placed alongside key operating results for this to be effective.
5. *Support.* Support is more than just providing resources and recognizing those who achieve results; it also means supporting the programs, encouraging people to be involved, and encouraging others to take action. This shows that leaders genuinely support these programs and their success.
6. *Long-Term Thinking.* Engagement cannot be seen as a fad that comes through the organization only to be abandoned for the next fad. Too often this occurs in

organizations—executives work on "engagement" this year, and "lean thinking" the next year, and "open-book management" the next. The key is to stay with it and make it work.

7. *Reference.* Refer to engagement often, as a driver of gross productivity, a driver of sales, and a driver of profits. Making reference to engagement regularly in meetings, reports, press releases, and annual shareholder meetings brings the importance of the process into focus. Collectively, these efforts from top executives, which are often coordinated by the chief human resources officer, will make a difference in the success of the engagement effort.

Empower Managers and Leaders to Build Engagement

First-level managers are key in the organization. They are in the position to make or break engagement, and they have to be prepared for it. The first step is to conduct learning programs where the issue of engagement is discussed—how they can encourage it, support it, and build it in their work teams. This provides not only awareness of engagement but skill-building around the components of engagement to make the process successful in the organization.

Most important, first-level managers must understand why engagement makes a difference. They must become role models of engagement and take an active part in ensuring that employees are empowered, are involved in key decisions, and assume ownership and accountability for what they do. Managers must demonstrate what has to be done to make the engagement process work, and they must genuinely support it. They must reinforce the concept of engagement, reinforce what it means to them, and reinforce their roles in the process.

Much of this involves learning—learning what engagement is about and what makes it work but also learning what it can do for the organization. Position engagement as a process similar to sales training for a sales team, or production training for the production group, or IT training for the IT staff. This is an important process that managers must learn, apply, and use to drive results. This also means that they have to redefine success. Success is not just knowing something but making it work and have an impact. Making it work involves the behaviors that are exhibited as people collaborate to complete projects, but the impact must show up in improved measures of productivity, innovation, quality, and efficiency.

First-level managers are critical, as they must use all the tools generated around engagement. The HR team offers the many processes and tools to be implemented, but the frontline leaders can make the difference in the success of the process by using the tools appropriately, following up to make sure they work, and reporting issues and concerns back to the HR team.

Measure the Progress and Impact of Engagement

Measurement for this process involves several issues. The first one is measuring the progress with engagement through an annual survey. This assesses the actual perceptions of employees about the progress they are making. The annual survey must include several major elements to make it successful.

- It must be carefully planned, sometimes even with input from those who are being assessed.
- The data must be collected anonymously or confidentially. This is a time to collect candid feedback on the progress being made.
- The data must be reported back to the respondents quickly, so that they can see what the group has said locally and globally.
- There must be follow up, some immediately, some later—all in reference to the engagement program. This survey-feedback-action loop will ensure that the process is taken seriously.

Another measurement issue is linking the engagement scores to a variety of outcome measures such as productivity, sales, retention, quality, safety, and so on. This is covered in more detail in Chapter 14 and in other references. It is an important way for the organization, executives, and the HR team to see the value of this important process.

Success should also be measured in terms of individual projects, such as leadership communications, coaching, team building, management development, and leadership development. These are all programs that often involve parts of the engagement process. It is helpful to connect particular programs not only to engagement but to individual measures that may improve in this process. An example of this is a program involving managers at a retail fashion store where they were involved in a variety of leadership initiatives that also played into the engagement process.[42]

Finally, measuring ROI is the mandate for many top executives. If the CHRO can show executives the return on investing in engagement, it reinforces their commitment to make this process work, and it often improves not only their relationship with those involved in engagement but also their respect for the entire talent management and human resources function. Pushing at least some of the programs to the ROI level is very helpful, and ultimately it is possible to show the ROI of the entire engagement process. This is something that is covered amply in other resources.[43]

Implications for Human Capital Strategy

This chapter has highlighted the importance of engagement, which causes employees to become more involved in and committed to their work. Several elements affect employee engagement. The human capital strategy should consider these issues:

- The definition of engagement
- The role of engagement in the organization
- The organization's structure and process to drive engagement
- Responsibility for the implementation of engagement
- The engagement implementation model
- The measurement strategy for engagement
- Workplace design to enable engagement
- Alternative work systems to maintain engagement

CREATE A PERFORMANCE AND INNOVATION CULTURE

Developing and Sustaining a High-Performance Organization

Force 5: Performance and Innovation. Creating and sustaining a high-performance organization that focuses on innovation is the desire of most organizations. Unfortunately, many of them do not actualize it. Achieving a high performance level often requires constant reinvention, adaptation, and improvement. It requires serious innovation. This issue is facing every organization, and the human capital strategy is the best vehicle to address it.

The title of this chapter is very important, as the words *performance, innovation,* and *culture* are connected. To achieve high performance in an organization, it must be driven by a constant focus on accountability, with a culture that focuses on delivering results to the various stakeholders, including customers and investors. To sustain this over a period of time often requires constant review and improvement of products and services. Innovation is a constant in the process. Innovation can come from several sources, but most of it has to come from within, and this is where the focus on human capital strategy is so critical.

Figure 7.1 shows the intersection of having a focus on high performance, a culture of accountability, and a successful approach to innovation. Where they intersect, a very high-performing, sustainable organization is created. This chapter describes culture in terms of how it can help drive performance and accountability, and how a performance management system is needed as well. Let's face it, most performance management systems have failed to live up to expectations, and part of every human capital strategy should be to revitalize and improve those systems.

Opening Story: The Royal Bank of Canada

The Boston Consulting Group recently reported an excellent example of the impact of a performance management system.[1] The Royal Bank of Canada (RBC)—Canada's largest bank—had experienced a significant drop in financial performance. After

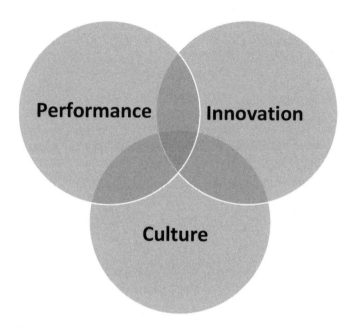

Figure 7.1.   Relationship of performance, innovation, and culture.

ten years of top-quartile performance, shareholder returns had fallen to the fourth quartile. Through careful analysis and by talking with employees from the front line through senior management, CEO Gordon Nixon recognized that fixing organizational and people issues would be critical for improving financial performance and competitive advantage.

Collaboration was poor across businesses. The executive team's decision-making discipline had slackened—decisions were made slowly and without consistent analysis and transparency. And the organization structure, which was costly, was also leading to low levels of employee engagement.

The senior leadership team created a comprehensive transformation program that addressed operations, culture, and structure. The bank's management ranks were restructured, and initiatives that focused on revenue growth and cost reduction were put in place. To ensure the success of these initiatives, each leadership layer created its own role charts, so performance expectations and accountabilities were clearly laid out.

The senior team clarified its expectations for leadership behaviors and revised the performance management system to reward achievement of financial targets and agreed-on behaviors (such as welcoming challenge, being solution oriented, and taking an enterprise-wide rather than siloed perspective). To keep the effort on track, the bank rigorously managed the three-year transformation by establishing clear targets and accountabilities.

The plan worked. Three years after the completion of the transformation, RBC's stock price had doubled, far outstripping the gains of its peers. In subsequent surveys, most employees agreed that the daily activities of the bank and its employees reflected the vision of the transformation and that leaders were behaving in accordance with the new values. RBC continues to monitor its performance across five organization and people dimensions, and it takes action when performance drops or the competitive environment changes.

High-Performance Organizations

Before discussing ways to improve performance, let's define a high-performance organization (HPO). Logically, most organizations want to become high performing, as HPOs create high-performance work teams, groups, and functions. But just what is meant by high performance? The Institute for Corporate Productivity (http://www.i4cp.com) describes high performance in the context of a market performance index (MPI). This measure is a self-reported rating encompassing an organization's performance in four key areas—market share, revenue growth, profitability, and customer satisfaction—as compared to the levels achieved five years previously. The average of the four ratings determines the MPI score. The institute regularly produces documents that compare low- and high-performing organizations and the various characteristics that define the two groups. Sometimes organizations are identified as being in the top 20 percent, a level desired by HPOs. Another organization, the HPO Center, defines a high performance organization as one that achieves financial and nonfinancial results that are exceedingly better than those of its peer group over a period of five years or more. The specific measures examined are detailed in Table 7.1. This is more comprehensive and precise, as seven financial measures and five important nonfinancial measures are compared. What is often missing, however, is the target level that must be achieved on each measure to be labeled high performing. Although some ranges are provided by the HPO Center for the financial measures, they are quite broad.

Culture

A clearly defined, strong culture of accountability can drive high performance in the organization and lead to its sustainability. While there are different definitions of culture, one of the best is offered by Edgar Schein in his classic work, as shown

Table 7.1. The high performance organization.
A high-performance organization achieves financial and nonfinancial results that are exceedingly better than those of its peer group over a period of five years or more.

Financial	Nonfinancial
• Revenue growth	• Customer satisfaction
• Profitability	• Customer loyalty
• Return on assets (ROA)	• Employee satisfaction
• Return on equity (ROE)	• Innovation
• Return on investment (ROI)	• Complaint handling
• Return on sales (ROS)	
• Total shareholder return	

Source: HPO Center. "The High Performance Organization Framework." Accessed April 2, 2015. http://www.hpocenter.com/hpo-framework/.

in Figure 7.2.[2] The first level of culture, at the bottom, comprises the underlying assumptions, perceptions, thoughts, and beliefs in an organization. These are formed and developed over a period of time and are often very difficult to change. Sometimes they are set in place by the original founders of the organization. It is the most difficult area for change. The next level comprises the values in an organization, which are often defined and documented. Some are very specific; others are vague. Usually a strong-culture firm really lives up to its values. Two examples of written values are shown in Tables 7.2 and 7.3. The Coca-Cola Company is a little vague but attempts to set the tone for how the organization should function. Wal-Mart gets more specific, as its values are explained. Wal-Mart has a history of delivering low prices, and they go to extremes to achieve that goal in working with suppliers and employees. It all starts with a value system that is fully communicated throughout the organization and often becomes integrated into the daily work of employees.

The top cultural level comprises artifacts—the visible structures and processes. This includes the language used, dress codes followed, jokes that are prohibited,

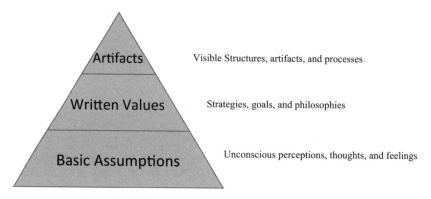

Figure 7.2. Three levels of culture.

Source: Adapted from John P. Kotter and James L. Heskett. *Corporate Culture and Performance.* New York: Free Press, 1992.

Table 7.2. The Coca-Cola Company values.

- Live our values
- Our values serve as a compass for our actions and describe how we behave in the world
- Leadership: The courage to shape a better future
- Collaboration: Leverage collective genius
- Integrity: Be real
- Accountability: If it is to be, it's up to me
- Passion: Committed in heart and mind
- Diversity: As inclusive as our brands
- Quality: What we do, we do well

Source: "Mission, Vision, & Value." Coca-Cola Company. Accessed December 29, 2014. http://www.coca-colacompany.com/our-company/mission-vision-values.

Table 7.3. The Wal-Mart values.

Open door

Our management believes open communication is critical to understanding and meeting our associates' and our customers' needs. Associates can trust and rely on the open door; it's one of the most important parts of our culture.

Sundown rule

Observing the sundown rule means we do our best to answer requests by the close of business on the day we receive them. Whether it's a request from a store across the country or a call from down the hall, we do our very best to give each other and our customers same-day service. We do this by combining our efforts and depending on each other to get things done.

Grassroots process

Sam Walton's philosophy lives on today in Wal-Mart's grassroots process, our formal way of capturing associates' ideas, suggestions, and concerns.

Three basic beliefs and values

Since the first Wal-Mart opened in 1962, our culture has thrived by operating with three core beliefs: Service to our customers, respect for the individual, and striving for excellence.

Ten-foot rule

The ten-foot rule is one of our secrets to customer service. During his many store visits, Sam Walton encouraged associates to take this pledge with him: "I promise that whenever I come within ten feet of a customer, I will look him in the eye, greet him, and ask if I can help him."

Servant leadership

Sam Walton believed that effective leaders do not lead from behind their desks: "It's more important than ever that we develop leaders who are servants, who listen to their partners—their associates—in a way that creates wonderful morale to help the whole team accomplish an overall goal."

Teamwork

Sam Walton, our founder, believed in the power of teamwork. As our stores grow and the pace of modern life quickens, that philosophy of teamwork has only become more important over the years.

Wal-Mart cheer

Don't be surprised if you hear our associates shouting this enthusiastically at your local Wal-Mart store. It's our cheer, and while it might not sound serious, we take it seriously. It's one way we show pride in our company.

Source: Walmart.com. Accessed December 29, 2014. http://careers.walmart.com/about-us/working-at-walmart/.

trophies that are admired, special greetings that are provided, and even the arrangement of the offices, furniture, and other visible displays. For example, the offices at the headquarters of Wal-Mart, one of the largest and most profitable companies in the world, are very small and modest. Even the CEO's office is very small with very inexpensive furnishings.

While every firm has a culture, a strong culture is desired. If an organization has inconsistent assumptions, value systems, and artifacts, then the culture is irrelevant. For example, if the dress code varies dramatically from department to department, then effectively there is no dress code. So the key is to have a strong-culture organization. In most organizations, this starts with the founding leaders. Because they believe in the organization so much, the founders often communicate, reinforce, and reward individuals who adhere to their distinctive culture.

The challenge is that it becomes difficult to change this culture, often taking much time, as Figure 7.3 shows.[3] The underlying foundation (the beliefs, norms, and assumptions) is the most difficult to change. Change requires consistent core values and constant reference to them, role models from the top down reinforcing the values, and storytelling to explain culture in the organization. Strong-culture firms often have a vibrant storytelling tradition. For example, FedEx is extremely proud of some of the stories that have been generated over the years as individuals have made extraordinary efforts to deliver packages.

Behaviors, which become a visible part of a culture when people are actually practicing it, are easier to change, but still difficult. Selection and promotion systems must be aligned with desired behaviors. In some organizations, a culture-value instrument is used at the selection stage to determine if an individual's value systems are aligned with the organization. This is useful for selecting the right employee because it has been shown to be a very good predictor of success. Low scores mean individuals may leave soon because they don't like the culture. High scores mean that they will more likely stay with the firm because they find the culture to be a good fit. The performance review, evaluation, and management systems described later in this chapter should align with the culture that is desired and the behaviors that are reflective of this culture. Corporate communications should routinely refer to the culture.

At the top level of culture, executives can set strategy to make adjustments to the culture. Leaders can be trained to communicate the culture, support the culture,

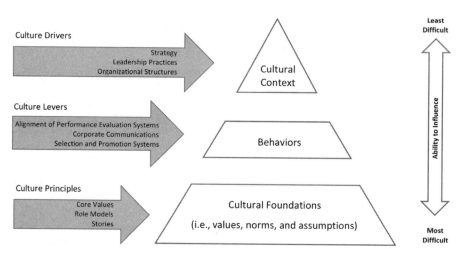

Figure 7.3. Degrees of culture change.

Source: Howard Thomas, Richard Smith, and Fermin Diez. *Human Capital and Global Business Strategy.* Cambridge: Cambridge University Press: United Kingdom, 2013.

and reinforce the culture. Even structures in the organization can be modified to fit the desired culture. For example, Google redesigned their offices to encourage collaboration because it is an important part of their culture. They purposely encourage chance meetings between engineering and sales staff, for instance. Cultural change can occur at a much faster pace, with quick results, at this level.

In summary, culture is often ingrained in the organization from its beginnings. Changing culture requires a determined effort. Some things are very difficult to change, some are easier, but either way, it will take determination and consistency to make it work. In the context of this chapter, the issue is to integrate high performance into the culture, so that individuals can see the need for the performance and understand the expectations and rewards for them.

Performance Basics

As a beginning point, it is helpful to understand some of the fundamental issues around employee performance: the measures of performance that really matter and the ways performance is actually delivered in work settings.

Fundamental Metrics

When determining the type of measures to use, reviewing metric fundamentals can be helpful. The first important issue is identifying what makes a measure effective; Figure 7.4 shows some of the criteria. Use these criteria as a checklist when considering which measures should be developed and added to the list of possibilities. Also stress the factual basis of the measure and distinguish between the various types of facts that go into it, such as anecdotal evidence from employees or empirical statistics. The basis for facts range from common sense, to what employees "say," to factual data.

- *No facts.* "Common sense tells us that employees will be more satisfied with their employer if they are allowed to have a flexible work arrangement."
- *Unreliable facts.* "Sales professionals say they are more likely to stay with the company if they are offered a pay-for-performance plan."
- *Irrelevant facts.* "We have benchmarked three world-class companies using cloud computing: a bank, a hotel chain, and a defense contractor. All reported good results."
- *Credible facts.* "A new procedure in the intensive care unit is reducing infections and operational costs."[4]

Performance Chain of Impact

How does high performance evolve at the individual level? Figure 7.5 describes the types and levels of performance data generated in the process.

Level 0 is *inputs* into the work environment. These are the tools, the resources, and the time needed to do the job—the necessary prerequisites for a person to be able to perform the work. The next four levels are outcomes that result from the individual.

Level 1 is *reaction.* Employees must see that their work is important, relevant, necessary, and maybe even exciting, motivational, or inspiring. This is essential because

Effective measures are ...	Definition: the extent to which a measure ...
Important	Connects to strategically important business objectives rather than to what is easy to measure
Complete	Adequately tracks the entire phenomenon rather than only part of the phenomenon
Timely	Tracks at the right time rather than being held to an arbitrary date
Visible	Is public, openly known, and tracked by those affected by it, rather than being collected privately for management's eyes only
Controllable	Tracks outcomes created by those affected by it who have a clear line of sight from the measure to results
Cost-effective	Is efficient to track using existing data or data that are easy to monitor without requiring new procedures
Interpretable	Creates data that are easy to make sense of and that translate into employee action
Simple	Is easy to understand from each stakeholder's perspective
Specific	Is clearly defined so that people quickly understand and relate to the measure
Collectible	Can be collected with no more effort than is proportional to the usefulness that results
Team-based	Will have value in the judgment of a team of individuals, not in the judgment of just one individual
Credible	Provides information that is valid and reliable in the eyes of management

Figure 7.4. Criteria for effective measures.

Source: Steve Kerr. "On the Folly of Rewarding A, While Hoping for B." *Academy of Management Journal* 18 (1995): 769–783; Andrew Mayo. *Measuring Human Capital.* Institute of Chartered Accountants research report, June 2003.

adverse reaction spells unsatisfactory performance. All those involved must make sure that the work is designed and communicated properly to obtain the correct reaction.

Level 2 is *learning* to do the work, which can occur primarily on the job, through the experience itself. It can occur through planned training, rotational assignments, or coaching, and it can also occur in a classroom or online. One way or another, the employee must learn to do the job properly. If there is no learning, or if the learning is inadequate, performance will be unsatisfactory.

Level 3 is *application*, where actual actions are being taken, projects are under way, technology is being used, and procedures are being followed. This is what is visible—what others see when people are working. Table 7.4 shows the types of action words that often describe the activity of doing the work, applying what is needed on the job. Although executives clearly see that this is a necessary step to achieve results, it can go astray through misguided actions or activities.

Level	Measurement Focus	Typical Measures
0: Inputs ↓	Inputs into the work, including indicators representing resource's scope, efficiency, and costs.	Access to tools, technology, materials, number of people involved, hours of involvement, budget.
1: Reaction ↓	Reaction to the work, including perceived value of the work.	Relevance, importance, usefulness, fairness, appropriateness, useful motivational, necessity.
2:Learning ↓	Learning to do the job including the confidence to be successful.	Skills, knowledge, capacity, competencies, confidence, contacts.
3: Application and Implementation ↓	The actions taken, use of tools, knowledge, materials, and system in the work environment.	Extent of use, task completions, frequency of use, actions completed, success with use, barriers to use, enablers to use.
4: Impact	The consequences of actions, use of the tools, materials, and system expressed as business impact measures of output, quality, cost, and time.	Productivity, customers served, revenue, accidents, incidents, quality, errors, cycle times, costs, project completions, efficiency customer satisfaction, employee engagement.

Figure 7.5. High-performance chain of impact.

The key is Level 4: *impact*. Managers may say they are busy, but are they actually getting results? The impact of each individual's work comprises personal productivity (output), the mistakes made along the way (quality), the time it takes to do the work (time), and the costs accumulated in the process (costs). Output, quality, time, and costs are the four major categories of impact. Although these data items roll up to the measures at the top—organizational production, sales, market share, and profits—it all begins at the individual level, driven by the chain of impact detailed in Figure 7.5. These levels of data are helpful because they show us the different points where things can break down. Part of the purpose of a performance management system is to understand what is working and what is not working. This leads us to a discussion of how performance management systems themselves are working.

Performance Management Systems

Performance management systems exist in every organization, ranging from loosely organized approaches in smaller firms to very detailed, documented, and

Table 7.4. Action words for performing.

Develop	Approve	Lead	Maintain	Publicize
Prepare	Control	Produce	Operate	Write
Assist	Plan	Coordinate	Direct	Reject
Perform	Administer	Evaluate	Select	Program
Recommend	Determine	Schedule	Establish	Hold
Review	Counsel	Analyze	Execute	Identify
Order	Allocate	Organize	Test	Correct
Assign	Improve	Interview	Initiate	Compare
Provide	Ensure	Compile	Inform	Purchase
Terminate	Issue	Authorize	Screen	Protect
Reboot	Negotiate	Arrange	Disburse	Guide
Meet	Formulate	Contract	Investigate	Report
Train	Account	Promote	Propose	Create
Change	Forecast	Acquire	Serve	Extend
Justify	Appraise	Contribute	Design	Collect
Consider	Activate	Remove	Interpret	Delegate
Release	Select	Audit	Request	Distribute
Upgrade	Handle	Transfer	Discharge	Replace
Sell		Recruit		Contact

bureaucratic functions in many large companies. Of all the human resources programs that are designed to improve performance, performance measurement systems probably stand out as the most disappointing processes. In far too many organizations, the process is not working, and it is disliked by the employees, who perceive themselves as victims of the process; the first-level managers, who see themselves doing something that is not necessary; and the executives, who are disappointed with the outcomes. It is rare to find an organization that is pleased with its performance management system, and such systems often go through periodic revisions, updates, and changes. Unfortunately, these changes are made by examining the old system and making minor, incremental adjustments. What is truly needed is to make a complete change in the system.

Things are improving in this area, and Figure 7.6 shows how performance management systems are shifting. This figure shows the previous approach and the approach that needs to be taken in the future. This shift has occurred in some organizations, but unfortunately, most have yet to achieve success in this area.

The first category is executive view. Too often, executives see this as something that is necessary—that must be done because everyone else does it. Executives often do not see this as a business driver. However, if the performance management system works, it should be driving the performance of the organization, and to achieve high performance, the system must work at its best.

The purpose of the system has been diluted and misguided, morphing it into a documentation process for defending the organization in case there is a challenge. It is perceived as a process for managing poor performance, and it is also perceived as a tool for documenting the rationale for pay decisions. It has rarely been perceived as a way to actually build the performance of the organization, taking average performers and moving them up to above average. Instead, performance systems often require managers to spend more time with the high performers (documenting

Issue	Traditional	New Approach
Executive view	A necessary process	A business driver
Purpose	Documentation, managing poor performance	Performance enhancement
Review frequency	Once or twice per year	Frequently
Rewards	Closely guarded, rare	Routine, transparent, based on performance
Design focus	Top down	Bottom up
Goals	Rigid and specific	Smart and flexible
Documentation	Bureaucratic and extensive	Simplified and flexible
Business alignment	Vague, top-level measures	Specific business measures at the individual level
Evaluation focus	Measure the process	Specific business measures at the individual level
Preparation	Training for managers	Training for managers, employees, and teams

Figure 7.6. The performance management shift.

why they are high performers) and the low performers (documenting why they are low performers and the actions planned). This does not leave much time for the average performers, where most of the improvement can occur.

The traditional way is to set goals and review them quarterly, or sometimes only once a year, with little formal feedback in between. The best approach is to have formal review sessions along with more frequent brief sessions about progress and feedback, so that it is not merely a once-a-year review.

The rewards and pay increases that come through the system are often closely guarded and rarely communicated within the organization. In more clever systems, rewards and pay increases are more transparent, and the pay-for-performance focus of the system is clearly described and reflected in the way it is managed and administered.

The design focus for many systems has been top-down, stemming from the executives who want to see it implemented. However, the design of the system should come from the bottom-up, with employees deciding what is feasible, what will work, and what is fair—understanding of these issues makes a system much more effective.

In traditional systems, the goals were quite rigid. When they were set for the year, employees and managers stuck with them. Sometimes they were nonspecific or vague. The new approach is to make sure goals are very precise, even in terms of application and impact. It is easy to see this precision in Tables 7.5 and 7.6. In addition to being precise, however, goals should also be flexible. As situations change, opportunities to improve may multiply or diminish. The key is to be flexible, smart, and clear.

Table 7.5.   Examples of application goals.

- Eliminate the formal follow-up meeting, and replace it with a virtual meeting by May 1.
- Continue to monitor the process with the same schedule previously used.
- Create a procedure by July 1 for clarifying physician orders in crucial situations.
- Use the new skill in every situation for which it was designed.
- Conduct a post-audit review at the end of each project.
- Submit a suggestion for reducing costs each quarter.
- Enroll in a fitness program by September 1.
- Respond to customer inquiries within 15 minutes.
- Continue networking with contacts on (at minimum) a quarterly basis.
- Increase the frequency of use of the physician portal.
- Decrease by 20 percent the number of times a particular process must be checked.

Table 7.6.   Examples of business impact goals.

- Incidents should decrease by 20 percent within the next calendar year.
- The average number of infections should decrease from ten to five per month.
- Sales should rise by 12 percent during the next calendar year.
- Operating expenses should decrease by 10 percent in the fourth quarter.
- Transaction errors should decrease by 25 percent in six months.
- Overtime should be reduced by 20 percent in the third quarter of this year.
- Complaints should be reduced from an average of twelve per month to an average of three per month.
- By the end of the year, the average number of product defects should decrease from twelve per month to four per month.
- Project time should be reduced by 10 percent in one year.
- System downtime should be reduced from three hours per month to no more than two hours per month in six months.
- Outpatient revenue should increase by 20 percent in one year.

The documentation of the performance management system needs to be as simple as possible. In far too many systems, it became complex, sometime with a complete book describing the process. Documentation should be informative for individuals and also amendable, if it is determined that it is not working well.

Alignment to key business measures has not been clear in many systems, prompting a common complaint, "How does this connect to the business of this organization?" A more effective way is to make sure that there is explicit alignment. As shown in Figure 7.5, connections can be shown to important business measures that roll up to critical measures in the organization. Alignment allows people to see how they fit in the organization, the difference that they make, and the contribution they can provide if they are successful with their goals.

The evaluation focus of the traditional system is to make sure that each employee follows the process, ensuring that all forms are completed in a timely manner, are accurate, and are properly stored in the system. A better focus is illustrating the contribution of the performance measurement system, showing top executives that there is a positive ROI on the implementation or revision of the system.

Finally, the preparation for the traditional system involves training only the managers. In better systems, the preparation involves training the managers, employees, and teams. Though managers still have the key role in the process and make the difference between success and failure, employees need to understand their role as well. Figure 7.7 shows the manager's role at Google. In this case, eight habits of highly effective Google managers are communicated throughout the organization and serve as a catalyst for many discussions. At the same time, Google presents three pitfalls of managers—things that get in the way of making the process work.

The legal issue is intentionally left out of Figure 7.6 because it is constant. It is important for the system to be defensible. Table 7.7 shows the various legal issues that must be addressed, based on actual case law.[5] Avoiding liability should not be the principle reason for meeting these basic requirements, however, as they are very logical and fair to all parties. Being able to defend the system is not the primary purpose of its design; it is just a secondary issue that is taken care of.

Take a fresh look at your performance management system as you develop your human capital strategy. Figure 7.8 provides sixteen steps to follow as the

---

Eight habits of highly effective Google managers

- Be a good coach.
- Empower your team and do not micromanage.
- Express interest in team members' personal success and well-being.
- Don't be shy; be productive and results oriented.
- Communicate and listen to your team.
- Help your employees with career development.
- Express a clear vision and strategy for the team.
- Demonstrate technical skills so you can help advise the team.

Google's three pitfalls of managers

- Have trouble transitioning to the team.
- Lack a consistent approach to performance management and career development.
- Spend too little time managing and communicating.

Figure 7.7. A manager's role in performance management at Google.

Source: Elaine D. Pulakos, Rose A. Mueller-Hanson, Ryan S. O'Leary, and Michael M. Meyrowitz. *Building a High-Performance Culture: A Fresh Look at Performance Management*. Alexandria, VA: Society for Human Resource Management, 2012, p. 4–5.

Table 7.7. Performance management guidelines based on case law.

- Evaluate employees on job-relevant factors.
- Inform employees of expectations and evaluation standards in advance.
- Have a documented process with specified roles for managers and employees.
- Train managers and employees on the performance management process and relevant skills.
- Document justifications for rewards/decisions by managers.
- Provide timely feedback on performance issues.
- Allow employees to formally comment on and appeal evaluations.
- Make sure evaluations used for decision making are consistent with decisions.

Source: Elaine D. Pulakos, Rose A. Mueller-Hanson, Ryan S. O'Leary, and Michael M. Meyrowitz. *Building a High-Performance Culture: A Fresh Look at Performance Management*. Alexandria, VA: Society for Human Resource Management, 2012.

1. Identify reasons for previous failures.
2. Start over with a blank page.
3. Explain importance of performance management.
4. Align performance to the business.
5. Obtain input from employees and managers.
6. Define roles of managers and employees.
7. Secure executive commitment and support.
8. Secure support and involvement from managers.
9. Define/describe performance.
10. Define measures and precision.
11. Make the process flexible, with ongoing expectations.
12. Require mutual agreement of performance.
13. Document with simplicity in mind.
14. Train managers, teams, and employees.
15. Ensure legal defensibility.
16. Measure the business contribution of performance management.

Figure 7.8.   Revitalizing the performance management system.

performance management system is redesigned and revitalized. Following these steps will ensure a system that is workable and appropriate for your organization.

Variable Pay Systems

Pay for performance is always an important topic. Actual pay level is not necessarily a motivator, but when a bonus is distributed based on performance, it becomes recognition, a powerful motivator. To achieve a high-performance organization, it is helpful to pay people for that performance.

The status of pay systems is outlined in Table 7.8, taken from the 2014–2015 salary-increase survey by Aon Hewitt.[6] Business incentives are the most common method. These are bonus plans that reflect all levels, from individual performance to top executives. Second are special recognition plans. These build on the importance of recognition as a motivator, and many such plans are designed to reward or recognize behaviors connected to business performance. Individual performance plans are third, still a very dominate method. An example would be a sales bonus for a sales person. Team awards, cash profit-sharing plans, and gainsharing/productivity plans are less often used but still important.

Variable pay plans have great promise, because if they are designed properly, they can deliver high levels of performance. If you really want to recognize performance, provide additional pay to reflect that. However, there are some very critical issues. The first one is defining the measures of performance, which need to be very precise. Alignment is critical, as the measures selected should be clearly connected to business goals, maybe directly to strategy. It should be possible to see the line of sight from a particular measure connected to the plan to the overall business goals in the organization. The next issue is determining who is eligible for the process. This must be very clear, as it could create confusion and upset some individuals if

Table 7.8. Status of pay for performance.

Incentive plan type	% of companies surveyed that have the following plan type, 2014, all industries
Business incentives—plans with combined financial and/or operating measures for the company, business unit, department, plan, and/or individual performance.	57
Special recognition plans—plans that are designed to recognize special individual or group achievements with small cash awards or merchandise.	50
Individual performance plans—plans whose payouts are based solely on individual performance criteria. Payout amount typically varies from one employee to another.	44
Team awards—designed to reward employees for the result/improvement in team results. Plans provide incentives to individuals on a project work team.	15
Cash profit-sharing plans—designed to award employees a percentage of the company's profits. Plans typically make equal payment (as a flat-dollar amount or percentage of salary) to all or most employees based on organizational profitability.	14
Gainsharing/productivity plans—plans designed to share a percentage of cost savings of a group, unit, or organization. The gains are typically shared uniformly among all participants.	6

Source: Aon Hewitt. "The Status of Variable Pay Systems. U.S. Salary Increase Survey 2014–2015." *Workspan Magazine*, November 2014.

they think they are eligible when they are not. Probably the most critical issue is funding—determining the maximum possible payout and making sure it is set aside and available for the individual payouts.

The plan features need to be clearly defined and followed. Targets should be realistic and achievable. Communication should be timely, routine, clear, and precise. Administration of the plan must be flawless.

Innovation

Innovation is critical for sustaining high performance—not just a matter of changing, but actually getting better. "Reinvent or die" does have meaning. If organizations do not adapt, they can easily fade away. Innovation means having more creative processes, solutions, and products, as well as more creative ways to deliver, service, and maintain them.

Innovation comes from many sources, as shown in Figure 7.9. The two most important sources are within the organization: the employees, purposely drawn to show their larger significance, and the top leadership, which provides the guidance for the innovation inside the organization. The collective energy, creative spirit, determination, and drive of the employees will make the difference. It is also helpful to work with the customers, to find out what they need or want. But sometimes

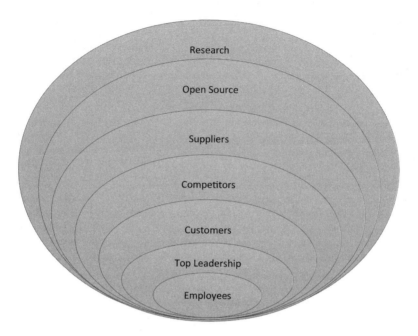

Figure 7.9. Where innovation comes from.

that is not enough. For example, many of Apple's products were not built on what customers needed or wanted, because Steve Jobs was interested in showing them a product that they had not even imagined, describing a need that they did not know they had.

Competitors are another source of innovation. It is always helpful to, as the old saying goes, "keep your friends (clients) close and your enemies (competitors) closer." Find out what they are doing and learn from them. Maybe your organization can do it better or build on what they have accomplished. If an organization doesn't do this, it may be accused of having its head in the sand. A creative spirit also comes from many suppliers. Honda, for example, requires that its suppliers be very creative in their work, changing and improving as they provide better quality products, with more features and innovations, as well as lower costs in some cases. In today's environment, good creative experiences are coming from crowd-sourcing opportunities, which let the public, or some segment of the public, offer suggestions and ideas on how things can and should be improved. Additionally, there is basic research developed by different organizations designed to help businesses improve. Many universities and research think tanks exist for this purpose. Incubators are designed to develop new products and services. Collectively, there are many ways in which innovation can occur, but for the most part, it is probably going to rest internally with employees.

The heart of innovation is capturing the creative spirit of employees. Employee programs range from classic suggestion systems to design thinking. In a suggestion system, employees are encouraged to provide suggestions for improvement and then are rewarded if their suggestion is accepted and implemented. Sometimes these cash awards can be very lucrative. This might also just involve a suggestion box, where employees make suggestions to management regarding how to change and improve things.

Sometimes, sessions are conducted to encourage brainstorming and other idea-generating processes. Some companies offer cash prizes for inventive concepts. Others source creativity and innovation through a pulse survey of all employees, who collectively, usually via a five-question process, provide input on ideas. These ideas are refined back through the employees, and actions are taken by different groups, where appropriate, to bring these ideas to fruition.

A more formal approach is a process called "design thinking," which is illustrated in detail in Table 7.9. This process involves groups and a lot of support, and it is designed to get people to radically improve the organization with a tremendous focus on innovation. Still others are using task-force approaches to bring groups together to develop particular projects. An interesting example of this is a process recently presented in *Harvard Business Review*. This process showed how a minimum viable innovation system (MVIS) can be developed in ninety days, when groups of people are assembled, possibilities are examined, and processes are developed. It becomes similar to an internal incubator for new product development, but it is quick, and that is key because development normally takes far too much time.[7]

In conclusion, it is helpful to put in context how an organization can turn employees into innovators using any type of process. Table 7.10 shows how it all

Table 7.9. Design thinking concepts.

Design thinking is . . .

A way to take on design challenges by applying empathy
An approach to collective problem solving
A framework to balance needs and feasibility
A means to solve complex or wicked problems
A mindset for curiosity and inquiry
A fixed process and a tool kit
A problem-solving approach to handle problems on a systems level
A culture that fosters exploration and experimentation
A design buzzword to suggest that designers can do more than just design
A management buzzword sold as the next strategic tool

Key words that describe it

Human-centric
Speed and agility
Adaptable and flexible
Inspired
Disruptive
Passionate
Purposeful
Creative and innovative
Connected and flat
Fun and playful
Committed
High energy
Risk taking

Table 7.10. Turning employees into innovators.

1. Define innovation.
2. Explain why innovation is important.
3. Teach employees how to be creative.
4. Involve them in creativity and innovation programs.
5. Expect creativity and innovation results.
6. Provide time to be creative.
7. Provide resources for creativity.
8. Measure success.
9. Provide feedback on progress.
10. Reward creativity and innovation.
11. Role model supportive behaviors.
12. Celebrate milestones.

works, from defining innovation to celebrating milestones. The challenge is to capture the creative spirit of employees, providing any needed resources or processes necessary to achieve this goal, giving feedback along the way, celebrating success at particular milestones, and rewarding employees when success is achieved.

Human Capital Strategy Implications

This important area of performance and innovation, achieved through shifting culture, sets several imperatives for human capital strategy:

- Define the goals of being a high-performance organization, and set target dates to achieve them.
- Redesign the performance management system.
- Adjust the culture to achieve the level of performance needed.
- Clarify the role of pay for performance in the organization.
- Implement a variety of creativity and innovation programs, and measure success along the way.

KEEP EMPLOYEES HEALTHY

**Controlling Health Status and
Healthcare Cost of Employees**

> *Force 6: Employee Health.* With the dramatically increasing cost of healthcare and the fact that in the United States, more than 40 percent of healthcare costs are paid by employers, a serious problem is developing. Companies can no longer sustain the projected increase in healthcare costs. At the same time, employees globally are increasingly unhealthy, creating problems with productivity, absenteeism, and accidents. Reducing or eliminating employee healthcare is not a viable option. New and creative solutions are developing that can help enable employers to control employee healthcare costs by shifting to employer-funded individual healthcare and taking dramatic and comprehensive steps to make employees more healthy. This is a critical part of human capital strategy, considering that healthcare is soon projected to cost $4 trillion in the United States, representing 17 percent of gross domestic product.

This chapter focuses on how employers can reduce the costs of healthcare and make employees healthier. Reducing costs is absolutely essential for the financial sustainability of many organizations. At the same time, the human resources function is in the best position to influence the behavior of employees who have developed unhealthy habits. For a necessary and dramatic shift in healthcare spending to be realized, employees must change their habits in terms of diet, exercise, and preventative healthcare. This chapter explores the current status and cost of healthcare, how it has affected employers, the deteriorating health status of employees, and some solutions that can make a big difference.

Opening Stories

The connection between health and job performance is widely known, and many companies are now realizing that success can only be achieved with a healthy workforce. The implementation of healthy-living initiatives benefit both employers and employees. A healthy workforce results in reduced downtime due to illness, improved morale, increased productivity, and higher employee retention, and employees get the benefits of increased job satisfaction and an improved ability to handle stress. Plus, getting a workout while getting some work done sounds good, too. Here's a look at three companies that are taking steps to improve employee health.[1]

Progressive Insurance

Headquartered in Cleveland, this national insurance company helps their twenty-five thousand employees stay healthy with an onsite fitness center, Weight Watchers reimbursement program, yoga and boot-camp classes, personal training, and smoking cessation program. Customer representative Carla Minichello lost 150 pounds after eighteen months using Progressive's fitness center.

"These amenities show Progressive's commitment to employees and their daily desire to be productive both in work and life," says Pamela Sraeel, senior manager of benefit services. Sraeel says making a healthy lifestyle more convenient and affordable for employees has resulted in a more motivated and less stressed staff. "When employees are healthy, they feel good. They innovate, solve problems, and take initiative, which is imperative in a tough global marketplace."

Twitter

This social media giant encourages the thousand employees at its San Francisco headquarters to stay healthy by offering onsite yoga, Pilates, Wing Chun Kung Fu, and CrossFit classes. Onsite massages and acupuncture sessions are also available for a fee.

"The attitude and energy we all bring to work is so important to our culture," says Amy Obana, HR and wellness program manager. "But such energy can make us susceptible to fatigue and burnout. Twitter aims to avoid this by offering diverse fitness and wellness programs to encourage renewal so that as employees we can manage our energy better and get more done in a sustainable way."

TELUS

This Canadian phone company has approximately twenty-six thousand employees in thirteen locations across the country and offers internal fitness facilities with cardio equipment, weight rooms, and group fitness classes, as well as on-site massage and reflexology practitioners, active living challenges, and mental health support.

Janet Crowe, director of wellness and work–life solutions, says encouraging employees to adopt healthy lifestyle habits is part of the culture of TELUS. "It's the overall strategy of TELUS to have a healthy work environment," she says.

Don't worry if these kinds of programs seem out of reach for your business. You don't have to build a gymnasium to encourage a healthy workforce. Crowe says wellness initiatives are possible no matter how big or small a company is, and having a healthy workforce begins with making health a priority in the workplace.

She encourages small businesses to begin by asking employees what initiatives would help them. "Don't assume what your team wants, ask them what they need to reach their goals," she says. Sraeel says reaching out to local gyms to negotiate a discount rate or hosting group lunch-hour walks is something every company can do no matter the size. Celebrate business goals with a healthy-cooking class or another activity staff identify as something they'd like to try. "Group activities can be empowering and team-building," says Sraeel.

The New Era in Healthcare

Healthcare reform is front and center in American society, the economy, and the political arena. Costs have grown annually, outpacing general inflation for decades, compounding the healthcare concern. The weight of this cost trend on Medicare has led Congress to pass landmark legislation that is the legacy of the Obama administration. The legislation addressed coverage for the uninsured, affordable health insurance for small businesses, and coverage for minors and those with pre-existing conditions. This legislation was sweeping in nature and has far-reaching implications. In other countries, where a larger share of healthcare costs are usually absorbed by the government, the healthcare systems face the same challenge: provide better patient outcomes, reduce costs, improve patient satisfaction, and serve more people.

Substantial Cost Impact

To pay for expanded coverage for the millions of uninsured Americans, a series of cuts in Medicare reimbursements to hospitals, physicians, and other providers from current levels were used as "prepayment." The expanded coverage and payments for the uninsured were designed to forestall the current practice of cost shifting by hospitals to commercial carriers to cover the uninsured. Hospitals have shifted the cost of providing uninsured care to commercially insured payers via increased pricing.

Healthcare reform also allows employers and individuals to purchase coverage through state-run insurance exchanges that bid competitively at lower prices to offer coverage. These declining Medicare reimbursement rates, which generally do not cover costs in most hospitals, are having a devastating impact on the viability of healthcare operations. Consequently, hospitals of all sizes will need to reduce costs by as much as 17 percent to break even on Medicare reimbursement.

Changing the Rules of the Game

Payment for services has traditionally been based on a fee-for-service model in healthcare. Healthcare reform includes modification to the model by shifting to a pay-for-value-added model via value-based purchasing, penalties for readmissions, and prices that do not cover excessive utilization but instead reward providers for managing population health. The overall concept of the "triple aim" focuses on the following:

1. Decreased costs
2. Higher value through improved outcomes and services
3. Expanded coverage to care for a population or community's health[2]

The "triple aim" approach is a radical modification of the current model for the healthcare enterprise. The healthcare system will shift accordingly with emphasis on accountable care.

Rethinking Organization of Care

Currently, analysts claim $365 billion of waste occurs in the healthcare system.[3] This waste is difficult to avoid in the current fragmented system, which is characterized by payers that cover the cost of care for users (patients) provided by an independent, fragmented market of providers (physicians and hospitals) that are not integrated with care models, information, or costs. The system is full of redundancies and inefficiencies of over- and undertreatment due to excessive, overlapping, and non-integrated processes, tests, and treatments. In the current environment, decisions for improvement are made incrementally by fragmented groups (physicians, hospitals, insurers, ambulatory centers, etc.), each maximizing returns at the expense of the others and at the expense of the patients in the system. Each exploits the other at the expense of the whole to maximize individual gains. This action drives costs of care up in a never-ending spiral. Each group also seeks larger scale to leverage negotiations, again at the expense of the others and the patients.

Generally, the system comprises tax-exempt organizations complemented by public institutions and independent physicians. Physicians are, however, rapidly moving away from independent practice and joining larger groups. These larger groups focus on the patient with a "do no harm" perspective with little or no business acumen in decision making. This process, therefore, makes limited use of financial or mathematical models to determine value added, even when investments are made with financial objectives.

In essence, the industry will not survive in its current form and must reinvent itself with new business models, systems of care, and processes. The system will evolve from care per incident, or pay for procedure, to care for a population and pay for value.[4] This evolution will require a model with lower-cost structures, medical management of care, intelligent information systems, and integrated networks of care and physicians, all accountable for population health. Employers are in the position to have an important role in this development.

The Challenges

Marshall Goldsmith's book *What Got You Here Won't Get You There: How Successful People Become Even More Successful* is especially appropriate for the healthcare industry.[5] This industry must transform fundamentally during a time when demand will increase significantly due to aging baby boomers, who are turning sixty-five in unprecedented numbers each year. This aging population puts enormous pressures on federal Medicare programs and radically shifts the mix of payers in the healthcare industry. As the baby boomers age, they enter the phase of life when the average individual consumes the majority of the medical resources a person uses in a lifetime. They also demand high quality of care.

More demand, lower prices, and higher expected outcomes and experiences require new skills in leadership and tools to permit the industry to determine added value of initiatives, interventions, and new methods. The American Hospital Association, among others, has highlighted topics and key skills for success, including physician relations, community health, critical thinking, financial and quality integration, and risk assumption. At the organizational level, boards of directors and trustees must apply knowledge and skills in healthcare delivery and performance, business and finance, and human resources. After all, success is achieved through people, and the cost of employees is the largest healthcare expenditure. To misjudge the impact and importance of these critical skills will negatively affect an organization's ability to survive during this time of accelerated transition.

The Cost of the U.S. Healthcare System Compared to Other Countries

The Organization for Economic Cooperation and Development (OECD) tracks and reports on more than 1,200 health system measures across thirty-four industrialized countries.[6] In a recent analysis, concentrated on OECD health data for Australia, Canada, Denmark, France, Germany, the Netherlands, New Zealand, Norway, Sweden, Switzerland, the United Kingdom, and the United States, healthcare spending in the United States towers over that of the other countries. The per capita spending of about $8,000 per year is about 60 percent more than the next country, Norway. Expenditures as a percent of GDP is at 17 percent, with France second at about 12 percent. Yet, the United States has fewer hospital beds and physicians and its citizens make fewer hospital and physician visits than in most other countries. Prescription drug utilization, prices, and spending all appear to be highest in the United States, as does the supply, utilization, and price of diagnostic imagining. U.S. performance on a limited set of quality measures is variable, ranking highly on five-year cancer survival, middling on in-hospital case-specific mortality, and poorly on hospital admissions for chronic conditions and amputations due to diabetes. These findings suggest opportunities for cross-national learning to improve health system performance.

How This Affects Employers

The total cost of healthcare was estimated to be $4 trillion in the United States in 2014, and 41 percent of this cost was borne by employers as they provided employee healthcare as part of their benefits structures.[7] Because of this financial burden on companies, many of them are declining coverage. From 1999 to 2013, the average annual premium healthcare companies charged for employee healthcare plans increased by approximately 182 percent to roughly $16,350 per family. For single coverage, the cost has increased about 168 percent to $5,884 per single.

During this period, many employers stopped providing health benefits entirely. U.S. jobs offering health benefits fell to 57 percent of all jobs in 2013, down from 66 percent in 1999. The future is not bright—the average cost of employer-provided health insurance is expected to reach approximately $20,000 per family and $8,000 per single employee in 2016. On average, employees will be paying more and getting less in terms of higher deductibles, higher copays, and higher out-of-pocket maximums.[8]

The trend of declining employer-provided coverage will continue, primarily because of the problems generated by employer-provided healthcare. Table 8.1 indicates the ten reasons employer-funded healthcare isn't working.[9] In essence, having employer-provided healthcare has caused many of the problems in the healthcare system overall, and it is not difficult to see why it works in an adverse way. For example, when employers pay for healthcare, insurance companies want to charge more, employees want to use the healthcare system more, and hospitals tend to do more testing, because, after all, the employer is paying for it. This has sparked excessive

Table 8.1.   Ten reasons employer-funded healthcare isn't working.

1. *It's temporary.* You lose your health insurance if you or your loved one gets sick.
2. *It's overpriced.* You pay $4,000 to $12,000 more than individual health insurance for the same coverage.
3. *It's risky.* Your coverage may be cancelled at any time without notice.
4. *It's limited.* You don't get to pick your doctors and hospitals.
5. *It's one-size-fits-all.* You don't get to choose your deductible or copays.
6. *It's unfair.* You are disqualified from receiving your $2,000 to $12,000 per year share of the trillion-dollar federal subsidy.
7. *It's unstable.* Your cost could double due to one employee with a million-dollar claim.
8. *It's bad for your career.* You may stay in a job that doesn't let you realize your full potential.
9. *It's bad for your business.* You spend time managing health insurance that should be spent on customers and products.
10. *It's bad for America.* Employer-provided health insurance is the top reason U.S. healthcare costs are almost $4 trillion, approaching one-fifth the size of the U.S. economy.

Source: Paul Z. Pilzer and Rick Lindquist. *The End of Employer-Provided Health Insurance: Why It's Good for You, Your Family, and Your Company.* Hoboken, NJ: Wiley, 2015.

costs through extra caution—or as some people refer to it, abuse by physicians, hospitals, clinics, and employees. More on this shift is covered later.

The Health Status of Employees

You don't have to look far in the United States, and even in some other countries, to see that the health of the population, and employees in particular, has decreased. Statistics are presented routinely about this trend. For example, these figures on obesity come from the National Institute of Diabetes and Digestive and Kidney Diseases (NIDDK):

- More than two in three adults are considered to be overweight or obese.
- More than one in three adults are considered to be obese.
- More than one in twenty adults are considered to have extreme obesity.
- About one-third of children and adolescents ages six to nineteen are considered to be overweight or obese.
- More than one in six children and adolescents ages six to nineteen are considered to be obese.[10]

Other statistics detail the increased prevalence of illness and injury:

- *Diabetes.* Obesity has contributed to more than eighteen million Americans having diabetes and another forty-one million over age forty having prediabetes. Most people with prediabetes develop type 2 diabetes within ten years. Diabetes virtually guarantees that you will have health issues requiring time away from work at some point in your life, and 65 percent of people with diabetes die from heart disease or stroke.
- *High blood pressure.* About sixty-five million Americans over age twenty have high blood pressure, a chronic disease requiring medication and one that

dramatically increases the chances of having heart disease during your working lifetime.

- *Cancer, heart attack, or stroke.* One in four men and one in five women will suffer one of these debilitating events before age sixty-five.
- *Car accidents.* More than three million people are hurt each year in auto accidents. Common injuries include fractures, broken bones, and spinal damage resulting in short- and long-term disability.
- *Other conditions.* Most Americans will develop some type of major medical condition at least once during a forty-five-year working life—a condition that could likely lead to job termination and loss of employer-provided health insurance.[11]

With this deteriorating health status and rapidly increasing healthcare costs, solutions that have been developed must become more common, intensive, and comprehensive.

Health Status Solution: Health and Wellness Programs

There is no doubt that health and wellness programs are positive for health and well-being. The question may be, "What is the right type of program for my organization?" This is what the organization must evaluate, and the choices are endless. Many company campuses are equipped with weight rooms, tennis courts, and jogging trails. Some companies offer free gym memberships or encourage and sponsor competitive events. As with many of the newer health and wellness programs, isolating the value of a specific program becomes difficult. With current spending on wellness programs equaling approximately 2 percent of an average corporation's total insurance claims, defining that value becomes more important.

Health Screenings

One element of an overall health and wellness program is a health-screening plan. These are designed to provide baseline information about both new and existing employees' physical health. These programs supplement existing programs that ensure employees are physically capable of performing their jobs. For example, to operate an overhead crane, an employee has to meet certain correctable vision standards. Employees likely know if they have monocular vision. On the other hand, if employees are long-term smokers and have trouble getting up stairs, there is an opportunity to improve their health by encouraging a smoking-cessation program, additional medical treatment, and a very limited exercise program. Presented in a positive way, employees are encouraged to improve their heath, resulting in gains associated with healthy and productive employees.

Healthy Eating and Nutrition

As with exercise, the connection between good health and nutrition is well established. Companies are developing programs to encourage healthy eating both at home and in the workplace. Campuses with in-house dining services are offering healthier products. Some companies are simply buying healthy breakfasts and lunches for their employees. Another option is swapping out the traditional snacks in vending machines for healthier alternatives.

While promoting healthy eating is not an overly expensive proposition, it is still a program that someone in the organization must design, implement, and manage.

Smoking-Cessation Programs

The connection between smoking and poor long-term health is also well established. Most experts agree that smoking takes about a decade off a person's life. In addition, the habit is very expensive for employers. In some cases, smoking cessation in the work environment is fairly easy to implement: simply prohibit smoking anywhere in or around the facility. While there may be some pushback from a group that has been going to a smoking pit for the last few years, overall a nonsmoking facility is well received by staff and employees. For those with difficulties quitting, at least while at work, there are intervention options.

In addition to eliminating smoking from the workplace, companies are looking to provide financial incentives for employees to completely quit. While there are a few compliance hurdles, companies are establishing two-tiered health insurance programs. Smokers pay a substantially heftier premium than nonsmokers.

In addition to addressing smoking among existing employees, some employers today are refusing to hire people if they are smokers. Being a smoker is not a protected status, and companies that are serious about these issues are not hiring those who currently smoke. According to the CDC, smoking accounts for $96 billion in direct medical costs and another $97 billion in lost productivity and premature death.[12] Therefore business takes smoking seriously.

Obesity Programs

Foremost among the health issues plaguing this country and its workforce is the obesity problem. The health effects of obesity are well known. Obesity can lead to a number of conditions:

- Type 2 diabetes
- Heart-related illnesses such as high blood pressure and stroke
- High cholesterol
- Osteoarthritis
- Gall bladder disease
- Liver disease and other illnesses

Obese workers are less healthy, miss more work, and drive up insurance costs. Companies are implementing programs to combat obesity. One place to start is with an employee health-screening program. As a part of that program, encouragement to lose weight and to improve health can be initiated in a positive way with the privacy of medical staff. Other obesity program efforts include the following:

- Educational programs
- Fitness activities
- Individual treatment
- Moral support groups

All these programs are being used as obesity-reduction initiatives in the business community.

Industrial Hygiene

While the role of the industrial hygienist remains devoted to the anticipation, recognition, evaluation, prevention, and control of stressors arising from the workplace, a considerable amount of industrial hygiene work has moved from the shop floor to the main office. Today's industrial hygienist spends a great deal of time working on programs to prevent poor indoor air quality (sick building syndrome, second hand smoke), exposure to diseases such as AIDS and other blood-borne pathogens, and cumulative trauma disorders.

In addition to these newer programs, industrial hygienists continue to develop and initiate programs that include the following:

- Managing chemical exposures
- Detecting and controlling exposures in the areas of radiation (ionizing and non-ionizing), noise, and illumination
- Emergency response and hazard awareness

More than ever, the programs within the industrial hygiene field impact all employees.

Ergonomics

With the rising cost of healthcare and the increase in musculoskeletal disorders (MSDs) as a portion of workplace injuries, much focus has been placed on the field of ergonomics in the workplace. In fact, MSDs are the most common form of workplace illness in industrialized nations. MSDs include carpal tunnel syndrome, repetitive strain injuries, and cumulative trauma disorders.

Comprehensive ergonomic programs are being developed. These programs include extensive training for employees and management, surveillance of data to spot trends early, case management of all MSD illnesses, job analyses, and design to address ergonomic risk factors (force, repetition, awkward postures, static postures, vibration). While these programs address the multidisciplinary sciences addressing the interface between the employee and the work performed, the value of these programs is often unclear. Productivity improvements are hard to isolate. MSDs may also be caused or aggravated by activities outside the work area, and the treatment of these illnesses is different for each individual. While it is widely believed that a sound ergonomics program brings value to the business, determining that value is a difficult task.

Stress Management

According to the Institute of Stress, employers lose $300 billion annually due to excessive worker stress. This is before the impact of healthcare costs, which are nearly 50 percent higher for workers reporting high levels of stress. Given these numbers, stress management/reduction programs are getting ample attention in the business community. Companies are making various efforts to reduce stress in the workplace. Some of these programs include the following:

- Bringing pets to work
- Assistance with time management
- Classes on financial wellness
- Time off for exercise
- Time for meditation
- Mutual support pairings

While the value of some of these programs may remain questionable, employers have recognized that stress arising from the workplace impacts the bottom line and are taking action.

The Payoff of Investing in Employee Health

The landscape is covered with all types of healthy-living initiatives and projects. Health, wellness, and fitness programs are everywhere. They touch every part of a business's operations and each employee within the business. These programs must be integrated, managed, and properly implemented to reap the greatest rewards. There are several factors that help drive the changes that are taking place in the health and safety profession.

The most important point is that these programs work, but only if they are implemented properly. For example, Johnson & Johnson has reported dramatic results with their wellness program. Since 1995, the percentage of Johnson & Johnson employees who smoke has dropped by more than two-thirds. The number who have high blood pressure or who are physically inactive has also declined—by more than half. That's great, obviously, but should it matter to managers? Well, it turns out that a comprehensive, strategically designed investment in employees' social, mental, and physical health pays off. J&J's leaders estimate that wellness programs have cumulatively saved the company $250 million on healthcare costs over the past decade; from 2002 to 2008, the return was $2.71 for every dollar spent. Similar savings are reported in other companies such as Chevron, HEB, Lowe's, Nelnet, and SAS Institute.[13]

Investing in healthy living is not new. It has been practiced for many years, and it has developed in phases, as shown in Table 8.2. The initial investment was based on image, recognizing that it is good to be taking care of employees. The focus was the job satisfaction of the employees involved. Then it became a benefit, implemented to attract and retain employees. The measurement focus was job satisfaction, participation, and recruiting image. With healthcare costs increasing, these programs became focused on cost control. Healthy living is a way to control healthcare costs, improve productivity, reduce absenteeism, and prevent accidents. Health insurance plans provide coverage for preventive programs in the healthcare plan, and health and wellness programs are offered in the organization. The measurement focus was participation, healthcare costs, productivity, absenteeism, and accidents. In today's climate, healthy living has moved to more of a business focus, recognizing that improving employee health is a great investment when the economic benefits of these programs are compared to their cost. However, these improvements will not occur unless the programs are implemented with proper planning, leadership, and execution.

Table 8.3 shows the key ingredients for the success of health and wellness programs. Leadership is necessary at all levels, from those at the top throughout

Table 8.2.   The phases of investing in employee health programs benefits.

Phase	Rationale	Measurement focus
Image	"It's good to be taking care of our employees."	Job satisfaction
Employee benefit	"This will attract and retain employees."	Job satisfaction, participation, image
Cost control	"This will help to improve healthcare costs, absenteeism, and productivity."	Participation, healthcare costs, productivity, absenteeism
High ROI	"This is a great investment when the economic benefits are compared to costs."	Six outcome measures, including ROI, and intangibles

Table 8.3.   Making wellness work.

1. Leadership is needed at all levels.
2. Alignment with business goals is essential.
3. Programs must be relevant to the target audience.
4. Top-quality services must be provided.
5. Programs should be accessible to all, at some level.
6. Make low- or no-cost programs a priority.
7. Integration of programs is essential, because convenience matters.
8. Partnerships, internal and external, must be established.
9. Communication with all stakeholders must be routine.
10. Outcomes at the business level should be measured:
    - Lower health costs
    - Improved health status
    - Less absenteeism
    - Reduced accidents
    - Improved retention
    - Increased job satisfaction
    - Increased job engagement
    - Decreased stress

Source: Adapted from Leonard L. Berry, Ann M. Mirabito, and William B. Baun. "What's the Hard Return on Employee Wellness Programs?" *Harvard Business Review*, December 2010.

the management ranks. The program must be aligned to the business, with clear business goals. The programs must be designed and executed focusing on what is necessary, convenient, and important for employees. The programs must be successful in terms of participation rates and ultimate outcomes. But most of all, the programs should be accessible to all—at least in some capacity. Some programs are more accessible than others, obviously, but ideally they should be available to all employees when possible. Low-cost or no-cost programs are preferred, and having them integrated on site is a plus. Partnerships should be established with a variety of groups that are available to help, either internally to promote the group process, or externally with all kinds of organizations in the healthcare improvement field.

Communication with all stakeholders is critical, letting them know why the programs are being implemented, the importance of these programs to employees, and why the company is pursuing them in such an aggressive way. At the same time, the successes along the way have to be detailed. The outcomes must be developed at the business level, and the lower part of Table 8.3 shows an impressive list of possible outcomes. These are reported in a variety of documents. It is easy to find these kinds of programs available, and when implemented, they can have a tremendous impact on not only the health status of employees but ultimately the bottom line of the organization.

Wellness programs must withstand criticism. For example, in the carrot-and-stick approach, programs have "carrots" to entice people to join and also have "sticks" that force them to do so.[14] This is supported by the Affordable Care Act in the United States. For example, the state of Maryland said its wellness program, required as part of insurance coverage, could bring penalties of as much as $450 per person by 2017 for those who fail to undergo certain screening and fail to follow treatment plans for chronic conditions. The state said the program could save $4 billion over the next ten years, according to news reports.[15]

The "sticks" sometimes create problems, because some groups suggest that they may violate other laws that protect people with disabilities. In places where obesity is defined as a disability, it may be difficult to force people with obesity into this process. Nevertheless, these issues must be addressed in a very aggressive way by employers to reduce healthcare costs and improve the health status of employees.

Healthcare Cost Solution: Shift to Employer-Funded Individual Healthcare

A huge change is evolving in healthcare in the United States, as employees are shifting to defined-contribution health benefits. Instead of providing a healthcare plan that continues to increase in cost and be abused, an employer with a defined-contribution health benefit essentially provides money to employees, either taxable or tax free, for them to purchase individual healthcare coverage. This is consistent with the Affordable Care Act and seems to have great potential. Table 8.4 shows ten reasons to have individual health coverage.

Table 8.4. Ten advantages of individual health coverage.

1. *It's portable.* You keep your health insurance if you or your loved one gets sick.
2. *It's 20 to 60 percent less expensive.* You and your employer pay $4,000 to $12,000 less for the same coverage.
3. *It's permanent.* Your coverage cannot be canceled as long as your pay your premium.
4. *It's not limited.* You get to pick your doctors and hospitals.
5. *It's customizable.* You choose your deductible and copays.
6. *It's subsidized.* You may be eligible for a $2,000 to $12,000 per year share of the trillion-dollar federal subsidy.
7. *It's stable.* You're in a large group, and your after-subsidy cost can only increase with your income.
8. *It's good for careers.* You are free to change jobs based on what's best for your career rather than what's best for your healthcare.
9. *It's good for business.* You spend more time focusing on customers and products.
10. *It's good for America.* It empowers Americans to manage their own healthcare, and it makes American businesses more competitive.

Source: Paul Z. Pilzer and Rick Lindquist. *The End of Employer-Provided Health Insurance: Why It's Good for You, Your Family, and Your Company.* Hoboken, NJ: Wiley, 2015.

Table 8.5. Percentage of employers offering health benefits, 1999–2013.

Employer size	1999	2013
3–9 employees	55%	45%
10–24 employees	74%	68%
25–49 employees	88%	85%
50–199 employees	97%	91%
All small and medium employers (3–199 employees)	65%	57%
All large employers (200+ employees)	99%	99%
All firms	66%	57%

Source: Kaiser Family Foundation. *2013 Employer Health Benefits Survey.* http://kff.org/private-insurance/report/2013-employer-health-benefits.

With these many benefits for the employee and cost advantages for the employer, this inevitably will be a huge trend. For example, Table 8.5 shows that the percentage of employers offering healthcare benefits has been changing.[16] This will continue, and it is estimated that 60 percent of small businesses will switch to defined-contribution plans by the year 2018.[17]

This trend will evolve by necessity, but it is also a creative way of handling the problems of rising healthcare costs and declining employee health status. This is similar to the huge adjustment that was made in retirement plans in the 1970s and 1980s as employers switched from defined-benefits plans to defined-contribution plans. This follows the same concept and shifts the burden of healthcare evenly between employees, the government, and employers.

Implications for Human Capital Strategy

Several recommendations for human capital strategy emerge from the discussion in this chapter. As a preliminary step, you should have a full accounting of the current cost of healthcare and how it has changed in recent years. With that backdrop, it will be clear that individual strategies should do the following:

- Include more preventive coverage within the current healthcare plan until major adjustments can be made.
- Shift the coverage from employer-provided health insurance to employer-funded individual health coverage. Serious communications are needed for this shift, and sometimes negotiations with unions may even be necessary.
- Develop and implement comprehensive and sustainable health and wellness programs for all employees, and ensure that the programs are fully functioning in the organization.
- Promote healthy living routinely with reportable results.

9

EMBRACE DEMOGRAPHICS AND SOCIETAL CHANGES

Using Differences to Drive Value

··

Force 7: Demographics and Societal Changes. One of the most important forces that is affecting all workplaces is how the workforce has changed—how the lives of people making up the workforce have shifted. The principal drivers are the pronounced changes in the age, gender, race, and ethnic background of employees. The challenge of having five generations at work, the rising role of females in organizations, the migration of employees across cities and countries, the shifts in the makeup of families, various causes of distrust in institutions, and declining happiness dramatically affect the quantity and quality of members of the workforce. The way in which these factors are managed can make a major difference in the success or failure of an organization, and the human capital strategy is the starting point in addressing these major changes.

··

This chapter outlines six major shifts that have a dramatic effect on the success of the workforce:

- The increasing longevity of the workforce and the population in general
- The mixture of generations at work, including the emergence of Gen Y
- The growing role and power of women in the workplace
- The changing structures of families
- The evolving challenges and opportunities of racial and ethnic differences
- The increasing emphasis on trust, happiness, and work–life balance

The chapter ends by describing the way diversity must be approached in organizations so that it is managed for value.

Opening Story: Dropbox

Dropbox is a free service that lets you upload and store your photos, documents, and videos, access your files easily from anywhere and share them with just a few clicks. Dropbox was founded in 2007 by Drew Houston and Arash Ferdowsi, two MIT students who were tired of emailing files to themselves to work on across multiple devices.[1] Today, more than 300 million people across the globe use Dropbox to share files with family, friends, and work teams. A recent article in *USA Today* highlighted the struggle at Dropbox to confront diversity.[2]

Employees in the company's San Francisco headquarters have enjoyed many perks such as: a Michelin-rated chef, a music lounge for late-night jam sessions, and major-league views of the San Francisco Giants' ball park and the San Francisco Bay. Yet beneath the gleaming surface, the promising young start-up was wrestling with a serious problem. Like other major technology companies, Dropbox employed mostly white and Asian men.

"Press on the issue wasn't good, which further impacted morale on the topic internally," said Blaire Mattson, head of engagement and monetization at Dropbox. "There were a lot of people working on increasing diversity within Dropbox, and the efforts were showing results. So, for all the people who had worked really hard, the press was distressing."

Because of this, Dropbox's CEO, Drew Houston, resolved to change the culture of his own company much in the same way he changed the way to transport files seven years ago.

The founders had always envisioned Dropbox as a place where everyone would feel welcome, and with more than two-thirds of Dropbox users hailing from outside the United States, they knew they had to build a diverse workforce to design products and services that appeal to a global marketplace.

The CEO thought that Dropbox is still young and agile enough to make profound changes to how it recruits and treats employees, including building an inclusive community and culture. Dropbox is also determined to increase the number of women and underrepresented minorities going into technology.

For years, Silicon Valley companies have downplayed the racial and gender imbalance in the technology industry. But now they are serious about making their workforces more diverse. Silicon Valley has good reason to care about bringing more women and minorities into the fold: Studies show that companies with gender and ethnic diversity are more creative and more profitable. Yet reports from major technology companies like Apple, Facebook, and Google paint a sobering portrait of an industry with too few women and even fewer blacks and Hispanics in all roles and at all levels.

On November 5, 2014, Dropbox became the latest high-tech company to release its diversity numbers. The report shows that Dropbox looks much like other tech companies:

- More than half of the Dropbox workforce (nearly 56 percent) is white, and nearly a third (30 percent) is Asian.
- Women account for about a third (33.9 percent) of the Dropbox workforce but nearly 50 percent of staff in nontechnical positions.

- Women account for just 12.8 percent of staff in technical positions and about a third of staff in management (32.7 percent).
- The percentage of blacks is low even compared to other tech companies. Blacks account for 1 percent of the Dropbox workforce, Hispanics for 3.7 percent. In technical positions, 0.3 percent of the staff are black and 2.3 percent are Hispanic.

Company executives consulted leading experts in diversity, including Joan Williams from the Clayman Institute. They also spoke with prominent women in the technology industry who are passionate about the issue, notably Facebook's chief operating officer, Sheryl Sandberg, and Megan Smith, a former Google executive who is now the chief technology officer of the United States. In fewer than ten months, Dropbox doubled the percentage of women working in engineering and tripled the percentage of women working in design, according to Dropbox general counsel Ramsey Homsany, who also oversees public policy and people operations.

Today, diversity is part of everyday business at Dropbox, from all-hands meetings to hackathons. Dropbox has overhauled recruiting, promotion, compensation, engagement, and retention, said Mattson. From changing the questions it asks job applicants to training moderators to detect bias in the recruiting process, Dropbox is going for "an objective lens" when making hiring decisions, she said. Dropbox has also identified areas where bias may creep into performance evaluations and stymie career advancement. A new program called "Matchbox" pairs employees with mentors. "Droptalks" feature women and people of color, including Task-Rabbit Chief Operating Officer Stacey Brown-Philpot and Hewlett-Packard CEO Meg Whitman. Justin Bethune, an account manager who is African American, came up with the idea for a "Dropbox Dreamcode Tour" during hack week in the summer of 2014. Bethune is visiting high school kids in the Bay Area to share what it's like to work inside a tech company and to encourage them to explore tech as a career. He also led Dropbox's first tour of historically black colleges and universities. This brief story highlights the problems facing organizations that ignore diversity and inclusion. It also highlights the challenges they face to bring about the changes needed as described in this chapter.

Increasing Longevity

The average lifespan of people has changed dramatically in the past century. For example, in Western Europe in 1800, less than 25 percent of males survived to age sixty, while by 2010, that figure was up to more than 90 percent. A sixty-year-old man in Western Europe today has the same life expectancy as a forty-three-year-old man in 1800. In the United States, the portion of the population over the age of sixty in 2000 was 16.5 percent. In 2025, it will be 25 percent.[3] This collective aging has become a disruptive force in many countries and economies. For example, Japan's population by midcentury may reduce by half, and nearly a third will be over age sixty-five. Seventy-seven million American baby boomers born between 1946 and 1964 are now passing age sixty-five—nearly one every seven seconds. The expectations, experience, and value systems of these older people have changed. They usually have better health, more education, and more income than previous generations, and they expect improved quality of life from having access to healthcare, connecting to love ones, and remaining engaged in rather than retired from society. These dramatic shifts raise important issues for organizations.

Longer Careers

The trends are showing that more people want to work longer. Figure 9.1 shows how workforce participation is changing and has shifted dramatically. In 1992, 11.5 percent of the workforce was sixty-five and older. This will be doubled by 2022, when 23 percent will be sixty-five and older. This is being driven by several forces. First, there are now fewer restrictions on people working into old age. In the United States, for example, in most occupations, it is illegal to force a person to retire based on age; it has to be based on job performance and other objective issues. Second, it is well-known that a person who is active and continues to work will live longer. Retirement spells death for many individuals; working longer means a longer life. Third, the need for more money has prompted some individuals to continue to work. Retirement financial planning has not worked for many, as the lifestyles they enjoyed while working require an income stream. And finally, some people just enjoy their work. If you have enjoyable work and you want to stay involved, then why should you retire? This is a question faced by many knowledge workers and professionals who really enjoy the type and nature of the work they do.

Retirement Income

Longer lifespans mean that people need more retirement funds to survive. Unfortunately, not every individual has properly planned for this, and company pensions

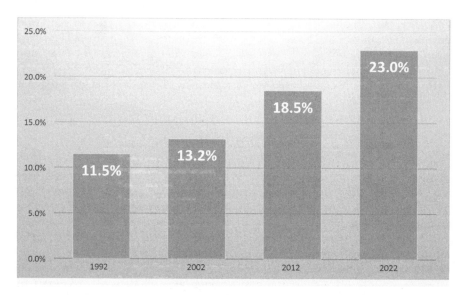

55 and older move from 29.7% to 41.5%
75 and older move from 4.5% to 10.5%

Figure 9.1. Labor force participation rates for age sixty-five and older.

are less than what they used to be. This often leaves huge gaps. Compounding this is the inability of many governments to continue to fund retirement benefits or increase retirement benefits to keep up with the rising cost of living. This means that many retirees are poor, and more of them will be poor in the future. This creates a huge burden for society and sometimes also for employers who provide fixed retirement benefits. In some extreme cases, bulging retirement costs have caused organizations to go into bankruptcy. Cities and counties in the United States have had to declare bankruptcy or default on bonds for the same reason. This generates a serious crisis for funding the lifestyles of people who are growing older.

The increase in longevity is driven in part by advances in healthcare technology, medicines, and new procedures. Increasing the average lifespan comes at a very high cost. The budgets of countries, organizations, and individuals are being strained to cover these increases in healthcare costs. This issue was explored in previous chapters.

Creative Solutions

With this myriad of retirement cost and income issues, many organizations are seeking creative solutions. It may indeed help to encourage the older members of the workforce (traditionalists and baby boomers) to work more years and to tap into their expertise and knowledge. They can serve as subject-matter experts. Traditionalists can work fewer hours on a part-time basis in lieu of full-time work. Employers can take advantage of their expertise and knowledge by assigning them to special projects in the organization. These could involve tackling a pesky problem, developing a new product, or implementing a new system. These employees can work on social-service projects while they are actually on the payroll instead of giving money to charitable trusts. This provides employment, either full time or part time, to this segment of the community and perhaps adds more value than a donation in money would.

These are only a few of the possible solutions that need to be explored as organizations try to maximize the contribution of the aging population as efficiently and effectively as possible. This all has to be accomplished with an eye on the unemployment issue. After all, millennials will quickly suggest that one way to improve the unemployment rate of millennials is to force baby boomers to retire. Both viewpoints have to be taken into account.

The Emergence of Gen Y

It is now possible for organizations to have five generations of employees at work at the same time. Figure 9.2 shows the breakdown of these different groups, ranging from the traditionalists to Generation Z. In 2005, the boomers were obviously a big part of the workforce, while Gen Z had not made it to employment age yet. In 2010, shifts started to occur. In 2015, Gen Z is included, and then the projections are that the millennials, Gen Y, will make up 75 percent of the workforce by 2020.

The millennials have been perhaps the most talked about group in organizations. They grew up in an environment connected to technology, are communicating in different ways, and have different value systems than previous generations. They have evolved with some very pronounced changes in the way they perceive

1. Traditionalists—Born before 1946
2. Boomers—Born between 1946 and 1964
3. Gen X—Born between 1965 and 1976
4. Gen Y— Born between 1977 and 1997
5. Gen Z— Born after 1997 makes up 75% of workforce by 2020

Figure 9.2. The five-generation workplace.

Source: Bureau of Labor Statistics and Chess Media Group. Adapted from Jacob Morgan. *The Future of Work: Attract New Talent, Build Better Leaders, and Create a Competitive Organization.* Hoboken, NJ: Wiley, 2014.

work and the kind of work that they want to do.[4,5] Although some would argue that millennials want the same qualities in a job as others do, the difference is that millennials put a much higher priority on these desired qualities than previous generations. Having a high salary and a prestigious title is of less interest to millennials. However, a work–life balance is very critical, and an opportunity to learn and develop one's own competencies is very critical as well. This means that millennials want to constantly learn from others. They also want to serve a greater good, and this often brings them into concerns about the environment and sustainability. Sometimes, this motivates them to work for nonprofits. Millennials also want to engage with the latest technology and devices. They grew up this way, and they want to continue to connect with others this way. They want to use text messages and social networks to communicate with others. They want a respectful workplace that will give them the autonomy and freedom to do their work without close supervision or micromanaging. They want a chance to be creative and challenge their intellectual capabilities.

The reality is that an employer must be willing to meet these requirements or risk having millennials leave an organization. After all, by the year 2020, these value systems will be held by 75 percent of employees.

Millennials also bring some new behaviors. While some of the classic behaviors are still very important, there are new behaviors particularly appropriate for millennials. As shown in Figure 9.3, these individuals want to be proactive and self-directed on their projects. Employers have to foster, reward, and encourage these behaviors. This generation needs to work independently, and this will need to be supported by the organization. Millennials need to filter information, because they are bombarded with so many different kinds of information. The ability to put filters on different information systems and processes will be an important skill set. Because there are so many possibilities, and so many things that would take their time, they have to constantly focus on what must be done. Some argue that millennials have a way of not following through with things, so this particular skill set helps them determine priorities. Since the workforce, the workplace, and the work itself are constantly changing, the ability to embrace change is critical, and it has to be supported and developed.

Finally, enhancing communication skills will be critical, as well as learning to learn. Although millennials communicate in different ways than other generations, they must have an outstanding communication skill set. They are often criticized as not communicating properly and sometimes not closing the loop in follow-up, so the critical issue is to make sure that these skills are properly in place.

There is no doubt that the millennials will create some challenges, but for some, these are necessary challenges. When managed and supported properly, millennials can add much value to organizations.

- Being proactive
- Operating independently
- Filtering information
- Focusing on important priorities
- Embracing change
- Enhancing communication skills
- Learning to learn

Figure 9.3. The crucial behaviors of millennials.

Source: Adapted from Jacob Morgan. *The Future of Work: Attract New Talent, Build Better Leaders, and Create a Competitive Organization.* Hoboken, NJ: Wiley, 2014.

Shifting Roles of Women and Men

The progress of women and their changing leadership roles are evident in all types of organizations. The German chancellor, the head of the International Monetary Fund, and the chair of the Federal Reserve Bank in the United States are all women. In Fortune 500 companies, the CEOs of General Motors, Hewlett Packard, IBM, PepsiCo, Lockheed Martin, DuPont, Oracle, General Dynamics, Duke Energy, and Xerox Corporation, among others, are all women. Today, 60 percent of the world's university graduates are women, and women control the majority of consumer-goods buying decisions. In the United States, women under thirty out-earn their male peers, and 40 percent of American households have women as their breadwinners.

With this tremendous progress comes some concerns. Women make up 51 percent of the U.S. population and 47 percent of the workforce, yet only 4 percent of CEOs and 17 percent of board members are women, according to Catalyst, a nonprofit market researcher. Women also earn, on average, 78 cents for every $1 men earn, according to the Institute for Women's Policy Research.[6] "Almost no one understands that women have made no progress at the top in 10 years—that is true of any industry and government," Sheryl Sandburg says. Sandburg is the chief operating officer of Facebook and author of the bestselling book *Lean In: Women, Work, and the Will to Lead.*[7] "I want to change the conversation from what we can't do to what we can do."[8] If nothing else, Sandburg wants to erase workplace stereotypes and dispel the perception that a woman can't have it all. One common theme in her book is the observation that as men advance, they are more liked, but as women make such strides, they are less liked.

While Sandburg's personal crusade has earned her much admiration, it has detractors. They reject what they deem the "Superwoman ideal," especially one that comes from an executive-suite mom who has the finances to afford child care and other amenities.[9]

Trends

Labor-force participation has changed. As Figure 9.4 shows, the labor-force participation of men has declined since 1992, and this decline is projected to continue

	Men	Women	
2022	67.6%	56.0%	(Projection)
2012	70.2%	57.7%	
2002	74.1%	59.6%	
1992	75.8%	57.8%	

Figure 9.4.   Labor-force participation of men and women.

Source: Bureau of Labor Statistics, U.S. Department of Labor. "Changes in Men's and Women's Labor Force Participation Rates." *Economics Daily.* Accessed December 29, 2014. http://www.bls.gov/opub/ted/2007/jan/wk2/art03.htm.

through 2022. For women, the participation rate is about the same, which means the proportion of female employees has grown. There are still challenges. While 57.7 percent of women participated in the labor force overall in 2012, in some companies, their participation was still very low, when it should have been much higher. For example, in 2014, when Goggle released its diversity report, 30 percent of its workforce was female, while 70 percent was male.

In terms of ascending to leadership roles, however, the progress has been very impressive. According to 2020 Women on Boards, the percentage of women on boards has steadily increased, as shown in Figure 9.5. For the Fortune 100, 500, and 1000 companies, there have been increases each year in the last four years where they have been reported. In 2015, twenty-five of the Fortune 100 CEOs are female, as well as twenty-eight of the Fortune 500 to 1000 CEOs, for a total of fifty-three women CEOs in the top 1000. Although this is progress, this is woefully inadequate when considering the number of women in the workforce.

Current female CEOs are making important strides to try to help with this situation. For example, Karen Abramson of Wolters Kluwer, a company with nineteen thousand employees in information software and services, indicates that their progress is very important:

> At Wolters Kluwer, we're very fortunate that, as a result of our efforts to bolster the senior team with women, today 50 percent of our senior team is female, and we really try to promote and foster female leadership. In accounting, 40 percent of the people coming into the field are women, but they account for only 14 percent of the people who have partnership and executive positions in the industry. The question is why. I think what we do differently at Wolters Kluwer is we foster general management skills by giving women P&L [profit and loss] responsibility. It's really important that women take the jobs that are going to get them noticed. Those are always the jobs that have clear P&L responsibility.[10]

Female board membership		Female board membership		Female board membership	
Fortune 100		*Fortune 500*		*Fortune 1000*	
2014	22.2%	2014	19.0%	2014	17.7%
2013	20.6%	2013	18.0%	2013	16.6%
2012	19.9%	2012	17.1%	2012	15.6%
2011	19.6%	2011	16.4%	2011	14.6%

Figure 9.5. Women on boards.

Source: Beth Kurth. 2020 Women on Boards Gender Diversity Index. Accessed April 3, 2015. http://www.2020wob.com/sites/default/files/2020GDI-2014Report.pdf.

Regarding some specific occupations, there is some good news as well. Since 1970, some dramatic changes have been made in female participation in certain jobs. For example, in accounting, the percentage of women in the profession moved from 24.6 percent to the current rate of 60 percent; for pharmacists, it moved from 12 percent to almost 53 percent; for physicians and surgeons, it moved from 9.7 percent to 32.4 percent; while for lawyers and judges, it moved from 4.9 percent to 32.4 percent. For positions that were predominately filled by women for many years, such as cashiers, registered nurses, and elementary and middle school teachers, female participation has declined, which is good news. This means that more men are moving into those jobs.[11]

Skills and Competencies

Do females have much better leadership skills than males? An article in the *Harvard Business Review* featured a study of 7,300 leaders and yielded interesting results.[12] According to the findings, women are rated higher than men in leadership effectiveness in every single stage of company growth, whether they are individual contributors, middle managers, or executives.

The article also went on to reveal that out of the top sixteen competencies that leaders exemplify most, women rank higher than men in fifteen of them, often by a considerable margin. These include things such as taking initiative, developing others, building relationships, innovating, developing technical and professional expertise, collaborating, and championing change. The only area where men narrowly edged ahead was "developing strategic perspective," where men scored a 51 and women a 49—but in every other area, women ranked higher.

The aim here isn't to say that women are better than men or vice versa. Instead, it is to point out that women are actually very valuable to the future of organizations and possess many of the desired skills and attributes needed to lead organizations. Men do as well, which is why it is important to have an equal balance.

The management consulting firm McKinsey has a group called "Women Matter." When this group asked business executives around the world what the most important leadership characteristics are, the top four attributes were intellectual stimulation, inspiration, participatory decision making, and setting expectations and rewards. According to Women Matter, all four of these qualities are more commonly found among women leaders.[13]

Dr. Alice Eagly, a professor at Northwestern University who specializes in gender differences and leadership styles, writes that there are several unique differences between men and women in terms of leadership.

Men's styles are characterized as the following:

- Task oriented
- Autocratic
- Command-and-control oriented
- Punishment oriented

Women's styles are characterized as the following:

- Collaborative
- Democratic

- Transformational
- Reward oriented

Clearly, this isn't to say that all men lean more toward leadership focused on punishment and all women toward leadership focused on rewards. However, this does provide some interesting things to think about and observe in the workforce. The future organization simply cannot be as competitive without having more women in senior leadership roles.[14]

Issues

This development of females and the need for more females to be in powerful roles has created some issues for organizations as well as family units.

The first is the role of the "balance male." It is estimated that 20 to 30 percent of households have females as breadwinners and males assisting in the classic, traditional roles of females. The stay-at-home "Mr. Mom" is not an unusual occurrence in many families. The stigma of this role reversal is being removed, and it is now often applauded instead of ridiculed.

Career development is another issue. As Sheryl Sandburg has highlighted, it is possible to be able to progress in a career and have a good family life as well. The CEO of Yahoo demonstrated that even childbirth is possible while you are a CEO. Career development policies need to be adjusted or modified to support some of the issues faced by females as they try to progress.

Another issue is changing the mindsets of individuals. Previously, men were taught to realize the differences between men and women and then ignore them or learn to work with them. The more proactive mindset is to understand and manage these differences in a way that helps all parties. Finally, showing the business value of women in the workplace is critical.

Shifting Families

The structure of families has shifted dramatically in the last two decades. The classic nuclear family (a married couple with a small number of children) now represents less than 25 percent of families. In 1970, it was at 40 percent.[15] Figure 9.6 lists the variations of the family and includes all kinds of arrangements, with or without children, with or without marriage, and including marriages of the same sex.

Although it may come in different variations, the family is still important, as illustrated in a study from the Harvard Medical School. This study, based on the lifetime health and happiness of thousands of people, revealed that those who are happiest in their lives are not the richest or the most accomplished. Research has found consistently that the greatest predictor of lifetime happiness is the extent to which people have close friends in their lives, while loneliness is associated with ill health. That is why easy, close, relaxed friendships have been described as such a key part of human mental health and happiness.[16]

Also, a study from the Pew Research Center showed that three-quarters of adults (76 percent) say their families are the most important element of their lives. Seventy-five percent say they are very satisfied with their family life, and more than eight out of ten say the family they live in now is as close or closer than the family

- Nuclear family
- Single, no plans to marry
- Blended family
- Same-sex couple
- Extended family
- Senior domestic partners
- Female-headed household
- Gay parents
- Single-mother household
- Living together anticipating marriage
- Single-father household
- Waiting for marriage
- Grandparents as primary caregivers
- Childless family

Figure 9.6. The new family.

in which they grew up. Interestingly, in this same research, 39 percent said that marriage is becoming obsolete.[17]

The changes in families will mean that organizations will have to provide different kinds of support processes and networks for these evolving lifestyles. Work–life balance becomes a critical issue for employees in these family arrangements, and considering many of the options that were covered in Chapter 6 may be helpful or needed here. Also, the health benefits that are provided can change dramatically because the makeup of the family has shifted.

Racial and Ethnic Diversity

The racial and ethnic makeup of organizations has changed dramatically, not only in the United States, but in other countries as well. Consider this statistic: the U.S. Census Bureau reported that 50.4 percent of children born in a twelve-month period that ended July 2011 were Hispanic, African American, Asian American, or from other groups, while non-Hispanic whites accounted for 49.6 percent of births during that period.[18]

Currently, 30 percent of the U.S. workforce comprises racial or ethnic minorities. It is projected that by 2050 about 50 percent of the workforce will be non-white. Hispanics have become the largest growing segment of American society. It is estimated that there are fifty-two million Latinos/Hispanics in the United States, including Puerto Rico, and that by 2017 Latinos will make up the largest bulk of entrants into the workplace. It is also estimated that by 2050 the Latino/Hispanic population will represent more than half of the U.S. workforce.

With 50 million, the United States has the second-largest population of Latinos/Hispanics in the world, after Mexico's 108 million. There are more Latinos/Hispanics in the United States than there are Canadians in Canada or Spaniards in Spain.[19]

Rates of migration across countries have also changed dramatically. In 1965, for example, 2.5 percent of the world population migrated across borders, representing about 75 million people. In 2010, the figure was 3 percent, representing about 214 million people, a much greater percentage of population becoming migrants. Figure 9.7 shows the racial and ethnic status of the U.S. workforce in 2012 according to the U.S. Census Bureau. When compared to the diversity makeup Google released in 2014, it is easy to see the underrepresentation of blacks and Hispanics.

While much has been gained in racial and ethnic progress, primarily because it has been such an important political and societal issue for many years, there is still room for improvement. This is particularly true for business, as people of color are underrepresented in many professional and managerial occupations. At the same time, people of color also are underrepresented in certain industries, such as the high-tech industry. One approach to correcting this is to constantly remind organizations of the business value of a diverse workforce. This is underscored by the Center for American Progress, which lists the top ten economic benefits of workplace diversity,[20] presented in Figure 9.8.

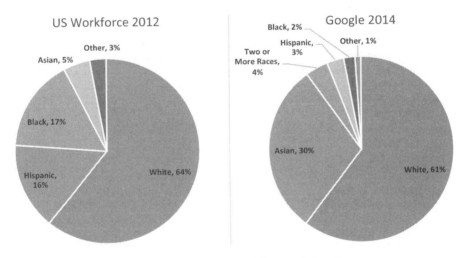

Figure 9.7. Racial and ethnic status of U.S. workforce and Google.

1. A diverse workforce drives economic growth.
2. A diverse workforce can capture a greater share of the consumer market.
3. Recruiting from a diverse pool of candidates means a more qualified workforce.
4. A diverse and inclusive workforce helps businesses avoid employee turnover costs.
5. Diversity fosters a more creative and innovative workforce.
6. Businesses need to adapt to our changing nation to be competitive in the economic market.
7. Diversity is a key aspect of entrepreneurialism.
8. Diversity in business ownership, particularly among women of color, is key to moving our economy forward.
9. Diversity in the workplace is necessary to create a competitive economy in a globalized world.
10. Diversity in the boardroom is needed to leverage a company's full potential.

Figure 9.8. Top ten economic benefits of workplace diversity.

Trust, Happiness, and Work–Life Balance

The final area to examine involves some interesting and perhaps disturbing trends that are evolving with the workforce. First, there is declining trust in institutions of all types. For example, we have been bombarded with data on the distrust of politicians. While this is a problem in almost every country, politicians currently have some of the lowest approval ratings in history in the United States. This distrust also moves to the leaders in companies. A study by the Davos World Economic Forum found that trust in leaders across all organizations is low and declining.[21]

There is also distrust in news sources and news reporting agencies, as well as banks, financial institutions, and stock-trading firms. There is a particular distrust in hospitals, as hospitals have the reputation of being one of the most dangerous places to be. This distrust will have to be addressed by organizations, particularly when they are working directly in that area.

Another trend is the decline in happiness. As far back as the 1990s, political scientist Robert Lane found that happiness had declined in many developing countries over the previous decade. Lane and others are trying to understand what defines happiness, and it is becoming clear that money or achievements are not necessarily what generates happiness. There has been a movement to actually redefine happiness on a national basis.[22] This effort is attempting to place more value on measures that relate to human development rather than just economic outcomes. For example, the United Nations measures three basic aspects of quality of life to develop a human development index: health and longevity, knowledge, and income. When these are adjusted for inequality, they show that the top countries in terms of human development are Norway, Australia, Sweden, the Netherlands, Iceland, Ireland, Germany, Denmark, Switzerland, and Slovenia. This is a dramatic shift in the idea of what makes a country truly outstanding.

A final issue is the increasing need for work–life balance. This was mentioned previously in this chapter, and Chapter 6 devoted much effort to this topic as well. In general, more efforts are needed to address issues around families, work arrangements, commute times, work places, and working hours. These issues have a significant effect on the happiness and well-being of employees.

Managing Diversity

This chapter has presented several issues about the diversity of the workforce, and this final section brings it all together in terms of how organizations must manage them. First, diversity must be defined to reflect all the issues in this chapter.

Global Diversity Definition

Diversity can be defined as a collective mixture characterized by differences and similarities that are applied in pursuit of organizational objectives.[23] *Diversity management* is the process of planning for, organizing, directing, and supporting this collective mixture in a way that measurably adds to organizational performance.

Diversity can be organized into four interdependent and sometimes overlapping aspects: workforce diversity, behavioral diversity, structural diversity, and business and global diversity.

Workforce diversity encompasses the group and situational identities of the organization's employees (i.e., their gender, race, ethnicity, religion, sexual orientation, physical ability, age, family status, economic background and status, and geographic background and status). It also deals with changes in the labor-market demographics.

Behavioral diversity encompasses work styles, thinking styles, learning styles, communication styles, aspirations, belief/value systems, as well as changes in employees' attitudes and expectations.

Structural diversity encompasses interactions across functions, across organizational levels in the hierarchy, across divisions and between parent companies and subsidiaries, and across organizations engaged in strategic alliances and cooperative ventures. As organizations attempt to become more flexible, less layered, more team-based, and more multi- and cross-functional, measuring this type of diversity will require more attention.

Business and global diversity encompasses the expansion and segmentation of customer markets, the diversification of products and services offered, and the variety of operating environments in which organizations work and compete (i.e., legal and regulatory contexts, labor-market realities, community and societal expectations/relationships, and business cultures and norms). Increasing competitive pressures, globalization, rapid advances in product technologies, changing demographics in the customer bases both within domestic markets and across borders, and shifts in business–government relationships all signal a need to measure an organization's response to and impact on business diversity.

Lawrence Baytos suggested that three *D*s have generated widespread corporate concern and interest in addressing diversity management issues, whether an organization has 100 or 100,000 employees. The three *D*s are as follows:

- *Demographics.* Females, minorities, and foreign-born personnel are projected to produce 85 percent of the net new growth in the U.S. workforce, while white males are fast becoming a minority in the workforce. In 1960, nine out of ten U.S. consumers were white. Currently, it is estimated that only six out of ten are white. The changing demographics of the workplace are also the changing demographics of the marketplace. Organizations are looking at ways to align themselves to the new realities of their customer bases.
- *Disappointment.* The traditional U.S. method for handling diversity was to bring women and people of color into the workforce under the banner of affirmative action. In doing so, it was often assumed that those individuals possessed some deficiencies and may not have been hired if not for affirmative action. It was also assumed that they should be willing to minimize their differences to better fit the norms of the majority group (usually white males) and thereby enhance their opportunities for recognition and advancement. In other words, to "make it," females and people of color would have to leave their needs and differences at the organization's front door. After a little more than two decades of affirmative action, it seems clear that this model has resulted in females and people of color being trapped in lower levels of the organizational pyramid. Turnover, discontent, and underutilization of talent are by-products of using this approach for more than two decades.

- *Demands.* The demands for new approaches to diversity come from employees, who have become less willing than their predecessors to minimize their points of difference in hopes of gaining the elusive acceptance into the club. Furthermore, the intense pressure of industry and global competition to reengineer the organization requires that organizations tap the full potential of all their human assets.[24]

The Phases of Managing Diversity

Figure 9.9 shows the different phases of diversity management and how it has evolved, particularly in the United States. As this figure shows, the early efforts in diversity were basic experiments of organizations trying to bring in females and people of color. Sometimes it was out of necessity, as when a company needed employees, but only black employees would take the job. The rationale for inclusion was, "Let's give this a try, and maybe the employees and customers will be satisfied." The measures were simply the number of people in the jobs and the success of those individuals. This was the early version of diversity management, before it became a political and legal issue.

When politics got involved and began to force organizations to prevent discrimination and to take affirmative action to make their workforce mirror the population in their particular area, this led to compliance: The point of diversity management was to comply with regulations and laws. The measures were the number of people in the jobs, recruiting efforts, retention, and complaints. The complaints were all varieties from internal complaints to charges, grievances, and even lawsuits. This approach worked for some, but it still did not lead to progress for most organizations, which lead to public pressure to bring attention to these issues. The major focus was employing more people of color and females in certain job categories and industries, though sometimes these efforts involved physically and mentally disadvantaged individuals as well. Companies and organizations often yielded to pressure tactics with exposure, and they began to measure diversity management in terms of people in jobs, progress made, their image, programs initiated, and even the job satisfaction of those in the organization, who often wanted to see an employee base more reflective of the general population.

Phase	Rationale	Measures
Experimentation/ necessity	"Let's try this, and maybe employees and customers will be satisfied."	Number of people in the job, success of those individuals.
Compliance	To comply with regulations and laws.	People in jobs, recruiting efforts, retention, complaints.
Public pressure	To yield to demands of customers and special interest groups.	People in jobs, progress made, image, programs initiated, job satisfaction.
Business value	To improve results of the organization.	Business measures such as productivity, retention, quality, and innovation.

Figure 9.9. Phases of managing diversity.

Finally, the most recent phase, which has been evolving for some time, is to show the business value of having a diverse workforce—how diversity improves the organization's effectiveness and efficiency. In this phase, measures of success include not only job satisfaction, complaints, absences, and turnover but also productivity, quality, and innovation. This is an important milestone, because moving in this direction can capture the attention of the executive group. When the issue of diversity is presented in terms of business value, most executives will understand that it is important and that they must take action to make it work. They see that in addition to it being a legal, ethical, and moral requirement, having a diverse and inclusive workforce actually leads to more productivity, better-quality products and services, and more innovation. When this occurs, you really have the hearts and souls of the top executives, and this is where diversity management has now come.

Building Centers of Diversity Excellence

Diversity management is a critical support to organizations. Learning to serve as a strategic partner within the organizational structure is not just a way for diversity practitioners to justify their existence or defend their turf. It has implications for the very survival of the diversity function and of the organization a whole. If the diversity function cannot show that it adds value, it risks being on the table for reduction—or worse, dismantling. With the right diversity mindset and measurement tools, implementing strategic business objectives for diversity can make the difference between being an organization that is just keeping pace with the competition or being one that is making major strides ahead. In essence, it requires creating centers of diversity excellence, using behavioral and technical measurement capability, demonstrating commitment, and building communities of practice to sustain it over time.[25]

In order for an organization to take full advantage of the potential wealth in its diversity mixtures, it must completely embrace the level of diversity required to meet critical organizational challenges head on. This occurs when organizations foster a climate and culture that values differences and maximizes the potential of employees through utilization—in other words, when the organization and the individuals within it operate in a mature fashion.

According to Dr. R. Roosevelt Thomas, diversity maturity requires both an individual and an organizational set of behaviors that drive success. He states that diversity-mature individuals do the following:

- Accept personal responsibility for enhancing their own and their organization's effectiveness.
- Demonstrate contextual knowledge (i.e., they know themselves and their organizations, and they understand key diversity concepts and definitions).
- Are clear about requirements and base inclusion/exclusion decisions on how differences impact an individual's ability to meet these requirements.
- Understand that diversity is accompanied by complexity and tension and are prepared to cope with these in pursuit of greater diversity effectiveness.
- Are willing to challenge conventional wisdom.
- Engage in continuous learning.

Diversity-mature individuals see themselves, not others, as responsible for addressing diversity effectively. They understand the impact of organizational culture on diversity-related practices, but they do not use it as an excuse for inaction and indifference.[26]

Implications for Human Capital Strategy

The material in this chapter clearly points out some great opportunities to improve the organization. The human capital strategy should involve several elements. These are consistent, for the most part, with what Jean Martin of the Corporate Executive Board recommends.[27] Develop a global approach to diversity, so that all business units are involved, but have local ownership within each unit.

- Reward progress made incrementally, and do not base judgment on the final outcomes that are desired.
- Expand the pool of diverse talent to include sources that are underrepresented and most trusted.
- Recruit aggressively with the diversity and inclusion targets in mind.
- Emphasize the importance of diversity with all of the employee database and at different timeframes.
- Make sure that diversity programs are aligned to the business needs.
- Ensure that high-performing employees from underrepresented groups are placed in leadership roles and are properly supported in those roles.
- Minimize, confront, and change the biases in talent management decision making.

10

Utilize Technology Effectively

Making Technology Work for All Stakeholders

....

Force 8: Technology. One of the most visible forces affecting organizations is the changing role of technology. Essentially, technology doubles its capability and power each year, following a concept called Moore's Law. Advances in technology bring significant improvements for organizations in terms of productivity, quality, time, convenience, and communication, among other things. At the same time, some concerns about technology and its proper use have evolved, including the critical issue of distracted employees. How technology is utilized is an important human capital issue, and the chief human resources officer must address it in concert with the chief information officer in an organization.

....

Everywhere we look, technology has rapidly changed and improved in so many different ways. New devices, software, and applications are literally being created daily, and their use radically changes organizations, the work that employees do, and the way in which employees communicate. This chapter explores the effects of technology in terms of learning and other HR functions in the organization. It also addresses many of the issues that arise with the proliferation of so many devices and possibilities.

Opening Story: NBC

Employees in many organizations are connected, wired, and tuned with all types of devices, apps, and favorite websites. Here is an account of a popular news anchor, Brian Williams, of NBC.[1] This story was written before he was forced to take a leave of absence for changing the facts about an incident in the Iraq War. We think it is still a great example of how technology is changing the workplace. Ironically, it was technology that exposed the contradictions of the incident. Brian Williams was the news anchor for the digital age, always plugged in and aware the latest apps and gadgets.

Williams was anchor and managing editor of *NBC Nightly News*, television's highest-rated newscast. With smartphone and table apps for both shows and a big social media presence, Williams was charged with bringing the television news audience into the digital age. "It's a Web-based job," different from the days of anchors Chet Huntley, David Brinkley, and Tom Brokaw. In those days, if somebody wrote a letter, there was a two- to three-day delay time. Now, the conversation starts after the newscast. The Twitter deck is monitored in the control room as a constant conversation. Williams has 160,00 twitter followers but has never tweeted. Williams said he doesn't do Twitter or Facebook because he hasn't found the time. He skips reading social media about himself because he would have no self-esteem and never leave the house.

He is a night owl, cruising various websites, looking for stories for the next day. He loves to be challenged by the staff and hates being the only one who brings a find to the afternoon story meeting. He follows his favorite websites—Buzz Feed, Daily Mail, and Gawker. Daily Mail is the No. 1 news site in the world, although most of it is fluff, once in a while they'll do a deep dive or gorgeous photos from the Smithsonian that will take your breath away. He starts his day with the big aggregators, *New York Times*, the *Washington Post*, and *Politico*. He is a nonfiction guy living in a nonfiction world.

At the time of the story, viewership was up over the previous year. People know they'll get a thirty-minute synopsis. The broadcast is old, turning sixty-five last year; however, it's every bit as vital today as in the past. It provides familiarity and quality, a sorting mechanism, a coffee filter to shake everything through.

Brian loves apps such as theBravest (a NYC fire department scanner feed) and SkyView (free), which is basically an app that explains the constellations and tracks the International Space Station and Hubble Telescope. He receives alerts from a great site (and app) called Satellite Flybys ($2.99) when the International Space Station is going fly by his ZIP code. He also likes Height Finder (free) to tell you what your height is above sea level wherever you are, Google Earth and photo apps Color Splash (99 cents) and Snapseed (free).

Most people in TV have twin devices, BlackBerry and iPhone. So many companies support the BlackBerry, and as many professionals need the keyboard for the constant emailing.

His other devices include a MacBook Pro and a "steam-powered" Dell both at home in the newsroom, wireless Beats by Dr. Dre headphones ("a game changer") and Bose in-ear headphones. He has an iPad but still is a paper book reader. He uses Shazam to find music "constantly" for his iPhone, which has 8,000 songs. His all-time favorite: Bruce Springsteen.

From his view, televisions are getting pretty great and they keep getting greater. Give him a NASCAR race on a Sunday afternoon on a fifty-five-inch screen and he's happy. The bigger the screen, the better the movie. He won't watch *Raiders of the Lost Ark* on his iPhone.

Trends in Technology

The use of all types of technology—devices, software, tools, processes, and applications—has increased at an amazing rate. In 2014, 45 percent of Americans had smartphones,[2] and there were 1.75 billion smartphone users worldwide. Globally, about 4.55 billion people were using mobile phones during the same year. Between 2013 and 2017, mobile-phone penetration will rise from 61 percent to 64 percent of the global population, according to emarketer.com.[3] By 2020, it is estimated that there will be 50 billion devices around the globe connected to the Internet. A third of them will be computers, smartphones, tablets, and televisions. The remaining two-thirds will be other kinds of things such as sensors, actuators, and newly invented intelligent devices that monitor, control, analyze, and optimize our world—the Internet of Things.[4] This trend has been decades in the making, but it has just now hit a tipping point. Figure 10.1 shows the top ten technology trends according to Gartner Research.[5] With these trends come some very interesting challenges and impacts in the organization.

Technology's Impact on Organizations

We can witness the tremendous impact that technology has had on organizations in our daily lives. For example, think about the gas stations where people purchase fuel for their cars. One of those chains, called Circle K, has five or six bays available for self-fueling of cars, where probably 95 percent of customers pay electronically. One employee manages the quick-stop store, which has groceries, supplies, and various items that automobile passengers may want. In the 1960s, a staff of five or six people would service the cars and run the store. Today it is one person.

Sometimes even one individual is not needed. At a fitness chain called Snap Fitness, when customers come to a location to participate in a fitness program, there is no one there. The customer uses a card to enter the door, and security cameras monitor everything that takes place. Some call centers are also completely automated, with few or no employees. Indeed, we have seen technology completely destroy some industries, like the video rental stores such as Blockbuster. Movie theatres may not be very far behind.

Productivity

Technology is a boon to many organizations. Improvements are made, tasks are much easier and faster to do, and productivity increases. The change can be dramatic in terms of how many employees are required to do the work. For example, the original Eastman Kodak Company employed forty thousand people at the height of its popularity and had a market value of $3 billion. This photograph company had existed since 1880. But when a new start up, Instagram, was sold to Facebook for about $1 billion in 2012, it had thirty million customers and employed only thirteen people. Although the companies are very different, they are both in the business of photography. A technology-based organization will naturally have dramatically less employees throughout the process. This dramatic shift has had a profound effect on employment levels in the United States.

Figure 10.2 shows what is happening to productivity and employment. In about the year 2000, productivity remained robust and growing, while employment basically tapered off and has continued to decline since. So what we have witnessed in the United States is technology rapidly displacing employees in large numbers. In a recent study, academics at Oxford University suggest that 47 percent of today's jobs can be automated within the next two decades. Consider the robot created by Kiva Systems, a startup that was founded in 2002 and bought by Amazon for

Computing Everywhere

As mobile devices continue to proliferate, Gartner predicts an increased emphasis on serving the needs of the mobile user in diverse contexts and environments, as opposed to focusing on devices alone. The combination of data streams and services created by digitizing everything creates four basic usage models—manage, monetize, operate, and extend.

The Internet of Things

The combination of data streams and services created by digitizing everything creates four basic usage models—Manage, Monetize, Operate, and Extend.

3D Printing

3D printing will reach a tipping point over the next three years as the market for relatively low-cost 3D printing devices continues to grow rapidly and industrial use expands significantly.

Context-Rich Systems

Ubiquitous embedded intelligence combined with pervasive analytics will drive the development of systems that are alert to their surroundings and able to respond appropriately.

Smart Machines

Prototype autonomous vehicles, advanced robots, virtual personal assistants, and smart advisors already exist and will evolve rapidly, ushering in a new age of machine helpers. The smart machine era will be the most disruptive in the history of IT.

Cloud/Client Computing

The convergence of cloud and mobile computing will continue to promote the growth of centrally coordinated applications that can be delivered to any device.

Software-Defined Applications and Infrastructure

Agile programming of everything from applications to basic infrastructure is essential to enable organizations to deliver the flexibility required to make the digital business work.

Web-Scale IT

Most organizations will begin thinking, acting, and building applications and infrastructure like web giants such as Amazon, Google, and Facebook.

Risk-Based Security and Self-Protection

All roads to the digital future lead through security. However, in a digital business world, security cannot be a roadblock that stops all progress. Organizations will increasingly recognize that it is not possible to provide a 100-percent-secured environment.

Figure 10.1. Top nine strategic technology trends.

Source: David Cearley. "Gartner's Top Strategic Technology Trends for 2015." *Forbes*, October 21, 2014. http://www.forbes.com/sites/gartnergroup/2014/10/21/gartners-top-10-strategic-technology -trends-for-2015.

$775 million in 2012. A warehouse equipped with Kiva robots can handle up to four times as many orders as a similar automated warehouse where human workers may spend as much as 70 percent of their time walking around to retrieve goods.[6]

Other Impacts

In addition to dramatic productivity gains, technology has had an important influence on quality. Electronic transactions are much more accurate than human

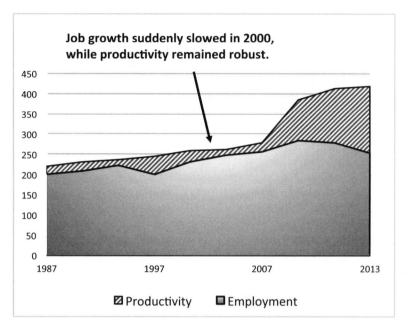

Figure 10.2. Decoupling productivity and employment.

transactions, and this is why technology has rapidly improved the quality of services. When combined with concepts like Six Sigma, large organizations can reduce transaction errors to one in nine million transactions, something that would be unheard of with human interactions. In addition, the time required to accomplish, process, or produce is greatly enhanced. For example, transactions involving the creation of one billion gigabytes of data would have taken over a thousand years to do using the technology of 2003. But by 2013, this same transaction took only ten minutes. This speed translates into all types of services in organizations throughout the economy. Because of the gains in productivity and time, technology has also led to a direct reduction in the cost of completing tasks.

Impact on Communication and Work Flow

The daily routine of a person in a tech-savvy world is wired and connected. The day may begin with a good-morning message on a social networking site and end with a good night on the same website. Emails, texting, video conferencing, tweeting, and other tools and processes may affect every aspect of the day's work. With the use of mobile devices and the Internet for communication, data and conversations flow quickly and easy. This connected type of workforce is alive and well in many organizations and is a rapidly growing trend in others.[7] These devices and processes also make it much easier for employees to work from home. As explained in Chapter 6, this is an important trend that will continue, thanks to technology.

Years ago, collaboration took place in cubicles, conference rooms, and formal meeting places. Today, it is all on documents being shared, discussed, and communicated all over the world at the same time. Employees are sharing their screens and chatting online in virtual teams. Good platforms enable employees to find the information they need and use it at work quickly, eliminating much of the time that was often spent trying to find information and send it to others. When using all these tools, however, it is important to take a balanced perspective. In Figure 10.3, Google's human resources director, Dr. Todd Carlisle, describes how Google is integrating technology and humanizing it in the workplace.[8]

Thoughtfully mix it up.

- Google employees who rely on one kind of communication—for example, texting or e-mailing—for everything and never meet with people in person tend to receive low engagement scores from their direct reports. Consequently, managers should be very thoughtful in determining the best way to communicate in every situation.

Let technology support employees in their personal lives.

- With global organizations, there is often a need to be online with the individuals who are in different time zones. Technology supports them to make these calls in the evenings or early morning to make it convenient for both groups. It also lets them take care of business in conjunction with something that is urgent and personal.

Leverage technologies to give employees a greater voice.

- Traditionally in business, an organization's policies and procedures were crafted and communicated by people in a Human Resources department, a process that excluded much, if any, involvement with line employees. Google sees its workers as the true subject matter experts, and purposely makes great use of its shared document technology to eliminate all "top-downness from decision making."

Go high-tech and low-tech.

- Almost every meeting held today at Google makes use of the Hangout program to accommodate employees unable to attend, or who work in other locations. Wherever they are, meeting attendees are able to use the camera on their phone or computer and talk face-to-face with every person participating.

Encourage people to disconnect.

- If you've ever checked email after waking up at 3 a.m. to go to the bathroom, or felt compelled to respond to a boss's inquiry on a Saturday afternoon, it's consoling to know that, at least at Google, people are giving thought to whether "always being on" is good for us or our organizations.

Figure 10.3. How Google humanizes technology.

Source: Mark C. Crowley. "How Google Humanizes Technology in the Workplace and You Can, Too." *Fast Company.* Accessed January 3, 2015. http://www.fastcompany.com/3028812/bottom-line/how -google-humanizes-technology-in-the-workplace-and-you-can-too.

Social Media

Social media represents an important opportunity and challenge for an organization. It is an opportunity to make the work much better, smoother, and more effective, and it is a great tool for connecting with customers, suppliers, and others external to the organization. According to a report in the *Harvard Business Review*, the strategies that are taken with social media often fall into one of four different categories, as shown in Figure 10.4.[9]

The "predictive practitioner" implements social media projects just for specific departments or groups, not company-wide or spread over large areas, and only in connection to existing business metrics. The "creative experimenter" works with social media on a similarly small scale but places less emphasis on predefined outcomes. The "social media champion" centralizes social media expertise and coordinates social media projects across the whole organization. Finally, the "social media transformer" integrates social media into all levels of business strategy and involves all stakeholders in the process, both internal and external.

One example of the applications of social media for business is the release of the Ford Fiesta automobile, detailed in the same *Harvard Business Review* report. In this release, Ford decided to lend a hundred Fiestas for six months to recipients who would use social media to discuss their experiences with the cars in an authentic, direct way. The company held online contests to select candidates with large social media followings. By the end of the six-month campaign, the drivers had posted more than sixty thousand items, which garnered millions of clicks, including more than 4.1 million YouTube views. The $5 million campaign created a prelaunch brand awareness of 37 percent among millennials, generated fifty thousand sales leads, and prompted thirty-five thousand test drives. To use traditional methods to achieve this success would have cost tens of millions of dollars.

Work Flow

In addition to making sure that people are connected and communicating properly using all the networks, devices, and tools, it is helpful to explore how the technology actually fits into the flow of the work. Figure 10.5 shows the approach suggested by Jacob Morgan in *The Future of Work*. Morgan's approach starts with thinking about individual values before corporate ones and always putting strategy before the technology. Too often it goes the other way. The remaining steps ensure that a technology is properly organized, executed, and measured as it is integrated in the flow of work.

Impact on Learning

Technology has dramatically changed how we learn at work. Much early training followed the traditional "knowledge broadcast" model, with the expert on the stage presenting what he knows. Early learning technologies such as projectors, digital presentations, and training videos fit this model well.

In the late 1990s, the rise of the Internet gave a huge boost to "digital content." Suddenly, it was much easier to create and share content around the world. This led to the growth of two very different types of stakeholders: content specialists, who developed and sold learning content in their areas of expertise (e.g.,

---

Predictive practitioner

Each of our social media projects is owned by a specific functional group or department.
There is little or no cross-functional coordination among projects.
Each project has a clear business objective.
We can measure each project's impact with existing metrics.

Creative experimenter

Our overall objective is to learn from our social media projects.
In particular, we aim to enable engagement and to listen and learn from resulting conversations.
We positon our projects as experiments within discrete functions or departments.
We are not overly concerned with predefining outcomes.

Social media champion

We have a centralized group and specific leaders dedicated to coordinating and managing
    social medial projects across departments and functions.
This centralized group develops policies and guidelines for social media use.
We enlist executive champions and other evangelists, including external influencers, to pro-
    mote and participate in our projects.
We share best practices and lessons learned from various projects throughout the
    organization.

Social media transformer

Our portfolio of social media projects involves both internal employees and external stake-
    holders, such as customers and business partners.
Our social media technologies are tightly integrated with how we learn and work.
Our projects typically encompass multiple functions and departments.
We have centralized groups tasked with thinking about how social media can inform our
    business strategy and culture in light of surprises and emerging trends.

Figure 10.4.   Four approaches to social media.

Source: Adapted from James Wilson, P. J. Guinan, Salvatore Parise, and Bruce D. Weinberg. "What's Your Social Media Strategy?" *Harvard Business Review*, July–August 2011, p. 24.

---

financial management), and systems specialists, who developed learning platforms or learning management systems (LMSs), which allowed companies to deliver online learning to employees around the world at any time.

Broadly, this was a success. Companies were putting more and more of their training online and were able to reach an increasingly diverse group of learners. The next ten years were vibrant days for learning technologists, with companies investing heavily in e-learning, excited by the potential cost savings of no more face-to-face training. During this time, hundreds of new e-learning companies formed, merged, and were acquired. Digital content became commoditized and was increasingly bought in segments, either by the hour or by the amount of content. However, there was little regard for the quality of the learning itself. Unfortunately, as with many new technologies, a large number of overly enthusiastic training departments forged ahead with this technology trend and mistakenly thought that some badly developed e-learning courses would somehow be as effective as expert face-to-face training sessions—they were not!

1. Focus on individual values before corporate values.
2. Strategy always comes before technology.
3. Learn to get out of the way.
4. Lead by example.
5. Listen to the voice of the employee.
6. Integrate technology into the flow of work.
7. Create a supportive environment.
8. Measure what matters.
9. Be persistent.
10. Adapt and evolve.
11. Understand that employee collaboration also benefits the customer.
12. Accept that collaboration makes the world a better place.

Figure 10.5. Integrating technology with work.

Source: Adapted from Jacob Morgan. *The Future of Work: Attract New Talent, Build Better Leaders, and Create a Competitive Organization.* Hoboken, NJ: Wiley, 2014.

From the mid-2000s, the e-learning market started to mature with the addition of three new ideas and associated technologies: talent management systems; increased use of blended learning; and virtual classrooms, video streaming, and collaboration tools. Figure 10.6 shows the various innovations in e-learning.

Most would agree that any large expenditure in an organization should in some way be connected to business success. Even in nonbusiness settings, large investments should connect to organizational measures of output, quality, cost, and time—classic measure categories of hard data that exist in any type of organization. In a review of articles, reports, books, and blogs about learning through technology, the emphasis is on making a business connection.[10] For example, in the book *Learning Everywhere: How Mobile Content Strategies Are Transforming Training* (2012), Chad Udell makes the case for connecting mobile learning to businesses measures. He starts by listing the important measures that are connected to the business. A sampling is shown in Figure 10.7.

Udell goes on to say that mobile learning should connect to any of these, and he takes several measures step by step to show how, in practical and logical thinking, a mobile-learning solution can drive any or all these measures. He concludes by suggesting that if an organization is investing in mobile learning or any other type of learning, it needs to connect the investment to these business measures. Otherwise, it shouldn't be pursued. This dramatic call for accountability is not unusual.

Impact on HR

The technology that has been integrated into HR has evolved over several decades. When considering how deeply technology has impacted the HR process, it is helpful to think of HR as being composed of two broad types of work: The first type is transactional work, and the second type is advice and execution work. Obviously, the transaction work has great potential for automation, but even the advice and execution work can be enhanced and augmented by technology.

Mobile Learning

Much hyped but only moderately understood, mobile learning involves mobile devices woven into a learning or training scenario. Often, but not always, the learners themselves are mobile.

Game-Based Learning

Game-based learning has been described as the next big thing for the past ten years. Two interesting and more successful models of this have emerged:

- Playing a real game, designed for entertainment, but setting challenges within it that build on learning.
- Doing real learning tasks, but using a badge system to show progress and gains. Mozilla's Open Badges framework offers good tools for this.

Bring Your Own Devices (BYOD)

BYOD refers to initiatives that allow employees to use their own personal mobile technology devices at work as part of their day.

Massive Open Online Course (MOOC)

A MOOC is a web-based course, often free, designed to offer learning to many thousands of students at the same time. Although they have been around since 2008, they have received a lot of attention since 2012, thanks to recent backing from some notable schools (Stanford, Princeton, and MIT, for example) and high-profile start-ups.

Flipped Classroom

If so much information is available online, and quality time with an expert facilitator is hard to find, why waste the time you have together by sitting quietly in your chair and listening to a lecture? It is far better, perhaps, to watch the recorded lecture before you come into class and then spend the face-to-face time discussing it, asking questions, and doing activities.

Figure 10.6. Evolution of learning through technology.

- Decreased product returns
- Reduced incidents
- Increased productivity
- Decreased defects
- Increased accuracy
- Increased shipments
- Fewer mistakes
- On-time shipments
- Reduced risk
- Decreased cycle time
- Increased sales
- Less downtime
- Less waste
- Reduced operating cost
- Fewer accidents
- Fewer customer complaints
- Fewer compliance discrepancies
- Reduced response time to customers

Figure 10.7. High-level business benefits from mobile learning.

Source: Adapted from C. Udell. *Learning Everywhere: How Mobile Content Strategies Are Transforming Training*. Nashville, TN: Rockbench and ASTD Press, 2012.

Prior to 1990, automation was very small scale, limited by the computer power that was available at the time. Much of the work was, essentially, done in a word-processing format. Many organizations around this time began to change their label from *personnel* to *human resources*. From 1990 to 2000, human resources evolved and the personal computer made processing much easier, and automation became a big part of employee records, benefits administration, and so forth. This decade also brought saw enterprise-wide human resources information systems for the HR staff.

From 2001 to 2010, talent management evolved and a variety of platforms and tools were created to help the organizations recruit, develop, track, and monitor talent. Many tools and processes were automated and connected to focus on the critical part of the organization. From 2011 on, the focus has been using the latest tools to not only facilitate the administrative transactional processes but help show the value of the human resources function using big data, predictive analytics for forecasting, and prescriptive statistics—all aimed at making the HR function more efficient and effective.[11]

Technology has radically changed all the classic functions of HR, from recruiting, which is now highly automated through e-recruiting, to benefits and compensation processing. Transactional processes have been automated, outsourced, or moved to other parts of the organization. Much of on-boarding and learning and development have been shifted to blended learning, e-learning, or mobile learning, as described earlier.

Issues with Technology

Technology can create problems if not properly addressed. There are many well-known examples of such issues, and they are often collectively referred to as the *dark side* of technology, which creates problems on the day-to-day scale of the workplace and the broader strategic scale of the organization.

Workplace

The first workplace issue is the concept of being always connected. Sometimes employees are expected to be on call at all times, constantly plugged into their devices. They are now on the job twenty-four hours a day, seven days a week. The stress from these extended hours might cancel out the benefits of the technology. Many organizations are establishing policies to discourage or prevent this situation. Some countries, such as Brazil and the Netherlands, have laws prohibiting sending business emails at night unless the employees are being paid for it. Indeed, part of the problem with emails is often the overwhelming number of them, with many employees receiving two to three hundred emails a day. The issue here is having an effective email policy and preparing individuals to manage their email.

Another issue is privacy, a concern for all employees, particularly with so many devices at work. A survey conducted by Harris Interactive involving 2,100 adults showed that 99 percent of users are now concerned about their online privacy.[12] Figure 10.8 shows their various levels of concern for particular online platforms. Privacy will continue to be a huge issue as employee's emails, personal material, information, and ID numbers such as social security numbers may be obtained by others.

66%	Social media networks
56%	Email
52%	Web browsers
45%	Search engines
35%	Social photo sharing
30%	Mobile apps
27%	Dating apps
23%	Instant messaging apps
23%	Microblogging

Figure 10.8.   Privacy concerns of online platforms.

Source: "71% of Americans Care Deeply about Their Online Privacy amid Recent Privacy Concerns." Businesswire.com, July 29, 2014. Accessed January 4, 2015. http://www.business wire.com/news/home/20140729006077/en/71-Americans -Care-Deeply-Online-Privacy-Privacy#.VR7pSvnF8gk.

Another challenge is using all the devices properly and efficiently. With so many new devices available, with so many apps, significant portions of time may be lost exploring new possibilities, trying to get current devices to work, trying to decide what was needed, or trying to locate the information that was desired. This problem is amplified by the need to stay abreast of what is available.

The issue that causes the most concern is the loss of focus and attention in an ever-connected environment. The constant connection to technology causes people to lose social interaction, and it requires multitasking. Many studies have shown that multitasking increases the occurrence of errors, which can be disastrous. This is particularly critical when there is a need for individuals to put down their mobile devices and have a face-to-face discussion. In some cases, people have become addicted to technology, which can give way to many personal and social problems.

Finally, there is the issues of technology abuse, as employees use their tools and devices for personal activities, lowering their contribution and productivity for the organization. All these issues will have to be managed properly through the human capital strategy to ensure success.

Organization

As mentioned earlier, job losses from productivity improvements represent a problem for organizations. Many organizations take pride in being labeled a great place to work, and they work hard to try to avoid having to lay off their employees when there is a needed reduction because of productivity improvement. For example, when a warehouse switches from people to robots, what are the implications for the employees that are being displaced? Although sometimes technology is integrated slowly and normal attrition can take care of it, there are times when many employees are suddenly no longer needed.

From a social perspective, an outstanding employer is one that is not only profitable and sustainable over a period of time but also a company that actually creates jobs. When companies have that goal, they can use displaced employees in very creative ways. They can be redirected to take care of growth, involved in other projects, or trained for other occupations that are needed. A variety of possibilities exist, and this perhaps is the biggest challenge that arises from the impact of technology— how to deal with zero or even negative job growth. This becomes quite noticeable when companies go through mergers. The total employment, for example, in the pharmaceutical industry has been declining because of mergers and consolidations of the different pharmaceutical companies. While this is helpful for the balance sheet, it is not good for growing economies.

Another issue is intrusion into systems and databases. Cybersecurity is one of the most talked-about areas in technology, and if not properly addressed, the results can be devastating to an organization. For example, the hacking of Target's database of customers and credit card numbers had a very negative effect on the company.[13] Not only did some executives lose jobs, but the brand and image of the company declined. Share prices declined, and revenue declined as well. Ultimately, this led to fewer employees, at least for the short term. This is only one of many examples that are routinely occurring. The challenge is to not only prevent the attacks but also have mechanisms in place to properly deal with them.

The velocity of change is another issue that affects organizations, as there are so many different technology options. Among the top challenges for chief information officers is simply trying to understand what is available, what is necessary, and what will work.

Finally, the last issue is the need to show the business value of technology. Many technology implementations go astray and do not add the value that was anticipated. Overall, the IT function has not stepped up to the issue of showing the value of technology investments, particularly before they invest. This is a huge problem for many.

Implications for Human Capital Strategy

The human capital strategy needs to address the technology issues covered in this chapter. It needs to be developed in concert with the chief information officer, chief technology officer, or another appropriate head of technology in the organization. Ideally, the strategy should address these six areas:

- The use of technology in terms of the systems, processes, tools, and platforms at the worksite along with ways to ensure that they are used properly and protected.
- The use of social media and how it should be protected. Some organizations do not allow employees to have access to Facebook at work, while others use it in their work. The strategy may be controversial either way, but the issue must be addressed to take into consideration productivity, efficiency, and effectiveness, while also making the organization a great place to work at the same time.
- The consequences of productivity improvements caused by technology enhancement. Although these improvements are needed and desired to have

an efficient and effective organization, there is also a need to ensure that employees are not always dismissed when they become redundant. Employees may be trained for other assignments, helped through the transition, or assigned to other projects—all to make sure that the total employment doesn't necessarily decline. This is approached in the spirit of having a company that is not only profitable and sustainable but one that generates job growth.

- A cybersecurity policy that not only protects databases and the privacy of data from employees, customers, and suppliers but includes a mechanism to control and minimize the impact of cyberattacks.
- The alignment of technology to business needs before adoption. If a clear line of sight to business measures cannot be determined, then perhaps the technology is not needed.
- The evaluation of major projects all the way to impact and ROI level, showing that the technology is working and is adding business value.

CONFRONT GLOBALIZATION

Maximizing the Value of Human Capital

> **Force 9: Globalization.** The international integration of goods, technology, labor, and capital is everywhere to be seen. Globalization has had tremendous impacts on countries and organizations. No medium- to large-size organization has escaped the effect, either positive or negative, of globalization. The challenge is for organizations to take advantage of the positive aspects of globalization and prepare for the negative consequences of globalization. This is best achieved through the development of human capital strategy.

This chapter describes the phenomenon known as globalization, which has had both positive and negative impacts on most organizations around the world. Globalization affects organizations directly in terms of selling goods and services to international markets, outsourcing work to other countries, or insourcing work from other countries. It has an effect on the pricing of products, the flow of capital and investments, and more important, it has an important impact on employment, job creation, inequality, and environment degradation, among other things. This chapter defines globalization, how it affects countries around the world, and how it affects organizations. Next, it describes how multinational companies become global in the first place. Most start off very small and eventually evolve into global powerhouses by passing through phases described in this chapter. The chapter ends with how globalization has affected the human resources function and the implications for human capital strategy.

Opening Stories

K'Nex

As every American child knows, toys come from the North Pole—or more likely, China. But K'Nex Brands LP, a family-owned company in this Philadelphia suburb, is trying to prove they can still be made in America.[1]

Over the past few years, K'Nex has brought most of the production of its plastic building toys back to its factory in Hatfield from subcontractors in China. To make that possible, the company has redesigned some of the toys and even handed over to kids a bit of the assembly formerly performed by hand in China.

"In the long term, it's much better for us to manufacture here," says Joel Glickman, chairman of K'Nex and its manufacturing affiliate, Rodon Group. The two companies have combined sales of more than $100 million, making them small players compared with American rivals Hasbro Inc. and Mattel Inc., neither of which has announced plans to shift production to the U.S. By moving production closer to U.S. retailers, K'Nex said it can react faster to the fickle shifts in toy demand and deliver hot-selling items to stores faster. It also has greater control over quality and materials, often a crucial safety issue for toys. And as wages and transport costs rise in China, the advantages of producing there for the U.S. market are waning.

But K'Nex has found it impossible so far to produce 100 percent U.S.-made toys, the firm's goal. The K'Nex experience shows both the attractions of "reshoring" production and the difficulties of making that happen.

Lining up suppliers has been a complicated chore in the U.S. where toy-making skills have faded. China, by contrast, has a vast, efficient network of suppliers and skilled labor. "In China, you can go over with just a drawing and say, 'I need a million of these,'" says Michael Araten, chief executive of K'Nex. That helps account for a huge U.S. deficit in the toy trade. In 2012, U.S. imports of toys, games, and sporting goods, mostly from China, totaled $33.5 billion, or about three times U.S. exports of such items. The roots of K'Nex go back to 1956, when Irving Glickman set up a small factory to make plastic items, such as protective caps for chair legs. In the early 1990s, his son, Joel, invented K'Nex toys to diversify the product line. By the late 1990s, K'Nex was following the fashion among U.S. companies of moving production to China. The affiliated Rodon Company continued to make such items as plastic window parts and coffee filters, requiring little manual labor at the Hatfield factory.

When the U.S. economy slumped in 2008, demand for products made by Rodon fell so sharply that the company couldn't keep all its workers busy. To avoid major layoffs, the Glickman family decided to begin moving production of the K'Nex toys back to Hatfield.

The Glickmans were confident that Rodon, whose slogan is "Cheaper Than China," could use its highly automated processes to mold plastic parts at a competitive cost. The challenge was that making K'Nex toys also involves manual labor, which is still much more costly in the U.S.

Toys had to be reimagined in some cases. K'Nex roller-coaster tracks were held together with metal pins, inserted by hand in China. The company redesigned the tracks so they could snap together. A tiny hubcap for K'Nex car wheels used to be attached by workers in a Chinese factory. Now it is included as a separate part in K'Nex kits, and children who get the toy have one more piece to snap into place.

Last year, K'Nex took over production and sales of Tinkertoys under license from Hasbro, which used to make them in China. Tinkertoys, a century-old product, were originally made of wood and later included both wood and plastic parts. To reduce costs and make U.S. production economical. K'Nex last year switched to plastic for the remaining wooden spokes.

K'Nex also makes Lincoln Logs, likewise under license from Hasbro. It considered transforming them to plastic, but research showed the public wasn't ready for plastic log cabins. So K'Nex continues to have the logs made in china, though Mr. Araten hopes to find a U.S. furniture company to produce the tiny logs in America.

K'Nex still imports small battery-powered motors for its toys from China because it hasn't found a competitive U.S. supplier. Also still imported from China is the head of the Angry Bird toy that requires a rubberized coating that would be expensive to replicate in the U.S.

To increase U.S. content, K'Nex has had to make compromises. Joseph Smith, the chief development officer at K'Nex, points to a little car with a shiny metallic finish that zips around on one of the company's roller coasters. The car's silvery finish is "a neat look," Mr. Smith says, but the process used to apply the coating is "expensive, it's dirty, and we can't do it here, so we designed it out of the product." Instead of the shiny coating, K'Nex may supply decals, to be applied by the cars' owners.

K'Nex is getting kudos for its made-in-U.S.A. efforts. President Obama paid a visit to the Hatfield plan in November 2012. Total employment at K'Nex and Rodon has grown to about 200 people from 150 four years ago. Wages at the nonunion plant range from about $12 an hour for the least skilled machine operators to more than twice that.

K'Nex recently bought a $30,000 Baxter robot from Rethink Robotics Inc., Boston. For now, Baxter is performing simple packaging tasks. Eventually, Mr. Araten hopes that more sophisticated versions of the robot will help K'Nex move more assembly work back to the U.S.

ROI Institute

The ROI Institute, founded in 1993, is a global leader in measurement and evaluation with the emphasis on measuring the return on investment in noncapital investments. Based in the United States, this small organization has grown incrementally to the point where most of its revenues are now derived from partners located abroad. The company has employees and independent contractors in the United States as well as international partners. The company delivers consulting services, showing the impact and ROI of many types of projects and programs. Workshops and ROI certification are also offered to build capability inside organizations. The target audiences are human resources, technology, marketing, and quality assurance functions. The types of organizations vary considerably, with about half of the market made up of businesses and the other half comprising governments, nongovernmental organizations, universities, and nonprofits. The ROI institute delivers services and products around five competencies:

1. Consulting directly with organizations in the form of impact/ROI studies
2. Teaching individuals to evaluate their own projects and programs
3. Documenting successes of ROI analysis through books, articles, case studies, and blog posts
4. Conducting research to understand the successes and the opportunities available
5. Speaking to groups to explain the need for this level of accountability and how the process works

From the very beginning, the ROI Institute wanted to operate globally, perceiving that the need for these products and services exist in every country and culture. The first assignment was in South Africa, the second in Malaysia, and the third in Canada. Since then, the company has placed a premium on working across borders, initially through offices in Europe and Asia but now through partners situated in thirty-five countries and serving a total of sixty countries. These partners operate much like franchisees and offer the same products and services to their countries.

When considering the issues of globalization, it is helpful to assess the impact of the ROI Institute along several dimensions. Although it is a small enterprise, when this impact is multiplied by the literally millions of other small enterprises, it is easy to see how even small organizations can drive globalization.

Regarding trade, the ROI Institute began by selling its services outside the United States, and it migrated to selling them through partners, so that the transactions flow from the home headquarters to different countries. Now there is even more trading across borders as a partner in one country applies the same process in another.

Regarding global consciousness, the ROI Institute attempts to customize its services based on the context, culture, and language of the customers. Instead of merely translating books (although the books have been translated into thirty-eight languages), the institute prefers to coauthor a book with a partner, bringing the culture, context, and examples from that country into the marketplace.

The ROI Institute's employment has grown each year of its existence. Although the number of employees and contractors in the United States is still around fifty, external growth has been more impressive. In the last ten years, the partnerships have grown from twenty to thirty-five, collectively employing seventy full-time individuals. Jobs were created in all involved countries, and no jobs were lost in the process.

Regarding financial flows, revenue flows into the United States from different partners, and various procurements are made abroad, causing revenue to flow from the United States to the different countries as well. Travel, scheduled routinely with the executives of the ROI Institute, is adding to the revenues of different hotels and airlines outside the United States. A software company based in Amsterdam has developed software for this process, so there is also a flow of investment into the Netherlands.

In terms of prosperity, the jobs created are high-wage jobs, and in most countries they are in the upper tier of the wage scale. In addition, the business model of the ROI Institute is to provide a process through which organizations can become more effective and efficient, which contributes to the economies of their respective countries.

Regarding mobility, some partners have moved across borders to work with the ROI methodology, and two people have transferred to the United States to work at the ROI Institute headquarters.

These two examples of K'Nex and the ROI Institute show how globalization is working. In the first example, a medium-size manufacturing organization is struggling with globalization and reversing previous moves of outsourcing to relocate production back to the United States. This is in response to a problem that has occurred with globalization as more jobs have been outsourced from the United States than have been created through this process. The second example shows how a small business can be a global organization as well and benefit from global trade. The success of the ROI Institute is, for the most part, based on its work outside the United States, although it has a large domestic presence.

While we could have featured large multinational organizations in the opening stories, such as Nike, McDonalds, or Coca-Cola, it is helpful to see how globalization is affecting the majority of organizations, which are small to medium in size.

Defining Globalization

Globalization has different meanings depending on who you ask, but its presence is very obvious. In any large city, in any country, Japanese and German cars are in the streets. An email or text message can arrange a purchase of products on another continent. Most local businesses around the world could not function without computers assembled in other countries or the Internet that connects them. In many countries, foreign nationals have taken over a large segment of service industries. Over the past twenty years, foreign trade and cross-border movement of technology, labor, and capital have been massive and irresistible. During the same period, in the advanced industrial countries, the demand for skilled workers has increased at the expense of less skilled workers, and the income gap between the groups has grown. Globalization is a force that commands much attention, and it is in the news almost every day.

One definition of globalization comes from Wikipedia: "Globalization is the process of international integration arising from the interchange of world views, products, ideas, and other aspects of culture. Advances in transportation and telecommunications infrastructure, including the rise of the telegraph and its posterity and the Internet, are major factors in globalization, generating further interdependence of economic and cultural activities."[2]

Other examples are also available:

- "Globalization can thus be defined as the intensification of worldwide social relations which link distant localities in such a way that local happenings are shaped by events occurring many miles away and vice versa." (Anthony Gliddens, former director of the London School of Economics)
- "Globalization may be thought of as a process (or set of processes) which embodies a transformation in the spatial organization of social relations and transactions—assessed in terms of their extensity, intensity, velocity, and impact—generating transcontinental or interregional flows and networks of activity, interaction, and the exercise of power." (David Held, professor of politics and international relations, Durham University)
- "Globalization as a concept refers both to the compression of the world and the intensification of consciousness of the world as a whole." (Roland Robertson, emeritus professor of sociology, University of Aberdeen, Scotland)[3]

Along with the different twists in the definitions, there are both supporters and critics. In almost any dimension, there are proponents of globalization who see the positive aspects and ignore the downsides. Then there are critics that focus on the downsides and miss much of the positive aspects of globalization. The reality is that globalization has both positive and negative outcomes. Globalization is not a new phenomenon. It started with the very beginning of civilization as the first humans migrated from the African continent to all the other continents in the world. Even after most human settlements became fixed, trade between territories began and people continued to migrate from one continent to another. The process has evolved over time; some would argue that it is inevitable. The first major push for globalization in the modern era occurred with the easing of tariffs and the promotion of trade at a conference organized by the United States near the end of World War II in the New England town of Bretton Woods. Under the leadership of the United States and Great Britain, the major allied economic powers agreed to make some changes in their protectionist policies. This ultimately led to a treaty called the General Agreement on Tariffs and Trade (GATT) in 1947. In 1995, the World Trade Organization was founded to continue to address trade issues. All types of organizations have continued to work at making globalization a reality.

Table 11.1 shows the various elements of the globalization process with both the supporters' view and the critics' view. For each dimension, it is probably easy for you to see the importance of the issue. Indeed, the critics' view is sometimes a painful reality that most can relate to. In almost every study, there are inconclusive or conflicting results. It is a fact that there is more trade thanks to globalization, and that more people have access to products and services. Some wages have increased, and many jobs have been created. On the downside, things have not always worked to benefit everyone involved, and the remainder of this chapter examines some of the key issues involved in the formal globalization process since its beginnings in the 1940s.

Table 11.1.   The globalization debate.

Issue	Supporters' view	Critics' view
Social inter-dependence	Growing economic interdependence leads to social interdependence. Social processes are leading to more global integration.	There is no empirical data that confirms this. People do not feel a part of a global family.
Poverty	More people will move out of poverty in the least-developed countries. Free markets lead to jobs, more wages, and lower consumer prices.	The reduction of poverty has largely occurred in China and India, through their economic policies and growth and by shifting production and service facilities out of developed countries.
Employment	Employment in the least-developed countries will increase and the employment in developed countries will also increase as the demand for goods and services increase.	There is little evidence that employment has increased in the least-developed countries because of globalization. In the developed countries, employment growth is stagnant.
Prosperity	Globalization makes the world's people more prosperous. The purchasing power for the least-developed countries will improve. Household incomes will improve.	The least-developed countries have become poorer. The bottom billion are losing ground and are highly unstable.
Inequality	Globalization should reduce the gap between the rich and poor.	Since 2010, household income in the poorest half of the world has decreased. The top eighty billionaires have more wealth than the bottom half of the world's population combined (3.5 billion people).

Table 11.1.   The globalization debate (*continued*).

Issue	Supporters' view	Critics' view
Global integration	More people are integrated into the global capitalist economy—more than 90 percent of the world's population since the 1990s.	The global capitalist economy is dominated by the rich members of the Organisation for Economic Co-operation and Development (OECD).
Global trade	More global trade than ever before is occurring. Reduction in air travel and shipping costs has facilitated a significant expansion of cross-border trade.	Most trade is not global but takes place regionally. International trade has not increased dramatically since the twentieth century. In the least-developed countries, the share of world trade decreased by 50 percent.
Global financial markets	Growth in global financial markets and the global circulation of currency will boost the economies of the least-developed countries	Capital outflows are mainly short-term speculative investments, not productive investments. The increasing volatility of financial flows helped to create the global financial crisis in 2008.
Mobility	Increased mobility of people creates a more migrant labor force around the globe.	Most people stay home, and most labor is not mobile.
Environment	Globalization will create new sustainable energy innovations and foster a willingness to comply with planetary sustainability goals.	The earth's environmental decline has been unprecedented. The effects of overconsumption and population growth have been disastrous, with food shortages, extinction of species, and excessive pollution.
Global companies	A new type of global company has been created with products, employees, R&D, and shareholders all over the world.	Most multinational companies retain national management, R&D, and investments. They are more imperialistic than truly global.
Global conscious	There has been an intensification of global consciousness. People are becoming global thinkers.	Although there is more global awareness, there is no shared cosmopolitan consciousness.
Nation states	A "borderless" world will be created where political power is located in global formations and global networks—not in territorially based states. Nation states will lose their dominant role in the global economy.	Territory still matters. Conventional political units are still relevant. Local political decisions control global economic activities and policies.
Control	No one is in charge of globalization. It cannot be dominated by only one nation.	The United States is the strongest economic and military power, and the largest global organizations are based in America. The substance and direction of globalization are shaped by American domestic and foreign policy.

Source: Manfred B. Steger. *Globalization: A Very Short Introduction.* Oxford, UK: Oxford University Press, 2013; Frank J. Lechner and John Boli, eds. *The Globalization Reader*, 5th ed. West Sussex, UK: Waley Blackwell, 2013; Winnie Byanyima. "Richest 1% Will Own More than All the Rest By 2016." Oxfam.org. Accessed April 3, 2015. https://www.oxfam.org/en/pressroom/pressreleases/2015-01-19/richest-1-will-own-more-all-rest-2016.

The Impact of Globalization on Countries

Referring to Table 11.1, it is helpful to understand some of the issues in a little more detail to see how they affect countries and organizations. It is easy to see why trade is a critical beginning point. Prior to the efforts in the 1940s, international trade was very difficult and expensive. The bureaucracy, documentation, and tariffs involved made trade almost impossible in some countries, but with the treaty developments of the last century, trade has become much easier. Tariffs have been reduced and sometimes completely removed for some items. However, because of the recent global financial crisis, some tariffs have been reinforced or reinstated, reversing some of the earlier trends.

Global financial markets were created to make it easy for money to flow across borders into all types of organizations. The International Monetary Fund was created to ease some of the issues on money flows and investments and provide assistance and support where necessary. In addition, the World Bank was created to help the least-developed countries. Foreign investment into countries was promoted and increased to the point where it became a critical issue with many organizations. Almost every country wants foreign investment, not just for job creation, but also for gains in productivity, advanced manufacturing techniques, research and development—and consequently, higher wages. Even the highly industrialized and developed nations are very eager to capture foreign direct investment.

For example, in 2014, for the first time, foreign investment in China exceeded foreign investment in the United States. In fact, the investment in the United States was only slightly more than the investment in Singapore. Table 11.2 shows the top destinations for foreign investment in 2014. The problem is that direct investment is not occurring in the least-developed countries, at least not enough to create enough jobs to bring them out of poverty. An obvious reason is that these countries are often unstable and deteriorating, making them unattractive targets for investors.

Table 11.2.   Top destinations for foreign direct investment in 2014.

Country	Investment in billions of dollars
China	128
Hong Kong	111
United States	86
Singapore	81
Brazil	62
United Kingdom	61
Canada	52
Australia	49
Netherlands	42
Luxembourg	36

Source: United Nations Conference on Trade and Development. "World Investment Report 2014: Investing in the SDGs: An Action Plan." Accessed January 31, 2015. http://unctad.org/en/PublicationsLibrary/wir2014.

Employment is the term that is most often used in connection with globalization. There has been tremendous job growth in India and China, as many manufacturing and service industries have outsourced an enormous amount of work, creating jobs and raising the wages in those countries. For the same reason, job creation has been relatively flat in the United States and the European Union. This creates issues for politicians and policy makers. Table 11.3 shows the effect of globalization on unemployment trends and projections. Total unemployment is increasing, as the unemployment rate is projected to be fairly stable through 2018. This means that not enough jobs are being created to keep up with population growth.

The environment is an area where globalization was once thought to have a positive impact. The assumption was that having products and services cross borders could help organizations in the least-developed countries become more efficient, reduce their pollution, and moderate their effects on the environment. It was also thought that through a global community, there would be pressure on the primary culprits who are destroying the environment to actually improve their practices. This has not happened as expected. Figure 11.1 shows the consequences of global environmental degradation caused in part by the globalization effort.[4] More specifically, in terms of the total emissions of carbon dioxide, China remains the biggest culprit, followed closely by the United States, India, and the Russian Federation. However, on a per capita basis, the United States is much worse than China. Globalization's effect on the environment is a serious problem, as we have consistently seen the destruction of biodiversity, food shortages, unusual weather patterns, and the general warming of the climate. This is perhaps one of the most serious issues that we have to address as a global community.

Finally, regarding poverty and inequality, globalization is not working as it should be. The rich are becoming richer and the poor are becoming poorer. A recent

Table 11.3. Global unemployment trends and projections, 2003–2018.

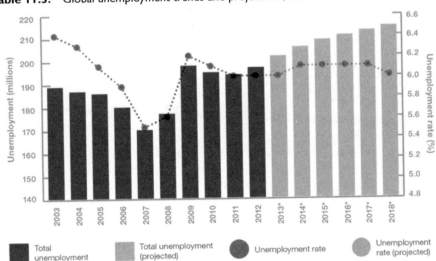

Source: ILO, Trends Econometric Models, October 2013

Figure 11.1. Major manifestations and consequences of global environmental degradation.
Source: Manfred Steger. *Globalization: A Very Short Introduction.* Oxford, UK: Oxford University Press, 2013.

report from Oxfam shows that the richest 1 percent is likely to control half of all global wealth by the end of 2015.[5] In 2014, the eighty wealthiest billionaires in the world all together had $1.9 trillion in wealth, nearly the same amount shared by the 3.5 billion people who occupy the bottom half. The year before, it had taken eighty-five billionaires to equal that figure. The same report indicates that there are more than 1 billion people who live on less than $1.25 per day. The reality is that the bottom billion people are getting poorer, while the upper 1 percent is getting richer. These serious issues show the downside of globalization.

The Impact of Globalization on Organizations

Just as globalization affects countries and the global community as a whole, it also affects individual organizations as they participate in globalization. There are five important issues beyond the impacts described in the previous section.

The first issue is pricing strategies. When work from highly developed countries is outsourced to less-developed countries, it can be performed much cheaper. For the most part, this is passed onto the consumer with lower prices. To remain competitive, organizations have to meet those low prices, which means either finding efficiencies to lower costs or participating in the same type of outsourcing. In addition, consumers can easily compare prices using the Internet—in some cases, instantaneously on their mobile devices. Globalization has a tendency to take pricing out of the mix, constantly driving prices down or at least keeping them under control and very near to the competition. This makes more products and services available to consumers, including in some of the least-developed countries. At the same time, it places pressure on companies to increase efficiency and effectiveness. Only the strong and determined survive in this kind of environment.

The second issue is trade. Imports and exports are always critical for a country. In an ideal situation, a country exports more than it imports. But many countries are out of balance, and it becomes a major problem when trade is severely out of balance. The goal for all is to develop more goods and services and trade them all over the world. The challenge is to make sure they flow in the right direction for a given country.

The third issue is foreign direct investment, which is important as companies seek assistance to invest in another country. For example, incentives are often provided to attract investments. In a highly developed country like the United States, lucrative incentives are provided to foreign companies to build plants and service facilities—sometimes excessive enticements. To try to balance this and encourage foreign direct investment into the least-developed countries, assistance and support is provided through organizations such as the World Bank and the International Monetary Fund.

The fourth issue is employment, the globalization issue affecting organizations the most. The definition of a good employer is one that not only keeps jobs but creates jobs, while becoming more efficient and profitable so that they can be sustained over a period of time. To increase efficiency and profitability while creating jobs is difficult, but some of the best are doing it. The challenge is to ensure that globalization does not have an adverse impact on the right kind of job growth.

In theory, when a massive number of jobs are relocated to another country, new jobs will be created in the outsourcing country that will be higher skilled and higher paid. For example, in the United States, the textile industry has mostly been relocated to Asia, displacing millions of Americans from textile employment. It was assumed that these people would move into other jobs or be trained for higher paying jobs. This has not happened in many cases, creating real problems for unemployment. As of 2015, the U.S. unemployment rate is 5.8 percent, but some argue that the real employment rate is more than 12 percent because so many people are underemployed. There are many stories about waiters with bachelor's degrees, taxi drivers with PhDs, and landscapers with engineering degrees. These individuals do not appear in the official unemployment rolls because they are not drawing unemployment benefits. Nevertheless, they are victims of a massive but hidden problem called underemployment.

The fifth issue is inequality—an issue for countries, but also an issue for companies. For the United States as a whole, Figure 11.2 shows the lowest income of the top

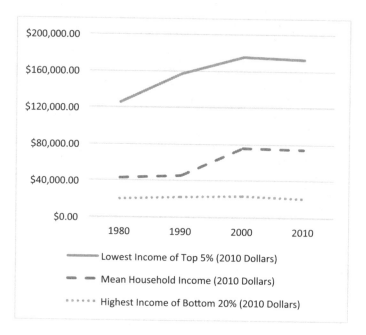

Figure 11.2. The divergence of the rich.

Source: United States Census Bureau Historical Income Tables: Household. Accessed January 10, 2015. http://www.census.gov/hhes/www/income/data/historical/household/index.html.

5 percent compared to the highest income of the bottom 20 percent, as well as the mean household income. This shows a tremendous gap between the rich and poor.

Figure 11.3 shows the growth of gross domestic product per capita compared to the growth of household income. In the last twenty-five years, household income has been stagnant, whereas GDP has grown significantly.

For companies, this is connected to the salary gap, the difference in the pay between top executives and low-level employees, which has been widening rapidly. Some organizations have set ratios that they try to maintain between the higher paid and the lower paid. To keep demand for goods and services growing, household incomes must increase. Individual organizations must do their part by taking action to correct inequality.

How Organizations Become Global

Most global organizations started out as home-based organizations in one country that then grew to another country and another until they become global power-houses. McDonalds started with one restaurant in California, and Coca-Cola started with a few customers in Atlanta. Now both of these companies dominate the global landscape. Yet, they started slowly and grew incrementally over a period of time into the global powerhouses that they have become.

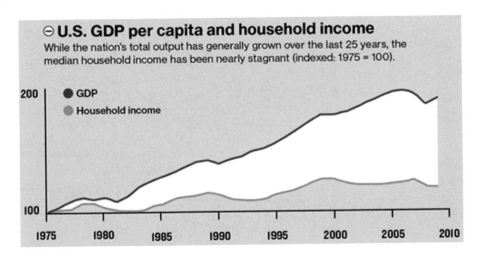

Figure 11.3. U.S. GDP per capita and household income.

Source: David Rotman. "How Technology Is Destroying Jobs." *Technology Review*, June 12, 2013. http://www.technologyreview.com/featuredstory/515926/how-technology-is-destroying-jobs.

Table 11.4 shows the typical phases of a firm's evolution in globalization. This chart shows how globalization affects several dimensions of business, such as expanding sales and locating manufacturing or support facilities in other countries. It also shows how procurement flows are gradually shifted, research and development moves to other countries, and management becomes permeated with individuals from all over the world. The company's national identity is sometimes even lost purposely. While stakeholders are initially based in the home country, global organizations have a global shareholder base.

Almost any firm in the international context is positioned at some point on this process with the goal of being a truly global organization. We are not suggesting that it is best to be a truly global organization, but some firms want to become so much a part of local communities that even the local communities identify with them. A good example is trying to understand where a company is based. In some companies, this is not a secret, and it is actually part of the market strategy. For example, Volkswagen will always remind its audience that German engineering is a part of their company. An Italian fashion designer will always remind you that it is an Italian company. A French wine estate will remind you that it's French. However, to truly get the local acceptance of a product or service, some companies prefer not to be identified with a particular country. For example, it is difficult to figure out exactly where many pharmaceutical companies are based. The same is true for the "Big Four" global consulting and accounting firms: PricewaterhouseCoopers, Deloitte & Touche, Ernst & Young, and KPMG. In our own work with those organizations, we have found that even many of their own consultants are not sure where their company is based. Different employees give different responses. Can you guess where they are based? PwC and EY each have dual headquarters in London and

Table 11.4. A firm's evolution in globalization.

Phase	Sales of products or services	Investments in other countries	Manufacturing and/or support facilities in other countries	Procurement flows	Research and development	Management	National identity	Shareholders
1 Exporting products and services	Sell through distributors/partners	None	None	Home	Home	Home	Home	Home
2 Exporting sales	Dedicated sales team	Offices, contract employees	None	Some local	Home	Some local	Home	Home
3 Exporting international operations	Dedicated sales team	Offices, company employees	Limited operations	More local	Home	Local/home	Home	Home
4 Major operations	Dedicated sales team	Offices, company employees	Major operations	Limited, across borders	Some local	Local	Home/local	Home/local
5 Global scope	Dedicated sales team	Offices, company employees	Major operations, regional headquarters	Across borders	Mostly local	Open to all	Home/local	Home/local
6 Truly global	Dedicated sales team	Offices, company employees	No single region is dominant	Across borders	Local with home coordination	Global mixture	No national identity	Global

Influencers: Standardization, Integration, Efficiency, Culture

New York. Deloitte is based in New York, and KPMG is based in Amsterdam. But because consultants operate in their particular countries, they each feel part of that country and may not realize their company is based elsewhere. It is important for some companies to have an image that is not attached to a particular country or culture but becomes a part of each local context to the greatest extent possible.

HR in a Global Company

It is one thing to sell products and services to a global market base when the need is there and the consumers want the product, but it is another thing entirely to employ a foreign workforce to make that happen in each country. From the very first time that a company has employees in another country, it faces many issues. There are ten very important challenges that are faced by most multinational companies:

1. *Compliance with labor laws.* Every company finds a challenge in working with laws, regulations, and rules in another country. These vary dramatically from one country to another, and companies often need the help of good advisors to unravel and comply with the different rules and policies.
2. *Talent acquisition.* It is critical to acquire the right people at the right time, but finding the right talent for a "foreign company" is sometimes a difficult task. Even simply identifying and recruiting individuals can be a challenge in another country.
3. *Developing agile leaders.* An organization needs flexible leaders who can adapt to the changes and challenges of operating in a global environment. They must be able to bring the local context and culture into their decisions and relationships within each country.
4. *Balancing local and home issues.* Deciding which decisions must be made locally and which must be made at the headquarters is critical. For example, financial accounting may be kept at headquarters, while succession planning may need to be more at the local level.
5. *Building capability.* Employees must understand the products and services and how to produce or sell them. They must understand how to communicate and integrate with others across borders in the cultural context. Learning and development can be different from one country to another. For sustainability, capability must be enhanced routinely in the organization.
6. *Efficient coordination and collaboration.* A global company must be connected and orchestrated in its work. Employees must be synchronized in their projects and efforts, and they must collaborate on a routine basis. This gets more difficult when different languages and long distances are involved.
7. *Retaining critical talent.* Some individuals in the organization are considered critical talent, and these are the people who make the most difference. It is not always an executive or a manager. It might be the IT team, the direct sales force, the store managers, or the research and development professionals. The challenge is to retain this critical talent in the organization. High turnover can be disastrous.
8. *Sharing knowledge across borders.* Knowledge management and knowledge sharing are important, particularly in a knowledge-based company. Using all

the tools for collaboration and sharing is essential. Building databases that easily integrate with each other is also important.

9. *Operating efficiently.* The products and services delivered must be produced at a low cost to the organization; otherwise, competition will have an advantage. Efficiency is king, and delays and bottlenecks have to be removed to make a smooth work machine.

10. *Improving productivity.* In addition to lowering production costs, there must be more output. The gross productivity of a firm, revenue divided by employees, must be continuously improved as technology is used, capability is enhanced, and engagement and motivation kick in to deliver a very powerful workforce.

These challenges are consistent with those found in many studies. For example, IBM's most recent "Global Chief Human Resources Officer Study" identified developing agile leaders, retaining critical talent, improving productivity, and sharing knowledge as very important challenges for today's environment.[6]

Implications for Human Capital Strategy

The human capital strategy should direct some very important, and sometimes sensitive, issues:

- Determine the policy and philosophy for outsourcing. It is obvious that too many outsourcing decisions have been made based on short-term cost savings alone. Sometimes a longer-term view is needed, and often a consideration of the human capital aspect needs to be a part of this decision.
- Focus on employment and job creation. To be a good citizen, the firm should aim to keep jobs as much as possible, redirecting people to other work as efficiencies are gained. But firms also need to look at job-creation efforts, so that higher-paying jobs are created to add value to the country as well as the company.
- Pursue innovation. As described in Chapter 7, innovation is the best way to make sure that new jobs can be created and that new products and services can be developed. Innovation also helps deliver a lower price with top quality so that a competitive edge can be gained.
- Address inequality at the firm level. This issue can be addressed in two ways. First, make sure that the firm moves beyond the minimum wage, if employees are at that level. If organizations boost their low-level employees, the increased household income of that group will drive demand for goods and services. At the same time, it is important to be mindful of the differences between executive pay and regular employee wages, perhaps setting a particular ratio that makes sense to the organization and the shareholders.
- A communication strategy should be developed for globalization issues. When the organization is drastically impacted by events outside the home country, employees must understand why. For example, if the employees' 401(k) plans have been reduced because of the debt default of Greece or falling oil prices, the organization needs to be proactive in explaining this. This requires very important communication efforts.

12

PROTECT THE ENVIRONMENT

Implementing Green, Sustainable Projects

- -

Force 10: Environmentalism. This important force involves protecting the environment. When the issue of global warming first surfaced in the 1980s, it stirred up much public debate and concern throughout the world. However, business leaders resisted the issue of global warming, expecting they would have to pay a lot of money to address the problems causing it. While most agreed that climate change was occurring, views differed regarding its origins, and finding solutions was not a priority to the business world at large.

Today, most (if not all) businesses recognize that climate change is a problem, and some businesses are making attempts to solve it, resulting in a wave of sustainability and environmental projects. However, too many organizations are currently caught in what may be called a green slump, struggling to engage in green projects and making far less progress than is actually required.

From an organizational perspective, going green offers employees, contractors, volunteers, and members the opportunity to influence the green movement through involvement and contribution. The challenge is to create the correct approach to involve these people—one that includes teaching, convincing, communicating, enabling, supporting, and encouraging participation in the green process. The best way to accomplish this is through the human capital strategy.

- -

This chapter shows the importance of protecting the environment with a variety of green sustainable projects. The sheer number of potential green projects and initiatives, and the fact that not everyone is buying into the issues, brings into focus the need for this chapter. Many individuals do not see the need for action because they do not understand the issues or know what they can do to help. Some people do not understand green projects and sustainability efforts, feel inconvenienced by them, believe they are negatively affected in one way or another by project out-comes, or perceive projects to require unrealistic investment.

This chapter presents the many facets of the green revolution and how organizations are managing to go green. It explores the value of green projects and what must be accomplished by the CHRO to deliver results to protect the environment.

Opening Story: Interface

Interface Inc. began in 1973 when founder and chairman Ray C. Anderson recognized the need for flexible floorcoverings that would facilitate the emerging technologies of the modern office. Over the years, Interface grew its core business and expanded through more than fifty acquisitions to become the world's largest producer of modular carpet, with manufacturing on four continents and sales in more than 110 countries. Today, Interface is a billion-dollar corporation, named by *Fortune* magazine as one of the "Most Admired Companies in America" and "100 Best Companies to Work For."

In 1994, while preparing remarks on Interface's environmental vision for a company task-force meeting, Ray Anderson experienced a fundamental perspective change. Seeking inspiration for his speech, Ray read Paul Hawken's "The Ecology of Commerce" and was deeply moved—an experience he described as an epiphany. It awakened Ray to the urgent need to set a new course for Interface toward sustainability.

In that year, Anderson set a daring goal for his commercial carpet company: to take nothing from the earth that cannot be replaced by the earth. At the time, carpet manufacturing was a toxic petroleum-based process that released immense amounts of air and water pollution and created tons of waste. In the fifteen years since Anderson's call for change, Interface has accomplished the following:

- Cut greenhouse gas emissions by 82 percent
- Cut fossil fuel consumption by 60 percent
- Cut waste by 66 percent
- Cut water use by 75 percent
- Invented and patented new machines, materials, and manufacturing processes
- Increased sales by 66 percent, doubled earnings, and raised profit margins

The journey to a fully sustainable Interface is like climbing "a mountain higher than Everest"—difficult, yes, but with a careful and attentive plan, not impossible. Interface created a framework for the climb called "Seven Fronts on Mount Sustainability":

Front #1—Eliminate Waste: Eliminate all forms of waste in every area of the business.

Front #2—Benign Emissions: Eliminate toxic substances from products, vehicles, and facilities.

Front #3—Renewable Energy: Operate facilities with 100 percent renewable energy.

Front #4—Closing the Loop: Redesign processes and products to close the technical loop using recycled and bio-based materials.

Front #5—Efficient Transportation: Transport people and products efficiently to eliminate waste and emissions.

Front #6—Sensitizing Stakeholders: Create a culture that uses sustainability principles to improve the lives and livelihoods of all our stakeholders.

Front #7—Redesign Commerce: Create a new business model that demonstrates and supports the value of sustainability-based commerce.

As part of its Mission Zero commitment, Interface has set a goal to source 100 percent of energy needs from renewable sources by 2020. To achieve this, Interface has a simple strategy—improve energy efficiency and increase use of renewable energy. They have taken an aggressive approach to reach this goal, installing renewable energy systems at factories and purchasing renewable energy for facilities around the world. By 2013, five of its seven factories operated with 100 percent renewable electricity, and 35 percent of its total energy use was from renewable sources.

The vision and mission of Interface focuses on sustainability.

Interface Values

Vision

To be the first company that, by its deeds, shows the entire industrial world what sustainability is in all its dimensions: People, process, product, place, and profits—by 2020—and in doing so we will become restorative through the power of influence.

Mission

- Interface will become the first name in commercial and institutional interiors worldwide through its commitment to *people, process, product, place, and profits.*
- We will strive to create an organization wherein all people are accorded unconditional respect and dignity; one that allows each person to continuously learn and develop.
- We will focus on products (which includes service) through constant emphasis on process quality and engineering, which we will combine with careful attention to our customers' needs so as always to deliver superior value to our customers, thereby maximizing all stakeholders' satisfaction.
- We will honor the places where we do business by endeavoring to become the first name in industrial ecology, a corporation that cherishes nature and restores the environment.
- Interface will lead by example and validate the results, including profits, leaving the world a better place than when we began, and we will be restorative through the power of our influence in the world.

Ray Anderson and Interface have been featured in three documentary films, including *The Corporation* and *So Right, So Smart*. In 1997, Anderson was named cochair of the President's Council on Sustainable Development, and in 2006, he served on the national advisory committee that helped guide the Presidential Climate Action Project, a two-year, $2 million project administered by the Wirth Chair School of Public Affairs at the University of Colorado. He and Interface have been featured in the *New York Times, Fortune, Fast Company,* and other publications.

Anderson died on August 8, 2011, twenty months after being diagnosed with cancer. On July 28, 2012, Anderson's family relaunched the Ray C. Anderson Foundation with a new purpose. Originally created to fund Ray Anderson's personal philanthropic giving, family members announced the rebirth and refocus of the foundation on Anderson's birthday, nearly one year after his 2011 death. The purpose of the Ray C. Anderson Foundation is to perpetuate shared values and continue the legacy that Anderson left behind. The Ray C. Anderson Foundation is a not-for-profit 501(c)(3) organization whose mission is to create a brighter, sustainable world through the funding of innovative projects that promote and advance the concepts of sustainable production and consumption. The world needs more leaders like Ray C. Anderson and organizations like Interface.

The Green Revolution

A green revolution is occurring throughout the world, and this effort toward fundamental change is particularly pervasive in the United States. Perhaps Thomas Friedman captures this revolution best in his bestselling book *Hot, Flat, and Crowded*, in which he makes the case for a green revolution that should sweep through organizations, cities, communities, and governments to create what he describes as the Energy Climate Era.[1] Here are a few examples of green initiatives.

Green Cities

Discussions about environmental issues often dwell on cities, focusing on their congestion, inefficiencies, and unmanageable challenges. Tall buildings, consuming enormous amounts of energy, and heavy traffic, inundating the environment with carbon emissions, are obvious environmental hazards. The cities themselves have taken the brunt of many of the social ills that stem from poverty, illness, crime, pollution, open sewers, and exhaust fumes. Despite these burdens, however, cities—with their great density—offer perhaps the best opportunities for environmentally friendly places to live and work. For example, the population density in Manhattan is sixty-seven thousand people per square mile, more than eight hundred times the nation as a whole and roughly thirty times the city of Los Angeles. In dense cities, residents can often live without the convenience of an automobile. Working near home allows people to live without the ecological disasters of cars, in contrast to workers who live in rural or suburban areas and have to use an automobile for every trip. In cities, people can engage in environmentally friendly habits such as bicycling, using mass transit, and walking while supporting each other as a community. Some cities are working hard to increase their residential appeal, which reduces the environmental burden caused by the mass exodus of the workforce commuting home at the end of the day. Some cities, airports, and ports are striving to be the greenest in the world, with much progress.

Green Organizations

The starting point for most organizations is to organize properly for green initiatives. This process begins with a mission statement, a vision statement, and a value statement that all incorporate green issues and sustainability efforts. This also involves the assignment of specific responsibilities to individuals involved in green projects. Role definition for all organizational stakeholders is a must if involvement, support, encouragement, and accomplishment of green objectives is the goal. An executive should be assigned the responsibility of environmental and sustainability efforts. Ideally this should be the CHRO. Figure 12.1 highlights the seven actions that must be taken to create a green organization.

Employees must understand the necessity for green projects and be aware of important environmental issues. Formal and informal meetings and communications using the plethora of social media tools can help. Learning programs make employees aware of the issues and the necessity to make improvements and adjustments. Brochures, guides, fact sheets, program descriptions, and progress reports help promote and encourage green project participation.

Organizational leaders must "practice what they preach" through visible and substantial green projects. These projects should be communicated to the organization, and their successes should be clearly documented. An example of a highly visible project is one that has been undertaken by Hewlett-Packard. A problem exists with the mountains of consumer electronics being disposed of in landfills. To set an example in this important area, HP has collected more than three billion pounds of e-waste (the weight of three thousand jumbo jets) since 1987. More than 75 percent of ink cartridges and 24 percent of HP LaserJet toner cartridges are now manufactured with "closed loop" recycled plastic. HP remanufacturing programs give IT hardware, such as servers, storage, and networking products, a new lease on life, reducing environmental impacts from disposal.[2]

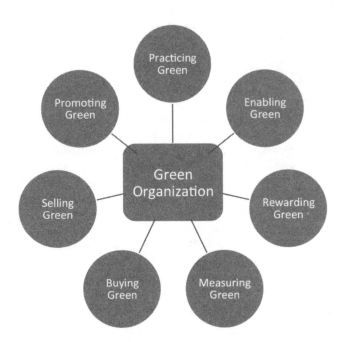

Figure 12.1.   Becoming a green organization.

Organizations are enabling stakeholders to be involved in green projects in their communities and in their personal lives. Organizations assist employees with recycling programs and support employees in a variety of ways to understand, promote, and be involved in green initiatives. For example, eight communities across the United States joined to create Climate Prosperity Project Inc., a nonprofit organization to address climate change and pursue economic development. The communities—Silicon Valley / San Jose, CA; Portland, OR; St. Louise, MO/IL; Denver, CO; Seattle, WA; Southwest, FL; Montgomery County, MD; and the State of Delaware—are convinced that climate change presents not only an environmental imperative but also an extraordinary economic opportunity.

Progressive companies are rewarding stakeholders for being involved in green efforts. For example, Southern Company has launched EarthCents programs, which include new and existing programs and educational efforts to help reduce residential and commercial energy consumption. The benefits of EarthCents include not only wise use of energy but also reduction of costs that hit the pockets of their customers. In addition, shareholders are rewarded because corporate costs are reduced and capital expenditures are avoided.[3] Through EarthCents education programs, employees have an opportunity to engage in stewardship that is highly valued and recognized by the organization. Some organizations provide quarterly or annual awards for green efforts by employees or groups of employees. Others provide bonuses for green ideas.

It is important for green-project success to be monitored and adjustments to be made along the way. Results must be communicated to stakeholders even if they show processes are not working well. The lobby of the International Fund for Agriculture Development (IFAD) boasts a large chart showing the progress of green projects. Measurement is a critical part of accountability, and making adjustments as measures are taken is a great way to keep projects on track.

Green organizations purchase green materials and supplies through their procurement functions by specifying and requiring green products. This is important with cleaning materials, for example, which can be toxic and hazardous to the environment. Purchasing green paper products is a highly visible way to contribute to the green movement, because it touches so many employees and stakeholders.

Progressive green organizations ensure that their products and services are sensitive to environmental issues and support sustainability efforts. This may mean that new products are developed to support the green movement. For example, Office Depot/OfficeMax researched how to transform its market based on creating a green office. These offerings include a green book catalog as well as a green office website. This site provides customers with definitions of terms and certifications, such as postconsumer recycled content. Through its effort, Office Depot/OfficeMax reinforces to businesses that there are real cost-saving opportunities with green products.

Collectively, these efforts are being taken up by thousands of organizations. If implemented properly, they can make significant progress with sustainability efforts. The important point is to make sure the value and success of these projects are known to stakeholders responsible for the design, implementation, and funding of projects.[4]

Green Buildings

Green organizations should be housed in green buildings, which represent another important opportunity and challenge. The opportunity exists because there are more than thirty million buildings in the United States, most of which are anything but green. These buildings consume about one-quarter of the global wood harvest, one-sixth of its fresh water, and two-fifths of the material and energy flows. They account for about 40 percent of primary energy use.[5] A typical house in the United States produces twenty-six thousand pounds of greenhouse gases each year, enough to fill up a Goodyear blimp. The challenge is that becoming a green building is not easy.

The good news is that major building projects across the country are now largely adhering to new benchmarks with environmentally sustainable construction standards, focusing not only on recycled building materials but energy efficiency as well. At the center of this movement is a certification program offered by the U.S. Green Building Council (USGBC). This program, known as Leadership in Energy and Environmental Design (LEED) certification, is a third-party verification system to show that a building was designed and built using true environmental standards, including energy savings, water efficiency, and CO_2 emissions reduction. Almost all the large-scale commercial projects in the United States are now LEED projects, and given that more than half of greenhouse gases come from buildings (compared to 9 percent for passenger vehicles), this is huge step in the right direction.

Green Workplaces

When people are not at home, they are usually at work, so the workplace represents another important area of focus for green initiatives. The workplace provides an opportunity for people to function in a green environment, learn about green issues, experiment with green projects, and observe cost savings at the same time. Figure 12.2 shows opportunities to make a workplace green.

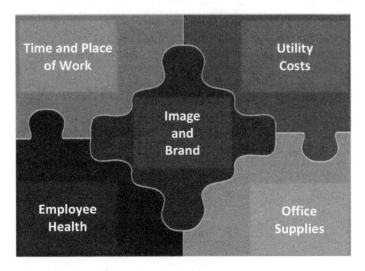

Figure 12.2. Making a green workplace.

Perhaps the greatest opportunity to save money and have a positive impact on the environment is to take advantage of the many possible options to let people work at home. Some organizations allow two or more employees to use a single assigned workplace and rotate schedules. Sometimes several people share office space close to their home at a reduced cost. Of course, the greatest environmental benefit comes from working at home full-time. One study revealed that 1,478 tons of carbon dioxide was prevented from being released into the environment each year when 350 employees were allowed to work at home.[6] Many organizations have been using telecommuting practices for years. Not only does the practice contribute to the environmental good, but many find that allowing employees to work at home creates a significant savings in real estate costs, as they are able to give up office space when the leases expire. Companies also find that productivity increases, because employees working at home are able to maintain larger workloads. Other benefits include gains in retention, job satisfaction, and talent recruitment, as described in Chapter 6.

Another important savings at the workplace can come from the reduced use of water, electricity, and natural gas. Although technology, design, and control mechanisms can make a difference, behavior change by the workforce can have the greatest impact. Many cost-saving processes can lower utility bills and help the environment. Simply shutting down computers at the end of the day and using motion-detection lighting can have a big impact on energy usage and operating costs.

Since the 1980s, businesses have been exploring ways to maintain a green workplace, from paper and toner cartridges to almost every office product category. Unfortunately, the traditional perception of making an office green is that costs will increase. This is not necessarily true. Even when items cost more initially, there is often a payback in the long run. Improvements have been made in the production of green office products. Businesses need to recognize that there is a green cost continuum. Some products, such as remanufactured ink or toner cartridges, are greener *and* less expensive. Also, investments in durable items rather than disposable ones, as well as in reusable and energy efficient items for the office, can mean dollars added to the company's bottom line due to decreased operating costs and repurchase costs.

Maintaining a green work environment creates an important image for consumers, employees, and others who care about the green movement. Consumers are attracted to companies that are environmentally responsible, and employees often want to work for companies that put the environment first. This can be an attractive recruiting tool, particularly for younger employees who want to work in this type of environment.

Indoor air quality is also a critical issue for employee health and well-being. Mold in the workplace—along with exposure to laser toner, cleaning agents, carbon monoxide, aerosols, and other items—can lead to a variety of ailments for employees, such as asthma and nasal irritations. The proper use of cleaning products and regular heating, ventilation, and air conditioning maintenance will make a difference.

The workplace is a fertile ground for green initiatives. It represents a major opportunity to shape employees' behavior. To do so will require a systematic approach to show the value, importance, and success of a variety of green initiatives.

Green Meetings

One of the top offenders to the environment is the meetings and events industry, rated only second to the construction industry. Each year, tens of thousands of meetings are organized globally where people convene to discuss all types of issues. Long-distance travel, large meeting places, and constant hotel stays have a huge impact on the environment. For example, the annual conference of the Society for Human Resource Management (SHRM)—the world's largest association of human resources professionals with about 275,000 members—attracts HR specialists, managers, and executives from around the world. A recent meeting in Las Vegas drew approximately 12,000 participants, about one-fourth of them from outside the United States. Everyone travels to the meeting; most of the travel is by air, and many flights involve long distances. The conference accommodates nearly 2,000 exhibitors, and some exhibits are so large that they need to be trucked in prior to the conference. Attendees take up thousands of hotel rooms, consume a tremendous amount of local transportation, and then travel back to their original destination. The effect this one meeting has on the environment is significant. Multiply this by all types of private company meetings, professional associations, trade shows, and special events, and it becomes clear why this industry is destroying the environment.

A few experts in the green and environmental movements suggest that, for the most part, these large-scale meetings should go away. In this era, such conferences add little to knowledge and understanding, they damage the environment, and much of what they do can be accomplished in other ways. While this is a harsh position, the industry is facing challenges on several fronts. Technology has enabled people to meet more conveniently and without the cost of the travel. Many executives are questioning the value of this expenditure. The recent global recession has put many of these events in the crosshairs of cost-cutting CEOs.

Green Energy

Many observers see green energy as the key to solving the climate-change problem. They posit that clean energy is the solution to all environmental ills. The topic of clean energy garners much attention, focus, and money, although some projections are bleak as energy demand increases. There are many projects and programs in place to tackle the issue.

Suppliers of energy realize that the best way to address the crisis is simply to save energy. This is why electrical power companies and other energy providers are advising consumers on ways to save electricity. Indeed, this may be the only way for them to meet the demand. This involves saving energy through efficient light bulbs, pumps, and motors; good building design; and refined processes.

A variety of new green power sources are being developed from solar, wind, small hydro, biomass, and geothermal sources. These are being funded in part by business energy users as they purchase renewable energy certificates (REC). With the RECs, businesses are buying power that is purchased from the new power sources and placed on the grid. It is impossible to hook a business up directly to a wind farm, but the business can purchase the equivalent of the power they need to be generated by the wind farm. It is like trading in the commodity market. This is providing significant funding for new sources of green power.

Green Technology

A bright spot in the green revolution is that the development of new technologies are, in some cases, central to green projects and sustainability efforts. Some advocates describe green technology as a huge growth opportunity for the next decade. Just as information technology exploded in the 1990s, green technology is set to be the next major growth sector. Renewable energy, sustainable agriculture, green-building design, environmentally friendly construction and retrofits, greater efficiencies in lighting and appliances, smart grids, clean-energy transportation—all are markets of promise to generate jobs and profits globally.

Green technology does not have to represent huge projects; small devices can make a difference. Consider, for example, power adaptors—the boxes on charging cords that that either sit between the plug and the mobile phone or are integrated with the plug. There are about five billion power adaptor devices in use worldwide. The function of the power adapter is to convert high-voltage alternating current into the low-voltage direct current that is used for charging mobile phones, tablets, and other electronic devices. Until recently, the conversion was made using copper wire, and as much as 80 percent of the power was lost in the conversion as waste heat. Now conversion can be made more efficiently with an integrated circuit, with as little as 20 percent of the power being lost. It took some time for manufacturers, utilities, and state and federal authorities to work together to adopt the new technology, but for consumers, the switches mean lower power bills and smaller and lighter power adapters. Although they cost a little more to produce, the savings are tremendous. For the world as whole, this has meant a drop in global power consumption that is worth about $2 billion per year and saves thirteen million tons of carbon emissions annually.

Technology projects are fast growing and almost limitless. Green technology patents are on a growth path, and the U.S. government is expediting the patent process, reducing the traditional time it takes for a patent to be processed from forty months to one year. Faster patent reviews mean that firms can arrange financing more easily. This action should generate additional research and development from private firms (large and small) and universities as well. New products will likely emerge, including patents for hardware, software, and communication devices to monitor commercial and home energy use. All types of technologies are being developed to cut carbon emissions.

Managing the Change to Green

The landscape is covered with all types of green initiatives and projects, and the CHRO should have the responsibility for these projects. Sustainability must be integrated, managed, and properly implemented to reap the greatest rewards. There are several factors that help drive the changes that are taking place in the green revolution.

The number one driver for implementing green projects is the image it presents of an organization. Green is in vogue in all types of organizations. Organizations recognize that it is in their best interests for their constituents, consumers, employees, stakeholders, and the general public to view them as environmentally friendly.

In 2009, when Mike Duke took over as CEO of Wal-Mart, the world's largest retailer, which uses more electricity than any other private organization in the world and has the second-largest trucking company, his message to employees in a time of recession covered the expected topics about providing good service, keeping costs low, and beating the competition.[7] However, he also talked about sustainability. Specifically, he described many of the environmental projects that Wal-Mart had undertaken to reduce transportation and energy costs. He emphasized that these sustainability efforts must be accelerated and broadened in the future, regardless of the recession.

Why would the world's largest retailer, with approximately $500 billion in net sales and eleven thousand stores in twenty-seven countries, focus so much on the green issue?[8] Wal-Mart sees this as a way to provide low prices as they manage and control costs, which enables them to stay profitable, drive innovation, and help many of their customers through difficult times.

Sustainability, which includes sustaining the life of an organization, the profits of the organization, and society at large, is a part of Wal-Mart's strategy. A green strategy often focuses on protecting and restoring the ecosystem, and it involves actions and conditions that affect the earth's ecology, including reduction of climate change, preservation of natural resources, and prevention of toxic waste hazards.

During the last two decades, organizations have begun to incorporate strategies for sustainability with tremendous focus on green elements. Like all strategies, these plans must evolve from a clear understanding of where the organization is and where it can go, and they require the input and buy-in of all stakeholders. Plans should show how the strategies can be implemented and achieved with effort, determination, and deliberation. Organizations must review these strategies occasionally to see how they are working and apply great leadership throughout the process to make sure that each strategy is challenging, feasible, workable, and successful.

There is often a perception that a clean environment is going to cost everyone— that green initiatives come with a premium. This is not always the case. In fact, there are more opportunities for positive ROI values with green projects than negative ROI values.[9] Smart, progressive companies use their environmental strategies to innovate, create value, and build competitive advantage, and the opportunities are endless. To convince a group of money-conscious executives to undertake green projects, a method must exist that shows there is value in these projects that will ensure continued funding and growth.

According to Andrew Winston, green projects may represent the best way to stimulate the economy and keep companies prosperous. He suggests four strategies to turn green into gold:

- *Get lean.* Generate immediate bottom-line savings by reducing energy use and waste.
- *Get smart.* Use value-chain data to cut costs, reduce risks, and focus innovation efforts.
- *Get creative.* Pose theoretical questions that force you to find solutions to tomorrow's challenges today.
- *Get engaged.* Give employees ownership of environmental goals and the tools to act on them.[10]

As we continue to work to manage the change to green, one of the main challenges is to convince a variety of stakeholders about the value that green projects deliver, up to and including the financial ROI.

Another important element of managing change involves taking advantage of the "green-collar" economy. This concept essentially addresses two of the biggest problems facing most countries: the economy and the environment. A green job is defined as one with "decent wages and benefits that can support a family. It has to be part of a real career path, with upward mobility. And it needs to reduce waste and pollution and benefit the environment."[11]

Development of new green products and services, such as new sources of energy and new technologies, leads to new jobs. These jobs are significant in number, and the investments are large enough to drive the economy. In addition to the bottom-line contribution, both to those who obtain the new jobs and the economy at large, green jobs ultimately have a positive environmental impact. In the United States, the best example of perpetuating a green-collar economy is the American Recovery and Reinvestment Act, which included more than $60 billion in clean-energy investment intended to help jumpstart the economy and build clean energy jobs for tomorrow. This investment is expected to easily generate a more than $500 billion return in new jobs, business startups, expansion, and energy savings.[12]

The fifty interviews conducted by MIT in its Business of Sustainability Initiative revealed significant behavior changes that have taken place and must continue to take place. As organizations work to address environmental sustainability projects, there are eight management behaviors for leaders to keep in mind:

1. Sustainability projects will find you; it is hard to escape it. It is best to plan for it now.
2. Do not be surprised if you see unexpected productivity gains from green projects.
3. Your reputation is at stake; not addressing the green issues could seriously tarnish your efforts.
4. Strategy is needed and must be executed to see the system as a whole and to connect the dots.
5. Sustainability challenges demand innovation that is more iterative, more patient, and more diverse.
6. There must be collaboration across all boundaries to be successful.
7. The fear of risks has skyrocketed, creating a need for any practice or behavior that would access risk and reduce it.
8. The first adaptors with particular processes will be the winners.[13]

With this push and need for sustainability, there must be a focus on changing the behavior of people involved in this process. Attitudes, perceptions, awareness, and the barriers to actions must be addressed. As illustrated in the next chapter, there are many obstacles that can kill a project before it has a chance to add value. The measurement process described in this book can be used to assess a project's success and allow leaders to make adjustments to drive results.

The Value of Green Projects

"Is it worth it?" When asked this question about new or proposed green projects and sustainability initiatives, many executives, government officials, community leaders, and others involved with the environmental movement will answer with a resounding "Yes!" Others, however, respond with hesitancy. Some need convincing that there is value in going green.

The ultimate payoff of green projects and sustainability efforts is addressing climate change, deforestation, famine, and many other issues we face. Unfortunately, progress is lacking. Even at the microlevel, as hundreds of green projects are initiated every day, progress is minimal.

The Green Killers

When we consider the problems facing the planet and its future state, the need for healing is evident. Unfortunately, there are some people who do not support sustainability efforts. While many individuals stand in the way of progress, much of their inertia is based on misunderstandings of the need to make improvements. The sad truth is that people struggle to change. Elected officials and business leaders are not highly respected these days, and so when they tell us, "Trust me, this is good for all of us, just go and do it," people tend to tune them out.

Defining Value

Figure 12.3 shows some of the questions and issues that often arise when people are first introduced to green projects and sustainability efforts. They represent less-than-supportive attitudes toward green initiatives. These "green killers" inhibit progress and success.

The killers are categorized along a five-level results framework that is fundamental to the ROI Methodology, which is described in more detail in Chapter 14. The levels of data follow a chain of impact that must be in place for a green project to add business value.

The first level of value is *reaction and perceived value*. As the "Reaction/Perceived Value" section of Figure 12.3 shows, many people are still apathetic or believe their actions can make no real difference. They seem to think that sustainability is someone else's problem or that the only way to change it is through regulations and laws tackling the energy companies and the big polluters. Because of these initial reactions to green projects, CHROs must position the projects so employees, customers, and suppliers can perceive them as relevant and valuable.

The second level of value is *learning*. Try this experiment. Take five of the important elements that describe climate change, such as change in average weather over time, increase in CO_2 in atmosphere, local species extinction due to global loss of biodiversity, variations in solar radiation, or abrupt climate change, and ask your friends if they understand their meaning. Chances are, out of ten people, only one will be able to describe all five. There has not been enough specific information offered about climate change, particularly for the population born prior to 1970. Sustainability issues are now a part of most academic course curricula, but for the majority of the world's population, there has been limited education.

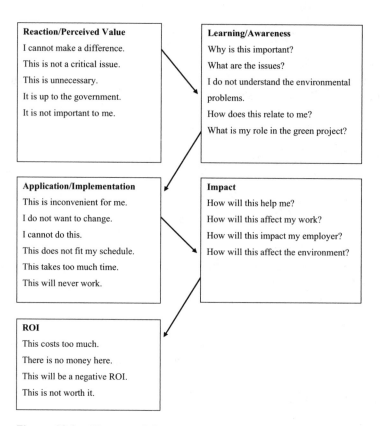

Figure 12.3. The green killers.

Consider the simple issue of changing to an alternative type of light bulb. In the United States, lighting represents about 20 percent of all electricity usage. A standard incandescent light bulb costs around $2 and uses about $20 of electricity per year. In contrast, a low-energy bulb costs about $8–$10 but only uses about $4 of electricity per year. With a cost reduction of $16 per year and an investment of $10, the benefits clearly exceed the costs.

While it makes sense financially, as well as environmentally, for people to change their bulbs, changing to energy-efficient lighting is a behavior many consumers cannot conceive. Manufacturers of energy efficient bulbs blame this on public apathy or lack of awareness. In this case, the public needs to be aware not only of how a particular green project can work but also of its benefits to the climate as well as the pocketbook. The learning that must take place is substantial. The more people know, the less resistant they will become. Even with government interventions phasing out the less efficient incandescent bulbs and offering only energy efficient bulbs, educating the public is essential.

The third level of value is *application and implementation*. Perhaps the greatest problem with green projects is people's inability to change current habits. Essentially, there is often limited application or implementation of processes focusing on green outcomes, at least at the level that may be needed to achieve desired results. Sometimes people do not do what is needed because it is inconvenient, it requires a change of habit, or they think they cannot do it. Others think that it may take too much time and see many barriers to the actual success of the project. Still others see that they can do it but need support. Consider this story:

> After much political wrangling, you manage to install energy-efficient lighting in a high-end hotel restaurant. The project will save thousands of dollars in electricity costs while preventing tons of carbon emissions from entering the atmosphere. It is the "rubber meets the road" of the sustainability movement, the blue-collar work of the climate battle. The restaurant opens, and the manager is put off by the sight of compact fluorescent bulbs. He removes the bulbs, throws them out, and replaces them with inefficient halogens. Not because he is ignorant or because he does not care, but because he has a business to run, and he is doing it the best way he knows how. His perspective is: you do not put energy-efficient fluorescent bulbs in a fancy restaurant any more than you would put Cool Whip on an éclair.
>
> Nonetheless, this is what your sustainability efforts have brought you: a wasted design and installation fee; inefficient lighting; the manager's loss of faith in green technology; hundreds of expensive compact fluorescent bulbs that, instead of being reused (at the very least), are now leeching costs for new bulbs and installation.[14]

There must be bottom-line consequences for many people to change their behaviors, particularly toward an outcome they believe is still somewhat elusive.

The fourth level of value is *impact*. Most individuals sponsoring green projects want to know the impact a project is going to have and the specific measures it will drive. Those involved want to know how it will affect them personally. Employees want to know how it will affect their work or maybe even their employer. Others want to know the impact on a community group or the city where they live. Some want to know what affect it has on the environment or how it helps the sustainability effort. Unfortunately, this evidence is often needed before the decision to begin is made. If the project involves savings in electricity usage, for example, some want to know before investing how much savings will occur. While there may be enough credible data to make a reliable forecast, the convincing needs to be strong. Some of the important impacts are energy use, carbon emissions, recycle volume, fuel costs, supplies costs, and landfill costs.

From our work at the ROI Institute, we recognize that impact data are the most critical data executives want to see. Executives are often willing to invest in green projects if there are intangible benefits that do not figure into the ROI calculation. So it is the impact data that are critical, and this must be developed for many executives to invest.

The fifth level of value is *return on investment* (ROI). Some people believe that green projects will result in a negative payoff. There is often an impression that a premium price is paid for anything that is green in nature. Perhaps this is based on a memory of when, years ago, recycled paper was expensive. In reality, most green products can actually save money in the long term, but the perception still exists that the cost of green outweighs the benefits, resulting in a negative ROI. As such, people conclude that green is not worth it. More examples are needed to show the costs versus benefits for a variety of projects.[15]

Change Toward Green

The green killers lead to inaction or inappropriate action affecting outcomes associated with green projects. While it is disappointing that attitudes, perceptions, lack of interest, and purposeful (or not) green washing seem to get in the way of making progress with sustainability efforts, these barriers exist with almost any type of change. For change to occur, employees must have a favorable reaction, understand the issues, and take appropriate action. The good news is that most people have a genuine interest in sustaining and developing our world. Research conducted at Wal-Mart and reported in the book *Strategy for Sustainability* describes some interesting findings.[16] The author interviewed Wal-Mart associates, exploring the basic concepts of sustainability and discussing what mattered to most of them. Here are some of the findings:

1. *They believe the environment is in crisis.* Once you removed the politics from the equation, people were ready to believe in global warming.
2. *They want to learn more about it.* Wal-Mart associates value learning, and any time they had the chance to learn something new that they could share, they were excited.
3. *They want to do something about it.* They lead busy lives with complex demands from family, work, religion, and hobbies. But if they could do something to help the environment that would also help them achieve their other goals, they were all for it.
4. *They have not made sustainability their top priority.* Sustainability does not work as another "thing" to care or worry about. But when the author presented sustainability as a framework that could help manage the other priorities in their lives, from personal health to finances, they were able to conceive of it as a matter of common sense.

Just as sustainability does not work for businesses unless it serves business needs first, sustainability does not engage individuals unless it first and foremost solves problems they experience in their lives.

The Chain of Impact for Green Projects

Sometimes it is helpful to think about the success of a green project in terms of a chain of impact that must occur if the project is going to be successful in terms of its business contribution. After all, if there is no business contribution, it is unlikely the project will be implemented. The chain of impact includes the five categories of data discussed in general terms previously. Together, these five levels form a chain of impact that occurs as projects are implemented.[17] But this chain of impact begins with the inputs to the process. Inputs, referred to as "Level 0," include the people involved in the project, how long it will take it to work, cost, resources, and efficiencies.

Obviously, these data are essential to move forward with a project, but they do not speak to the success of the project. It is through reaction, learning, and application of knowledge, skill, and information that a positive impact is made on business measures. Stakeholders realize how much impact is due to the project because a step occurs that will isolate the effects of the project from other influences. Impact measures are converted to money and compared to the cost to determine the ROI. In addition to these outcomes, intangible benefits are reported. Though they are not a new level of data, intangibles represent impact measures purposefully not converted to money and are always reported in addition to the monetary contribution of a project. Figure 12.4 represents this chain of impact that occurs through the implementation of green projects and key questions asked at each level.

Level	Measurement Focus	Typical Measures
0: Inputs and Indicators	Inputs into the project, including costs, project scope, and duration	Types of projects Number of projects Number of people Hours of involvement Cost of projects
1: Reaction and Perceived Value	Reaction to the project, including the perceived value of the project	Relevance Importance Value Appropriateness Fairness Commitment Motivation
2: Learning and Awareness	Acquisition of knowledge, skill, and/or information to prepare individuals to move the project forward	Skills Knowledge Capacity Competencies Confidence Awareness Attitude
3: Application and Implementation	Use of knowledge, skill, and/ or information and system support to implement the project	Extent of use Actions completed Tasks completed Frequency of use Behavior change Success with use Barriers to application Enablers to application
4: Impact	Immediate and long-term consequences of application and implementation expressed as business measures usually contained in the records	Productivity Revenue Quality/Waste Costs Time/Efficiency CO_2 emissions Brand Public image Customer satisfaction Employee satisfaction
5: ROI	Comparison of monetary benefits from project to the project costs	Benefit-cost ratio (BCR) ROI (percentage) Payback period

Figure 12.4. Levels and types of data.

Implications for Human Capital Strategy

Strong leadership is necessary for projects to work. Leaders must ensure that green projects and sustainability efforts are designed to achieve results rather than just to improve image. These projects and efforts must deliver the value that is needed by all stakeholders. Several actions must be taken to provide effective, results-based green leadership:

- Allocate appropriate resources for green projects and sustainability efforts.
- Assign responsibilities for green projects and programs, perhaps under the CHRO.
- Link green projects and programs to specific business needs.
- Create expectations for the projects' success with all stakeholders involved, detailing their roles and responsibilities.
- Address the barriers to the successful project early on so that the barriers can be removed, minimized, or circumvented.
- Develop partnerships with key administrators, managers, and other principle participants who can make the project successful.
- Communicate project results to the appropriate stakeholders as often as necessary to focus on process improvement.

13

Build Global Leaders

Developing Agile Leaders to Drive Business Results

> *Force II: Global Leadership.* Highly effective leadership is needed throughout every organization, from the first-level managers to the CEO. For international firms, a global perspective is critical, as leaders operate in a volatile, uncertain, complex, and ambiguous world. Even if an organization does not have a presence outside its initial borders, the global landscape will affect it in many ways. Understanding global dynamics and translating the information into excellent decisions and actions will determine the survival of the organization. The chief human resources officer must take the lead in developing leadership programs, processes, and events to ensure that leaders are ready and effective. This chapter takes a fresh a look at leadership and leadership development, detailing what has been achieved, what needs to be accomplished, and the next steps.

This chapter discusses the importance of developing global leaders and the human resources role in that challenge. Few things are more important to an organization than having great leadership, as leaders make the difference in the organization's success, sustainability, and impact on shareholders, customers, employees, and the community.

Opening Stories

Investment in leadership development is at a all time high. Here are three examples of leadership development approaches.[1]

Agilent Technologies

This manufacturer of instruments and equipment for life sciences, healthcare, and the chemical industry has introduced a leadership effectiveness analysis program, which has led to improvements across a number of key business outcomes. Introduced by incoming chief executive Bill Sullivan, the program has changed the strategic intent of the company through leadership excellence and created a set of expectations for leaders to fulfill.

The analysis takes the form of a leadership audit, with the questions adjusted over time to reflect not only changes in the business but also changes in leadership measurements. The results of the surveys are measured against external norms rather than against previous survey results. Once scores for particular traits have reached a level that is considered top quartile and it is clear that a particular leadership quality has become embedded in the company, new questions are introduced.

This leadership effectiveness analysis has enabled Agilent to develop different expectations of leaders at different levels, based on a "core" of expectations running all the way through the business. The analysis has become part of the DNA of the company and has a participation rate of 89 percent.

The program was implemented from the C-suite downward in order to ensure that when leaders began participating in the program, their own managers were already fully supportive of it. The analysis provides Agilent's twelve thousand employees with a reliable, consistent understanding of what leadership is and ensures that every business leader is following the same path. This has helped Agilent, which operates across many sites and has made a number of acquisitions in the past six years, ensure that its leadership is aligned across the company.

In addition to surveying its employees, Agilent also surveys its customers, and it has found that customers and employees give similar feedback, underlining the value of the program. It should come as no surprise that Agilent's customer loyalty and customer satisfaction ratings are better than those of its best-in-class competitors.

In addition, the program has helped to create a company-wide understanding of the direction of the company, as set out by the chief executive, and employee retention is better than the market average. The program has also helped Agilent attract new talent, with acceptance rates now above 90 percent. Ultimately, Agilent has seen a marked improvement in the leadership of the company, as the analysis has helped identify managers who are struggling to lead their teams effectively and the specific areas in which they are struggling. This has enabled HR to provide targeted support for these leaders, pairing them with mentors, teaching best practices, and working closely with them to improve their leadership skills.

PepsiCo

This food and beverage company based in New York is focusing heavily on leadership development programs to support its managers. While the company generally takes a top-down approach to training, the company found that new managers have a high risk of failure without the right support. This led PepsiCo to begin its leadership program with individuals assuming a management role for the first time.

The First Time Manager program was implemented because new managers benefit from greater support following their promotion. The program is a global one, and as the company works on a governance model, all the company's sector chief HR officers were in favor of initiating the leadership transition suite of programs by first focusing on the transition from individual contributor to manager. In addition, a global task force was set up to assist with the design of the program. It takes the form of a two-day residential course, followed by eighteen months of continuous learning, with participants undertaking regular tasks, readings, and so on to provide a combination of both active and passive learning.

The course focuses on teaching newly promoted managers the value of the role of a manager and adapting to a "manager mindset," and it provides guidance on how managers should adjust their time usage to ensure that they are properly delegating while at the same time building on the talent within their team.

PepsiCo has also introduced a Leaders of Managers program, as the second offering in its leadership-transition suite of programs, for the managers of managers. It covers a number of core skills, including business acumen, strategy, collaboration, talent management, and global mindset, and the course is a combination of leader-led learning and business simulation.

As a highly diverse company, both geographically and sectorally, with twenty-two billion-dollar brands, PepsiCo believes that the biggest impact of its leadership programs has been in helping managers to take a more global and cross-functional approach—giving them a greater understanding of the impact of decisions made at the local level on the rest of the company. The program has also assisted managers in building networks throughout the company outside of their own region and line of business.

IAMGOLD

IAMGOLD Corporation is a midtier Canadian gold mining company engaged internationally in mining and the exploration of gold. IAMGOLD has operations in North America, South America, and West Africa. The foundation of the company's culture is a belief in engaging, empowering, and supporting employees to build a company where the pursuit of excellence and an industry-leading vision of accountable mining exist in harmony. IAMGOLD was facing a typical challenge. Survey data taken from its employee engagement survey was much lower than expected, indicating that the first level of management needed leadership help and pointed to a need for formal leadership development.[2]

In response to this, IAMGOLD Corporation designed and implemented its comprehensive Supervisory Leadership Development Program (SLDP). The objective was to build a leadership pipeline while developing supervisory capabilities to engage, empower, and support employees. The program was highly visible, linked to key business objectives, and required substantial resources for the design and implementation, which covered a three-year timeframe. The project involved fourteens days of leadership development coupled with 360-degree feedback processes and a team of individuals to make it successful. In all, nearly 1,000 managers would be trained at a cost of more than $6 million. These factors and a need to measure program success and improvement opportunities led to an evaluation study using the ROI Methodology.

It is important to note that many of the supervisors in West Africa and South America lack formal education and many even have literacy problems. Consequently, SLDP was experiential in nature and offered creative, engaging activities for learners to explore and arrive at new meanings. Transfer of learning was built into the program, and each activity seamlessly linked to the next segment of learning. The program was delivered in three languages to meet the specific linguistic needs of each site.

The evaluation study found that the SLDP favorably impacted several of IAMGOLD's key business measures, and a positive ROI of 46% was realized. Other intangible benefits not converted to monetary value included improving supervisory effectiveness, which ultimately impacted employee engagement. From a program perspective, this evaluation highlighted the importance of top-down leadership development. With all of this in mind, IAMGOLD is now pursuing the development of a Manager Leadership Development Program (MLDP). As the MLDP is implemented, pieces of SLDP will also be redesigned for use with the general employee population, ensuring effective sustainability of the program.

Global Leadership Is Crucial

In a world of strident shareholder demand, shifting business priorities, disruptive innovation, rapidly changing demographic and geopolitical forces, regulatory changes, and increasingly competitive business environments, leaders who envision and execute today's strategy as well as anticipate and prepare for tomorrow's challenges are more critical than ever. Leaders are expected to demonstrate a deep understanding of their organization's business as well as its products and services, master the nuances of global markets, and conduct themselves in ethical ways. They must respond quickly to competitive maneuvers, foster innovation, communicate a compelling vision, and develop not only their globally distributed teams but also the next generation of leaders, all while delivering long-term value measured by short-term results. Becoming such a leader is like reaching the Mt. Everest of leadership development—and attainment is elusive. The results of failure to produce such leaders are often public, usually pronounced, and always profound.

Yet strong leaders can be developed *if* organizations, business leaders, and those who head leadership development functions create the systems, processes, involvement, and accountability that are crucial to success. Some organizations seem to have reached the summit. Others struggle against the vertical climb. Still others remain unable to gain a foothold. It's not going to get any easier.

Global Leadership Defined

What makes an effective, successful global leader? What does it take to be successful, and how is that success determined? Is the success to be evaluated quarterly and based on results delivered to the satisfaction of analysts and shareholders? Is it to be judged by results delivered during the tenure in the role, over the course of a lifetime of leadership, or ultimately by the future success of the company, business unit, or team after the leader has departed? What role does character play in this examination of business impact? What characteristics and competencies of a leader distinguish the "best" from the merely "very good"?

As a core criterion, the expectation of leaders has always been to "get the job done" by managing assets and people in a complex global environment. Often missing has been a more holistic view of the process in terms of how to motivate, engage, reward, and lead employees.

Twentieth-century research began to crystallize the way effective organizational leaders are viewed and subsequently developed. Few depictions of effective leadership have withstood the test of time as well as that of Peter Drucker, who articulated the eight core practices of the effective leaders he worked with over his sixty-year career. According to Drucker, effective leaders do the following:

1. Ask, "What needs to be done?"
2. Ask, "What is right for the enterprise?"
3. Develop action plans.
4. Take responsibility for decisions.
5. Take responsibility for communicating.
6. Are focused on opportunities rather than on problems.
7. Run productive meetings.
8. Think and say "we" rather than "I."

As he saw it, these questions "gave them the knowledge they needed . . . helped them convert this knowledge into action . . . [and] ensured that the whole organization felt responsible and accountable."[3]

Jim Collins offered that in addition to IQ and technical skills, these five emotional intelligence attributes characterize the true leader:

1. Self-awareness
2. Self-regulation
3. Motivation
4. Empathy
5. Social skill[4]

"Level 5 leaders," as he described them, credit others with success yet assume personal responsibility for failure. These leaders are characterized by humility and a will to succeed that does not tolerate mediocrity; they are quietly and calmly determined to succeed.

Over the years, we've seen the "one-minute manager" joined by the "situational leader" and the "servant leader" and by those leaders who are "values driven," "principle centered," and searching for "true north" or "multipliers." While definitions will undoubtedly continue to evolve, the fundamental description of a leader as one who delivers results in a way that affirms, engages, inspires, and respects others is unlikely to fade from view.

The Forces for Effective Global Leadership

Effective global leadership is critical to the success, and often the survival, of corporations. In recent years, we have witnessed the demise or serious crippling of companies because of the inability of leaders to competently and ethically lead, creating a breach of trust with the public as well as with employees. Newspaper headlines and, in some cases, high-profile trials remind us of the failures of leadership. They are not confined to a particular region or industry, as scandals surrounding such companies as WorldCom, Satyam Computer Services, Adelphia, Parmalat, Tyco International, Clearstream, Enron, Global Crossing, and Arthur Anderson can attest. While most companies do not make the headlines for their leadership failures, they are *all* accountable for business results.

CEOs Care About Leadership

In the years since the global financial crisis, companies and their leaders have been shifting from survival mode to a business growth approach. It is no wonder that leadership development was on the minds of CEOs around the world when they responded to The Conference Board's annual CEO Challenge survey.[5] When asked to rank their top challenges for the coming year, they ranked business growth first. The surprise was that, after an absence from the 2009 and 2010 "top ten" findings, talent emerged as the second-most important global challenge; Asian CEOs ranked it number one, ahead of business growth. CEOs thought talent, innovation, and cost optimization would fuel business growth. When asked about the strategies CEOs would implement to address the talent challenge, these were the top ten:

1. Improve leadership development programs; grow talent internally.
2. Enhance the effectiveness of the senior management team.
3. Provide employee training and development.
4. Improve leadership succession planning.
5. Hire more talent in the open market.
6. Promote and reward entrepreneurship and risk taking.
7. Raise employee engagement.
8. Increase diversity and cross-cultural competencies.
9. Flatten the organization, and empower leadership from the bottom up.
10. Redesign financial rewards and incentives.

Even a cursory read of the top strategies indicates a focus on internal leadership (improving the existing internal leadership base, especially at the top of the house; up-skilling all employees; improving leadership succession) before fighting for talent in the open market. In Asia, where talent was scarce before the global financial crisis, "hiring more talent in the open market" was ranked eleventh, with an internal development and retention focus being preferred, as qualified talent is both scarce and expensive. Asian leaders understand that they must build leaders faster than the global competition. Two things distinguish the approach of Asian companies: (1) attention to the specific developmental needs of the individual leader and (2) the speed with which they accelerate the development of key talent through experience, exposure, and customized training programs.[6]

Customers and Consumers Care About Leadership

We live in an age when maintaining an organization's reputation and brand management is a constant challenge. Of the many ways corporate reputations are made and lost, few factors are more important than the quality of their leaders. Consumers are negatively influenced by headlines of errant and unethical behavior and positively influenced by lists of most-admired companies, especially those touted for their strong managerial practices. Consumers and customers have strong brand affiliations, product dependencies (e.g., prescriptions or replacement parts), and business affiliations that would be difficult to replace, and they take note of leadership behaviors. Knowing that raw materials are harvested in a sustainable way, that clothing is not manufactured by the use of child labor, that executives are not "tone deaf" to the average citizen, and that the stock market is still a fair and level playing field is important to consumers. In a world of choices, they will provide feedback by remaining loyal to a brand or by choosing a competitor for essentially the same product. They often share their thoughts and feelings among the members of their social networks with messages and postings that seem to never fade from the Internet.

Shareholders Care About Leadership

Those shareholders whose investment dollars and pension funds balance on the edge and are subject to mismanagement, lost revenue, and missed opportunity costs pay close attention. They are looking for superior returns and believe that those returns are the result of well-run companies led by ethical leaders. Analysts agree. There is mounting evidence of a direct correlation between effective leadership and business results. In their examination of CEO performance at publicly traded companies, researchers found that the "best-performing CEOs in the world" came from many countries and industries, and on average, those CEOs delivered a total shareholder return of 997 percent (adjusted for exchange-rate effects) during their tenure. On average, these top fifty CEOs increased the wealth of their companies' shareholders by $48.2 billion (adjusted for inflation, dividends, share repurchases, and share issues). Compare that to the fifty CEOs at the bottom of the list, who delivered a total shareholder return of –70 percent during their tenure and presided over a loss of $18.3 billion in shareholder value. Industry, country, and economic factors were accounted for, and each CEO's background and the situation he or she inherited were certainly factors in judging success. Many on the list of successes are familiar names; numerous others are relatively unknown but tend to have been selected internally and have served longer in the role than the current average tenure of CEOs.[7]

Internal Stakeholders Care About Leadership

In an era of increased scrutiny of virtually all expenditures, accountability for the development of leaders, particularly at the top, will only increase. Significant resources continue to be devoted to developing leaders. The Association for Talent Development (ATD) estimates that, even in the midst of the global financial crisis, U.S. companies alone spent just under $126 billion per year on employee learning and development; slightly more than 10 percent of that expenditure was devoted to developing leaders and managers, and an additional 4 percent was expended on executive development.[8] The inability to determine whether or not resources have been expended wisely cannot be sustained in most corporate environments, even when we intuitively believe that leadership development (along with all employee development) is a noble pursuit.

Current and Prospective Employees Care About Leadership

Effective leaders create a culture that serves as a magnet for attracting top talent. With each generation entering the workplace, a greater emphasis is placed on continual development, as these new employees know that they are unlikely to stay more than a few years; it's about what they can develop, acquire, and take with them to the next stop in their career journey. We know that effective leaders are one of the most important influences on levels of engagement. Recent research reaffirms the correlation between engagement and leaders' ability to do the following:

- Develop a positive and significant relationship with each employee.
- Provide constructive performance feedback often.
- Coach employees.
- Provide opportunities to grow and develop.
- Set a clear direction—at whatever level is appropriate.
- Communicate not only corporate strategy goals but also progress toward those goals.
- Act in ways that are consistent with words.

Higher rates of engagement translate into higher rates of retention, an important factor in retaining talent in an increasingly competitive job market.[9] In a world in which fewer than one in three employees are engaged, trust in executives can have a significant impact on engagement.[10]

Other Stakeholders Care About Leadership

In an increasingly interconnected world, there are many stakeholders whose fortunes and fates are inextricably linked to successful leaders and the leadership development (LD) programs that create and support them:

- The families of employees who have offered their talents and energy in return for current compensation and, in many cases, future retirement and security
- Taxpayers called upon to "bail out" specific companies or even entire industries when economic stability hangs in the balance
- Industries that are enhanced by the reputation for good stewardship of outstanding executives or forever tarnished by the actions of a few highly visible transgressors
- Communities that stand to benefit from business profits that are poured back into the community in the form of goods and services purchased from local companies, as well as scholarships, endowments, and sponsorships
- National governments whose ability to gather tax revenue from profitable, well-run companies can mean the difference between national solvency and national bailouts

Current Status of Leadership Development

There is no doubt that leadership development is important, and it has changed dramatically in the past decade. Starting many years ago as typical classroom training on the principles of leadership, it has evolved into a critical part of organizational growth and development. How leaders are selected for programs and the specific ways in which programs are offered and structured are significant issues that define the current status.

How Leaders Are Selected for Development

Because leadership development can be one of the most expensive types of development (it is not uncommon for it to be four or five times the expenditure made for other employees), selection is usually a thoughtful process.

At higher levels in the organization, participants in LD programs are often selected by one or a combination of the following methods:

- Nomination by a manager
- Cumulative data from performance management systems and/or past talent review discussions
- Assessment results
- Individual assessment (including a 360-degree instrument and/or psychological profiles) and custom developmental plans based on the outcomes of that assessment
- Participation in an "assessment center" exercise
- Testing (the test needs to be subjected to validity and reliability checks to determine the value of administration)
- Behavioral or structured interviews

At lower levels, participants are often "selected in" versus "screened out" and enter into an LD program by virtue of a promotion or a change in job title. For example, all new supervisors may be automatically enrolled in a particular program.

How Leaders Are Developed

Lewis Carroll, in *Alice's Adventures in Wonderland*, wrote, "If you don't know where you are going, any road will get you there." This is also true with leadership development. Unless there is a clear road map, it is indeed a lovely journey but one without a destination or committed travelers. The methods for development are varied, and many are combined into programs and initiatives of infinite variety:

- Formal training, usually in a classroom (a virtual or "brick and mortar" one)
- Informal learning including self-guided or structured content (books, online learning, audio/video podcasts, etc.)
- Action learning (with a focus on strategic planning or innovation)
- Job shadowing
- Coaching (either internal or external)
- Mentoring
- Experiential learning
- Stretch assignments
- Simulations
- Community involvement
- "Community of practice" or network involvement
- Short-term rotational assignments
- Long-term international assignments

Years ago, researchers created *assignmentology*, a way of mapping standard leadership competencies to specific opportunities for development, such as serving on a task force, chairing a major initiative, or assuming a role with a greatly expanded scope. The science of knowing what developmental experiences will result in specific competency improvements (and, by extension, what will not) is an extraordinary global positioning system in a world of increasingly fewer marked paths.[11]

The Myth of 70–20–10

The time devoted to learning about leadership is a critical issue. For decades, there has been an assumption that 70 percent of the time should be spent on the job with actual experiences, 20 percent learning from others (usually through coaching, mentoring, shadowing, and role modeling), and 10 percent in formal leadership development programs (in the classroom, e-learning, or blended learning). This ratio comes from leaders who were asked to reflect on how they learned effective leadership. As you can imagine, there has always been a small amount of time in classroom leadership development, so their input naturally reflected a small amount in the formal learning category. The rest of it was their best guess of what has happened—it was never meant to be a prescription of what should be done! It's safe to assume that there is not enough formal learning provided during a person's career, at least in most organizations. A better approach is to ask leaders how they want to learn—what their preference is. A recent study by The Conference Board and Development Dimensions International (DDI) involved more than 13,000 leaders, 1,500 global human resources executives, and 2,000 participating organizations.[12] Figure 13.1 shows the results of this study. The 70–20–10 ratio is the perception, but the reality in terms of time spent for this group in learning about leadership is closer to 55–25–20. When this data was sorted for those individuals who have the highest-quality leadership, the ratio is 52–27–21. While this reflects the reality of what is happening in organizations, the important issue is what is preferred. This same group was asked to indicate how much additional time they would like to spend on leadership development per month. The average response was that they spent 5.4 hours per month now, and they desired 8.1 hours, with a difference of 2.7 hours, almost an additional week for a year. When asked how they would prefer to spend their time, 76 percent of them said on formal learning, whereas 71 percent said learning from others. Only 26 percent said they wanted to spend it on the job. These data clearly show what many have experienced: that the 70–20–10 rule does not reflect reality, and it should not be used to prescribe a process; it is merely a reflection on what has occurred in the past. It is much better to plan the proper mix around the needs of the organization and the needs of the leaders.

How Leadership Development Programs Are Structured

There will always be a need for a structured process of developing leaders. Simply dropping talented and successful individual contributors into the "manager's chair" robs them of the opportunity to continue to be successful in a completely new situation. It also runs the risk of doing not only professional harm to the individual but also organizational harm to those he or she impacts. This critical juncture in a career should be carefully managed, and all stakeholders need to be involved for mutual success to occur. Deploying new leaders to different environments or challenging situations without careful planning and support is not a recipe for success. Simply hiring a new CEO from the outside without considering the cultural assimilation challenges, as well as the internal communications and talent implications, is terribly shortsighted.

Most programs have one or more of these goals in mind for their leadership development programs and initiatives:

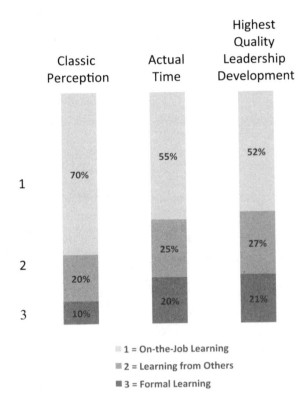

Figure 13.1. How and where leaders are developed.

Source: Adapted from Evan Sinar, Richard Wellins, Rebecca Ray, Amy Lui Abel, and Stephanie Neal. *Ready-Now Leaders: Meeting To-morrow's Business Challenges; Global Leadership Forecast 2014/2015.* The Conference Board and DDI research report, 2014.

- Assess the bench strength of the current leadership, and develop targeted plans to address deficiencies or placement issues for individuals as well as organizational talent gaps that could impact the execution of the strategy.
- Identify possible successors for critical roles.
- Enhance the effectiveness of current leaders by building specific competencies and/or reducing the potential for "derailers."
- Accelerate the development of high-potential and emerging leaders.
- Develop a strong leadership bench.
- Set standards of behavior and cultural norms.
- Leverage leaders' ability to develop and engage their employees, leading to increased levels of productivity, engagement, and retention.

The structure and effectiveness of LD programs is highly variable and, on the whole, disappointingly ineffective. Research indicates that these programs are "immature," according to a leadership development maturity model:

- "Inconsistent management training" is the lowest level of maturity, reflective of a program that lacks development process and has no involvement of business leaders but where content is available and viewed as a "benefit" to employees (47 percent).
- "Structured leadership training" is characterized by the development of competencies and a clearly defined curriculum, where management begins to embrace and support initiatives and programs (27 percent).
- "Focused leadership development" is culture-setting and future-focused, where individuals are assessed and thought of as corporate assets and where the organization's leadership needs are factored into the process (16 percent).
- "Strategic leadership development" is where development is championed by executives who take their own development seriously and all aspects of talent management are integrated (11 percent).[13]

So is anyone implementing leadership development well? Research by the Hay Group highlights many companies and their "best practices" approaches to leadership development, characterized by the following:

- Strong executive involvement
- Use of tailored leadership competencies
- Alignment with the business strategy
- A "leaders at all levels" approach
- An integrated talent management strategy in which leadership development plays an integral role[14]

These findings are echoed in *Fortune* magazine's list of the world's most admired companies, which provides insight into the choices these companies make about leadership development. The Hay Group's research also reveals the following about successful organizations:

- Ninety percent expect employees to lead, whether or not they have a formal position of authority.
- One hundred percent manage a pool of successors for mission-critical roles.
- Ninety percent collect leadership development best practices from subsidiaries and share them across the organization.
- One hundred percent give all employees the opportunity to develop and practice the capabilities needed to lead.[15]

The structure of leadership development will naturally shift to reflect the organizational models it supports. As command-and-control hierarchies intersect with social networks and team organizational structures, so will formal, rigid development programs morph into more flexible, customizable solutions for developing leaders. Rick Lash, director of the Hay Group's Leadership and Talent Practice and coauthor of the "Best Companies for Leadership" study, notes the "significant shift away from hierarchical organizational operating models. . . . Leadership in the twenty-first century is about leading at all levels, not restricting it to title. As organizations become flatter, the best leaders are learning they must check their egos at the door and become increasingly sensitive to diversity, generational, and geographical issues."[16]

One such customized approach can be seen at Bristol-Myers Squibb, which has found ways to customize leadership development through the use of blended learning, coaching, mentoring, and social networking.[17]

Managing Versus Leading

An important challenge in organizations is to increase the amount of time leaders actually spend on leading instead of managing. Leaders spend much of their time on classic management activities of planning, organization, and control. For example, developing plans, controlling the budget, and handling administrative work are all more managerial activities. Leading involves skill sets that include interaction with employees. Figure 13.2 shows a list of the critical skills identified in The Conference Board/DDI study mentioned earlier.[18] These are very powerful skill sets that can make a huge difference in organizations. The study found that leaders who spent more time interacting are more effective at these skills:

- Coaching and developing others
- Communicating and interacting with others
- Developing strong networks/partnerships
- Fostering employee creativity and innovation
- Identifying and developing future talent

This has been a classic issue with organizations that value spending more time on managing and less time on leading. In this particular study, 41 percent of leaders' time spent was spent on managing versus 25 percent on leading. However, leaders preferred to spend 22 percent on managing and 40 percent on leading. The

Communicating and interacting with others
Building consensus and commitment
Coaching and developing others
Managing and successfully introducing change
Developing strong networks/partnerships
Identifying and developing future talent
Inspiring others toward a challenging future vision
Fostering employee creativity and innovation
Leading across generations
Integrating oneself into foreign environments
Intercultural communication
Leading across countries and cultures

Figure 13.2. Critical skills.

Source: Adapted from Evan Sinar, Richard Wellins, Rebecca Ray, Amy Lui Abel, and Stephanie Neal. *Ready-Now Leaders: Meeting Tomorrow's Business Challenges; Global Leadership Forecast 2014/2015.* The Conference Board and DDI research report, 2014.

challenge for organizations, therefore, is to encourage, and build environments to support, spending more time on leading, which is where most of the payoff will be.

Global Versus Local Leadership Programs

For global organizations, an important challenge is to determine who controls the leadership development and talent development programs. In some organizations, the programs are dictated by the corporate headquarters to ensure consistency with the mission, vision, and values of the organization. At the opposite extreme, programs all are locally owned, developed in the countries where their leaders reside to address the needs and cultural issues in that area. Both of these extremes are not ideal. The better approach is to have a good balance of both corporate and local control. Certainly, corporate should be more involved in mid- to high-level leadership development, whereas frontline leadership development should typically be a balance between local and corporate control. Succession planning, on the other hand, is a local issue, involving candidates in specific areas, and local leaders often know their areas best. Balancing leadership development is an important consideration in the human capital strategy.

Common Challenges in Implementing Leadership Development

For those of us who have labored in the leadership development field for years, the challenges of getting it "right" at any company are at once unique and yet quite common. The details may be different at each organization, but these common challenges are ubiquitous:

- No clear vision of what individual leadership looks like at the organization now
- No clear vision of what organizational capacity looks like now
- No clear vision of what leadership should look like in the future
- Failure to gain consensus and commitment from senior leadership about the leadership model, behaviors, and pertinent corporate policies
- Absence of accountability of leaders to develop others and lead by example
- Lack of specific, descriptive behavioral anchors that help leaders clearly understand what is expected and accepted
- A patchwork of leadership development programs that do not link to each other or to other talent management practices
- Lack of clear definition of success for a program or initiative
- Absence of executive sponsorship, particularly by the CEO
- The perception that this is an "HR thing"
- Disconnection of leadership development from conversations and presentations about strategic direction and/or key performance indicators
- Lack of adequate resources to fully execute programs and initiatives
- An inability to articulate the impact of LD programs, initiatives, and resource deployments in business terms

The Success and Failure of Leadership Development

The success factors for leadership development are identified from the barriers and enablers of successful leadership development. When leadership development is successful, the enablers to that success are identified and isolated. When leadership development fails, the barriers that caused the failure are isolated as well. A failure does not necessarily mean that the program did not deliver a positive return on investment or even influence significant business impact measures. A failure is described as a program not living up to its expectations—not achieving the established impact or ROI objectives. It could have been more successful if adjustments or changes had been made; it will achieve success if changes are made going forward.

The data for the success factors are identified in a variety of sources. The most important sources are the ROI studies conducted by the officers, consultants, associates, and partners of the ROI Institute. Each year, this team is involved in approximately 100 to 150 leadership development studies, and each study reveals important issues about failure and success factors. In the case of disappointments, the data show the cause of the disappointment (i.e., barriers that must change in the program to generate more success). From time to time, the ROI Institute conducts reviews of these studies to determine the general barriers and enablers to success. Failure is divided into three categories. In the worst-case scenario, the studies are negative, delivering less value than the cost of the program. These are failures that present serious disappointments, and the lessons learned are very clear. The second category is when success has not been achieved at the minimal targets defined by the impact and ROI objectives. While these programs have positive results, they do not meet expectations; there are opportunities for improvement that will drive more success. A third category consists of programs that exceed the objectives and show additional potential. While these programs are successful, if adjustments are made, they can be more so. These adjustments are vital because maximization of the value delivered is always a goal of success.

These distinctions are made because the impact of leadership development, when properly designed and implemented, can be considerable, sometimes ranging from 300 to 1,000 percent return on investment. Consider the impact created when a leader changes his or her behavior and it affects the entire team. For example, for a first-level team leader in a call center with twenty direct reports, the impact would be the improvement of the team. If productivity (e.g., call volume) improves because of the leadership development, the team's productivity is measured. When the monetary value from the team's improvement is compared to the cost of the formal learning for the team leader, the ROI value can be significant. In our experience at the ROI Institute, when this leverage or multiplicative effect is explained to chief financial officers, they understand the value of leadership development. Consequently, we should expect high returns on investment from leadership development; if they are not there, we should determine what can be done to improve them.

In addition to examination of ROI studies, research began with an examination of the literature, probing into both the failures and the success factors of leadership development. Next, a survey was conducted with LD organizers: those who organize, coordinate, or facilitate leadership development and are often aware of the causes of failure. The survey data from 232 respondents are presented in Table 13.1. Barriers are ranked from most significant to least significant. For the most part, these results parallel what the ROI Institute team has uncovered in the analysis of its studies.

Table 13.1.   Reasons for leadership development program failures.

Reason cited	Ranking	Percentage
Not building data collection into the process	1	74
Not using the data routinely for process improvement	2	53
Failure to create application and impact objectives	3	51
Not assessing current leader behavior	4	49
Failure to secure commitment from participants	5	48
Not identifying the right data for analysis	6	47
Failure to secure management support for the program	7	46
Failure to remove or minimize barriers to application	8	43
Not assessing learning needs properly	9	42
Lack of business alignment	10	39
Improper program design	11	24
Taking all the credit for an improvement in business impact	12	17
Waiting for the request for impact and ROI analysis	13	16
Not including the right participants	14	13

Table 13.2 presents the success factors for leadership development in check-list form, in the order in which they normally occur in the LD process. Leadership development facilitators, developers, organizers, and supporters can use this checklist to ensure that the proper processes are in place for success. These factors are developed from literally hundreds of studies on leadership development and through other research. Usually, three to six items are missing for any given program design, and these are often critical enough to inhibit the results.

What Does the Future Hold for Leadership Development?

The ability to develop leaders more quickly and efficiently will become a competitive advantage for those companies who do this successfully. This concept of flexible and adaptive leadership is well suited for our turbulent times. One of the best crucibles for developing adaptive leaders is the military. Four principles have served military leaders well:

1. Create a personal link, which is crucial to leading people through challenging times.
2. Make good and timely calls, which is the crux of responsibility in a leadership position.
3. Establish a common purpose, buttress those who will help you achieve it, and eschew personal gain.
4. Make the objectives clear, but avoid micromanaging those who will execute them.[19]

Table 13.2. Success factors for leadership development.

1. Align the program to business measures in the beginning.
2. Identify specific behavior changes needed for the target audience.
3. Identify learning needs for the target audience.
4. Establish application and impact objectives for LD programs.
5. Involve the right people at the right time.
6. Design leadership development for successful learning and application.
7. Create expectations to achieve results and provide data.
8. Address the learning transfer issue early and often.
9. Establish supportive partnerships with key managers.
10. Select the proper data sets for the desired evaluation level.
11. Build data collection into the process and position it as an application tool.
12. Always isolate the effects of the program on impact data.
13. Be proactive and develop impact and ROI analyses for major programs.
14. Use data collected at different levels for adjustments and improvements.

Another core skill for future leaders will be the ability to thrive (not simply survive) in a permanent crisis; this VUCA world (VUCA is a term that originated in military circles, which means *volatile, uncertain, complex,* and *ambiguous*) means a never-ending series of strategy refreshes, setbacks, and unexpected opportunities. Many believe that effective leaders in this environment will need to foster adaptation, embrace disequilibrium, and generate leadership at all levels of the organization.[20]

Where will we find such leaders? Some suggest that we expand our search to include different markets, emerging economies, and differing cultural values—finding leaders who have forged their leadership skills in the crucible of resistance to apartheid, the growth trajectory of emerging markets, or during stints with mission-driven entities addressing humanitarian crises around the world.[21] The models are there; the largest India-based companies provide leadership lessons in terms of where and how they focus their energy and their emphasis on being transformational leaders.[22] So many types of experiential learning are finding their way into corporate leadership development programs at industry-leading companies such as UBS and IBM.

Leadership development will morph and adapt, just as the leaders it attempts to create must do. But one thing will remain constant: the need to articulate the impact of such a major investment. The journey is always the same for leadership development; at the end of the day, learning to effectively lead people remains a transformational process. It is always about how willing someone is to make himself or herself the lesser so that someone else can be the greater.

Many approaches can be successful, given the right support, the right timing, and the right alignment with corporate imperatives. While setting the course is difficult, attaining the results is even more challenging. One study of leadership competencies that matter most for growth (which, according to the authors, constitute "the Holy Grail of corporate strategy") reveals that great leaders are very rare indeed.[23]

Some companies have found a way. There is no one path; there is no one correct answer. There are, however, correct questions:

- What are you trying to accomplish?
- How aligned are you with the organizational strategy?
- Who will be the champion(s)?
- What specifically will you do? For how long? In what way? What methods will you use?
- Who will be selected to participate, and on the basis of what criteria?
- How integrated is this into every other aspect of talent management?
- How will you measure success?
- How will you articulate success?

Measuring the Impact and ROI of Leadership Development

In a survey of leadership development practitioners, 368 surveys were sent out and 232 were received, for a response rate of 63 percent.[24] Several lists of current practitioners were used to choose recipients who were actively involved in leadership development. In every case, the job title included leadership development or reflected a manager or director responsible for leadership development. Most of the organizations were global, representing both public and private sectors.

Table 13.3 shows where leadership development is being evaluated, using the levels of evaluation as a reference. These levels are described in more detail in Chapter 14. As this table shows, a surprising number of these evaluations are at the business impact and ROI levels, exceeding expectations. Part of this could be a function of the global recession. The recession has led some organizations to step up their evaluation efforts, pushing evaluation up the chain of impact to the impact and ROI levels.

Figure 13.3 shows today's ROI reality, as recipients responded to the question, "Is there an emphasis on ROI?" Surprisingly, 88 percent said yes. This dramatically underscores the concern about ROI during a global recession.

Table 13.3. Levels of evaluation for leadership development.

Level of evaluation	Percentage of programs evaluated at this level
1. Reaction—Measures reaction to, and satisfaction with, the experience, contents, and value of the program	88.9
2. Learning—Measures what participants learned in the program: information, knowledge, skills, competencies, and contacts (takeaways from the program)	59.1
3. Application/implementation—Measures progress after the program: the use of information, knowledge, skills, competencies, and contacts	33.9
4. Business impact—Measures changes in business impact variables such as output, quality, time, and costs linked to the program	21.3
5. Return on investment—Compares the monetary benefits of the business impact measures to the costs of the program	11.3

N = 232.

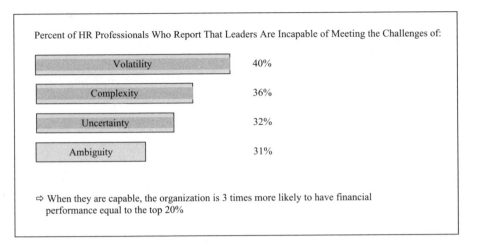

Figure 13.3. Today's ROI reality.
Adapted from "Ready-Now Leaders: Meeting Tomorrow's Business Challenges."

Figure 13.4 shows the drivers for ROI evaluation and represents data only from those who indicated there is a current emphasis on return on investment. Perhaps as anticipated, increased pressures for cost efficiencies dominated the rationale for ROI evaluation, which for the most part is a function of the current global competitive situation and the remnants of the economic recession. The cost of the program is the second driver, which is consistent with the work at the ROI Institute. An impressive 29 percent indicated that top executives are requiring this now, which is also consistent with ROI Institute data. This survey clearly shows that the need for ROI evaluation is here, and many organizations are stepping up to the challenge of showing the value of their programs up to the impact and ROI levels.

Can the Impact of Leadership Development Initiatives Be Measured?

We believe the impact of LD initiatives can and *should* be measured. What counts, however, are not our opinions but those of the business leaders who support all the human capital programs that professionals need. Increasingly, C-suite leaders such as CEOs and CFOs want to know the return on their investment in leadership development,

Is there an emphasis on ROI?	Response, %
Yes	88
No	12

N = 232

Figure 13.4. Drivers for ROI evaluation.

particularly the most expensive and higher profile LD programs. In a recent survey of Fortune 500 CEOs, 92 of 96 said that they wanted to see the business impact of learning programs, but only 8 percent see that happening at their companies now.[25] In the same survey 71 of 96 (74%) wanted to see the ROI, but only 4% see it now.[26] Other business leaders are increasingly interested in "people metrics" and the alignment between people-related data and business priorities, sales performance data, and revenue.[27]

Early research in human capital analytics paved the way for its application in the workplace. Some studied the impact of the consulting psychologist as a path to developing leaders who impact business results.[28] Others found that without the ability to articulate the business impacts of programs and initiatives, the human resources function would have a very difficult time playing a strategic role.[29] One study conducted research for The Conference Board with leading multinational firms, including BP, Colgate-Palmolive, Bayer, Unilever, AstraZeneca, and UBS, to determine the ways in which the profession could articulate the business value of leadership development. Two others state that even intangibles can be measured and used to support the impact discussion.[30] Research supports the critical need to demonstrate the return on investment of LD initiatives.[31]

This shift to analytics is well under way. At UPS, the use of metrics and data have driven decision making about programs and their effectiveness, as well as business impact.[32] Google's metrics-driven approach and analysis have helped create the culture-specific leadership model that is now the foundation for leadership development.[33] Companies as varied as Harrah's Entertainment, Starbucks, Procter & Gamble, Limited Brands, and Best Buy have determined that they can compete on talent analytics and win.

Measuring Progress

An important step is to assess where the organization is now regarding the measurement of leadership development and where it needs to be. Figure 13.5 shows the maturity stages for measuring the success of leadership development. Stage 1 focuses on measuring internal processes to make the leadership development more effective from the perspective of the designers, developers, or participants. The focus is on measuring who is attending, what topics are explored, and the time that they are allocating to the process (Level 0). This also includes measuring reaction to leadership development, ensuring that it is relevant, needed, and necessary (Level 1). It also measures the extent of learning of new skills and new approaches (Level 2). Most organizations are moving beyond stage 1 and are at stage 2.

Stage 2 is where the focus is on measuring behavior change. Typically, the approach is to use 360-degree feedback, where the current levels of behavior are measured going into a particular program and the changes are measured at some point later. This can also involve an organization-wide measurement, where the 360-degree assessments provide a profile of how others are perceiving the leadership behavior of managers and executives.

Some organizations have moved into stage 3, which connects leadership development to important intangible measures such as teamwork, communication, cooperation, and decision making. These are not necessarily business measures in the organization, but they are actual concepts. These perceptions can be very important. However, for most executives, this is not enough to see the value from their perspective.

Drivers for ROI evaluation		Response, %
Top executive requirement		29
The costs of the program		62
Increased pressures for cost and efficiencies		81
Competitive pressures for funding		48
Lack of success in previous efforts to show the value		38
Client requires it		14

$N = 204$

Figure 13.5. Maturity stages for measuring the success of leadership development.

Many organizations have migrated to stage 4, where leadership development is connected to standard HR metrics of retention, absenteeism, job satisfaction, job engagement, complaints, grievances, accidents, and other HR-related measures. This is pursued under the assumption that leadership development is more likely to translate directly into these "people-related" measures.

The ultimate approach, taken by a few organizations, is to connect leadership development to business unit measures. This measurement is based on the assumption that if leadership capability is enhanced, the team performance measures will improve. In essence, the programs start with the end in mind with clearly defined business needs. In the beginning of major leadership development programs, key business measures are identified that need to improve or change, using the leadership competencies with the team. Then it is the new leader behavior that drives up performance. This is a very powerful process and will be a major trend in the future. More detail on measurements are provided in Chapter 14.

Implications for Human Capital Strategy

This chapter identified issues that are critical for developing global leaders. Every human capital strategy should have a major component addressing the need for global leaders. This strategy should develop these key issues:

- Investment in leadership development
- Types of programs involved
- Target groups
- Succession planning
- High potentials
- Leadership culture
- Global perspective

14

Use Analytics and Big Data

Using Analytics to Drive Business Results

> ***Force 12: Analytics and Big Data.*** The evolution of comput-
> ing power with rapidly growing sets of data has created a need
> and an opportunity to use analytics and big data to help guide
> organizational decision making. Although most of the work in
> analytics was initiated in the marketing and technology areas, it
> has now moved in a big way to the human capital area because
> of the cost of human capital. With large numbers of employees
> and applicants, there are many big data applications. The chal-
> lenge for organizations is to develop a human capital analytics
> practice that exploits these opportunities and solves the vari-
> ous problems using a standardized, consistent methodology to
> drive decisions that affect the business. This is much easier said
> than done, and it starts with having a strategy connected to the
> issue of how to use analytics and big data.

This chapter addresses the issues of analytics and big data in organizations. It begins with a brief history of analytics and how it evolved in the human capital area. The good news is that this is not new to the human resources function, but previous applications have been narrowly focused in a few progressive organizations. The chapter describes the fundamentals and types of data, a maturity model, and an analytics model that is systematic and replicable. The chapter also discusses the various challenges and issues of working with big data and analytics, and it offers a prescription for how to make it work in an organization. This is an important but challenging issue that can have tremendous payoffs.

Opening Stories

Analytics is a hot topic for any function in any organization. This is especially true for the human resources function. Here are two examples of how HR is addressing the use analytics and big data.

Scripps Health

Scripps Health is a not-for-profit San Diego–based healthcare system that is successful on any dimension. The system, which includes five hospitals and 26 outpatient facilities, treats almost 2 million patients annually. Scripps employs more than 13,500 employees and has been named one of "America's 100 Best Companies to Work For" every year since 2008. The system also includes clinical research and medical education programs.[1]

Having enjoyed success over the past eighty years, Scripps is a financially sound and stable organization with AA-rated bonds, one of only four healthcare organizations in California to hold this distinction. The "people" part of their process is managed extremely well, enabling Scripps to provide efficient, quality healthcare. Scripps regularly appears on lists of admired organizations, the best places to work, and the best employer for certain groups. Executives place specific emphasis on corporate social responsibility with more than $370 million contributed to community service and charity care. Scripps is considered among the top providers of healthcare. For example, Scripps was named by Thomson Reuters[2] as one of the Top 10 health systems in the nation for providing high-quality, safe, and efficient patient care.

The success of Scripps rests on the quality of its leadership and the systems and processes in place to make it an outstanding healthcare delivery organization. Scripps focuses significant efforts on sound financial processes, process improvement projects, and a variety of initiatives to improve the quality of healthcare. Among the processes used by Scripps is the ROI Methodology, a process that shows the success of healthcare improvement projects using six types of data with standards and a process model. At least 20 of Scripps HR professional team members have achieved the designation of Certified ROI Professional as they continue to conduct ROI studies on a variety of HR processes to ensure that they are delivering value and quality healthcare and achieving a positive financial outcome.

Google

Google's HR function has established credibility by having a clear understanding of the company's functional, strategic, and analytic HR needs and by ensuring that the department is staffed accordingly, says Laszlo Bock, vice president of people operations.[3] When HR is compared to supply chain management, marketing, sales, and operations, there has not been as much rigor historically. In part, that is why the HR function has had a hard time getting a seat at the table.

Bock deliberately set out to hire staff with the skills that would allow the department to play both operational and strategic roles. One-third of the people come from traditional HR backgrounds. They're outstanding HR generalists and an outstanding compensation-and-benefits team.

The second third comes from strategy consulting firms. HR is seeking two things: great problem-solving skills—the ability to take a really messy problem, disaggregate it, and drive to data-driven answers—and really deep business sense, a deep understanding of how business actually works in the different functions.

This blend of specialists and generalists helps create powerful cross-pollination. The HR team learns a tremendous amount about business and problem solving from the consultants, and the consultants get very quickly up to speed on the pattern recognition you need to be successful on the people side.

The final third, according to Bock, are people with advanced degrees in various analytics fields—PhDs and master's degrees in operations, physics, statistics, and psychology. They let HR run all kinds of interesting experiments and raise the bar on everything HR does.[4]

A History of Human Capital Analytics

HR's need for data to influence decision making dates back to the 1920s, when personnel research set the stage for the development of measures of HR's activities and performance. In the 1940s and 1950s, about the time HR became a legitimate and essential part of organizations, practitioners and researchers began to explore ways of measuring its contribution. In the years that followed, HR practitioners wrestled with measuring contribution and using data as a strategic lever. By the late 1970s, data collection and analysis became a routine part of some HR departments. Considerable advancements in measurement and evaluation took place in the 1980s, and the 1990s saw more growth in this area. Since 2000, much progress has been made with HR relationship studies (macro), ROI analysis (micro), and predictive analytics.

Without question, the HR function, which includes a variety of activities, does contribute to organization success; the difficulty lies in selecting the right combination of measures and the best approach to develop an adequate analytics practice. When examining the history of ways in which organizations address this issue, the approaches vary, with some clearly more effective than others. Figure 14.1 shows the progression of approaches used to demonstrate HR's influence on

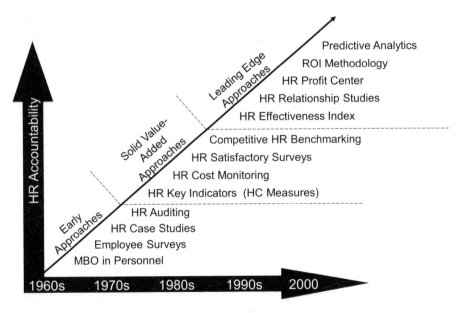

Figure 14.1. HR accountability progress: The evolution of analytics.

organizational success. Each one adds to the body of work, although overlap is present in the techniques, processes, and focus of some approaches. A detailed comparison of these approaches is available in numerous other publications, including the ROI Institute's website (http://www.roiinstitute.net).

The starting point in human capital analytics practice is to determine the specific human capital measures to monitor. These measures provide insight into the status and health of the human resources function. They signal when additional HR programs are needed, and they serve as the baseline for measuring the progress and payoff of investing in a specific program or project. The most common set of measures monitored by leading organizations is presented in Table 14.1. This list represents measures cited in over a dozen current studies on human capital measurement.

Some of the measures presented in this table evolved from the beginnings of "personnel administration" to what is today known as human resources or human capital management. They represent measures that were tracked during the field's infancy and are still tracked today. Although these measures have existed for some time, they are still important measures for understanding the nature, scope, and progress of human capital. The measures represent a balance of old-economy and new-economy organizations. Several measures are industry specific. For example, safety and health measures may be an important issue where employees are routinely at risk for accidents, injuries, and illnesses. Service and knowledge businesses, such as financial services and software companies, would not necessarily list

Table 14.1.   Common human capital measures.

1. Innovation and creativity	7. Productivity and performance
• Innovation	• Unit productivity
• Creativity	• Gross productivity
2. Employee perceptions	• Performance ratings
• Employee satisfaction	8. Workforce profile
• Organizational commitment	• Demographics
• Employee engagement	• Goals
3. Workforce stability	9. Job creation and acquisition
• Turnover and termination	• Job growth
• Tenure and longevity	• Recruitment sourcing and effectiveness
4. Employee capability	• Recruiting efficiency
• Experience	10. Compensation and benefits
• Learning	• Compensation
• Knowledge	• Employee benefits
• Competencies	• Variable compensation
• Education level	• Employee ownership
5. Human capital investment	11. Compliance and safety
• HR department investment	• Complaints and grievances
• Total human capital investment	• Charges and litigation
• Investment by category	• Health and safety
6. Leadership and succession planning	12. Employee relations
• 360-degree feedback	• Absenteeism and tardiness
• High potentials	• Work–life balance
• Leadership effectiveness	• Alternative work arrangements
• Bench strength	

these measures as a priority. Other measures, however, are critical to developing and emerging industries, such as innovation, leadership, and competencies.

Other references explore each measure category in terms of how it is developed and a few of the issues surrounding it.[5] This discussion is based on the assumption that anything can be measured, regardless of how subjective or soft it may be. The challenge is to increase the accuracy of the measurement, ensuring validity and reliability of the measurement process.

Human Capital Analytics Maturity

As reported in a state of human capital report titled "False Summit: Why the Human Capital Function Still Has Far to Go," human capital analytics is the linchpin of human capital investments.[6] While organizations are embracing some of the tried-and-true approaches described in the previous section, others have matured to a higher level of analytics by investing in capacity-building through hiring and developing skills as well as taking advantage of technology. Also, the business questions driving the need for HR to advance with analytics are changing.

The Conference Board's Human Capital Analytics (HCA) Research Working Group researched how organizations progress along the analytics continuum.[7] Using *MIT Sloan Management Review* / IBM Institute for Business Value research as the foundation for their own, the HCA Research Working Group developed a maturity model that reflects how HR functions advance in their human capital analytics practice.[8] The HCA Research Working Group found that maturity occurs as organizations identify challenges and opportunities, apply various frameworks and techniques, and ultimately align key measures to business outcomes. Successful maturity requires that HR professionals have a clear strategic context and engage with their key stakeholders. Even though an organization may reach the highest level of analytics maturity, it will always experience a need for the less mature practices. Organizations can identify with any position on a maturity model, with the true measure of progress defined by the human capital professional's ability to traverse the ever-changing analytics terrain. Human capital analytics maturity includes three types of analytics: descriptive, predictive, and prescriptive. Each type of analytics answers different business questions.

Descriptive Analytics

Descriptive analytics is the most fundamental level of analytics. It answers questions such as "What happened, and what is happening now?" Data from this type of analysis describe the conditions, people, and events as they were in the past or as they exist today. Descriptive analytics provides information useful in assessing the extent to which an organization is meeting its goals, as well as the extent to which employers are attracting the right candidates. An example of the use of descriptive analytics is the application of comprehensive talent assessments describing job requirements, preassessments, and postassessments that give organizations information on their workforce, which they can then benchmark against others.

At a solution level, descriptive analytics help determine the value of programs as well as provide suggestions on how to improve programs so that they can provide greater value. Descriptive data are often captured on scorecards and dashboards so that HR leaders and professionals can easily describe to stakeholders essential HR measures as well as connections to business measures that reflect the investment in human capital.

Predictive Analytics

As mentioned earlier, over the past decades, efforts have been made to develop statistical relationships between key HR measures and organizational performance measures. Using historical or existing data as the basis, predictive analytics moves the human capital practice further so that HR leaders can answer questions such as "What could happen, and when could it happen?" Data from predictive analytics describe conditions, people, and events as they could be in the future and when they are likely to be that way. It is useful in helping organizations determine possible outcomes of particular HR activities and influences the decisions of stakeholders.

Jac Fitz-enz's research places predictive analytics in the forefront of the human capital conversation. Since 2008, his HCM:21 model has evolved into a six-step approach that refines analysis and suggests effective actions:[9]

1. Assess the situation, external and internal.
2. Identify a key business opportunity.
3. Find the factors or forces that drive it.
4. Determine the scope: local or organization-wide.
5. Design an intervention or invest.
6. Evaluate, recycle, or move on.

Prescriptive Analytics

The ultimate level of maturity with human capital analytics is prescriptive analytics. This form of analytics helps organizations answer questions such as "What is the best course of action?" Prescriptive analytics makes predictions in decision making while taking into account the impact of those decisions. It describes what is possible given particular factors and what courses of action would be optimal given all the potential combinations of options and outcomes. An example of prescriptive analytics can be found in the literature on workforce optimization. In The Conference Board's research report, *Human Capital Analytics @ Work, Volume 1*, ABM, with the help of Mercer, developed a workforce-optimization model that describes the optimum number of employees and activities a manager can handle and still drive profitability for ABM.[10]

Figure 14.2 depicts The Conference Board's Human Capital Analytics Maturity Model as developed by the HCA Research Working Group. This model does not suggest that one level of maturity is better or worse than another. It simply demonstrates the continuum along which organizations are moving as they advance their human capital analytics practice. This chapter is an effort to help organizations develop along this progression.

Types of Data

Although most organizations use some approach to placing similar types of measures together, a logical data categorization framework is needed that uses levels

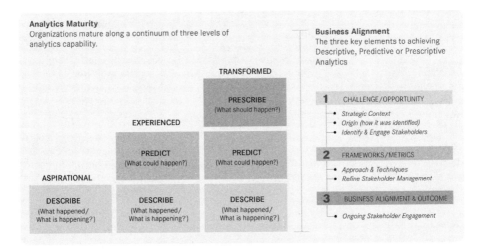

Figure 14.2. Human capital analytics maturity.

Source: This graphic representation was designed by several members of the research working group. The concept of the three levels of analytics capability is adopted from Steve LaValle, Eric Lesser, Rebecca Shockley, Michael S. Hopkins, and Nina Kruschwitz. "Big Data, Analytics, and the Path from Insights to Value." *MIT Sloan Management Review* 62, no. 2 (2011): 21–32; J. Fitz-enz, P. Phillips, and R. Ray. *Human Capital Analytics: A Primer.* The Conference Board research report, 2012, p. 15. Used with permission.

of data, recognizing that the next level is usually more valuable than the previous level from the perspective of the senior executive group. These levels are depicted in Figure 14.3.

Level 0 is *inputs*, which details the numbers of people and hours, the focus, and the cost of a solution. These data represent the activity around a human capital investment rather than the contribution of the solution. Level 0 data indicate the scope of the effort, the degree of commitment, and the support for a particular solution. For some, this information equates to value. However, commitment as defined by expenditures is not evidence that the organization is reaping value.

Reaction

Level 1 is *reaction*, which details how employees, associates, members, and other individuals connected to the organization react to a particular solution or project. These data, such as relevance, importance to success, appropriateness, usefulness, and intent to use, are important. They represent perceived value of a solution from the perspective of those involved in it in some way. Adverse reaction is often a clear indication that nothing will come of the solution—that it will serve merely as an expense rather than an investment. For example, an employee referral program as a recruiting source can be successful or unsuccessful, based on the reaction of employees to that solution. If they think it is valuable and important, and it is rewarding for them to make the referral, they will do it. Otherwise, they will not. Another example is the reaction employees have to a new diversity and inclusion effort. Positive reaction that reflects commitment to it is a good indication the process will be embraced as important to organizational strategy.

Level	Measurement Focus	Typical Measures
0 Inputs	Inputs into the solution, including indicators representing scope, volumes, costs, and efficiencies	Types of topics Number of programs Number of people Hours of involvement Costs
1 Reaction	Reaction to the solution, including the perceived value of the project	Relevance Importance Usefulness Appropriateness Intent to use Motivational
2 Learning	Learning how to use the solution, including the confidence to use what was learned	Skills Knowledge Capacity Competencies Confidences Contacts
3 Application and implementation	Use of solution and materials in the work environment, including progress with implementation	Extent of Use Task completion Frequency of use Actions completed Success with use Barriers to use Enablers to use
4 Impact	Consequences of use of the solution expressed as business impact measures	Productivity Revenue Quality Time Efficiency Customer satisfaction Employee engagement
5 ROI	Comparison of monetary benefits from the solution to solution costs	Benefit-cost ratio (BCR) ROI (%) Payback period

Figure 14.3.   Types and levels of analytics data.

Learning

Level 2 is *learning*. Measures of learning ensure that the individuals involved in a solution have the knowledge they need to make a solution, system, initiative, or project successful. These data may represent knowledge, information, awareness, and critical skill sets necessary for work to be done, programs to be implemented, and processes to be completed. Without the requisite knowledge, things can go awry. For example, almost 70 percent of employees in one of the largest healthcare organizations in Canada did not receive flu shots, although senior executives had requested flu shots for all employees. For a healthcare provider, it is important for employees to avoid the flu because they could be absent more frequently and may pass the flu along to their patients. At the same time, they may be exposed to the flu more than employees in any other occupation. Some analysis revealed that they did not pursue the flu shots because of some misunderstandings and misinformation about the shots and their effectiveness. When employees became more enlightened and the misinformation was clarified, the percentage of employees receiving flu shots increased significantly.

Application

Level 3 is *application and implementation*, also referred to as behavior and implementation, which measures people's actions, activities, and behaviors. Measures at this level are critical. Sometimes solutions break down or do not work because people do not do what they should to implement a solution successfully. Sometimes executives think that when something is not working, they want new behavior in place, suggesting that the new behavior will correct things, and often it does. An example is one describing Harrah's use of smile frequency as a predictor of customer satisfaction. This simple behavior led Harrah to implement a program and thereby drive a key organization outcome measure.[11] Behavior, action, and implementation represent critical measures that lead toward organizational performance.

Impact

Level 4 is *impact*. This category includes measures that are in the system and represent all types of business data. In most organizations, these measures exist by the hundreds, if not thousands, and they reflect the conditions of output, quality, cost, and time, which are major categories of any work in an organization. These measures usually define the problem or opportunity that initiates an analytics project. For example, an excessive number of patient accidents may be the driver for an analytics project at a healthcare firm. Reduction in customer satisfaction and new customer accounts may be the drivers for an analytics project for a large financial institution.

ROI

Level 5 is *ROI*, the measure that reflects ultimate accountability. It can be expressed as the benefit–cost ratio (BCR), the financial ROI expressed as a percentage, or the payback period (PP) that indicates how long it will take for the investment to pay for itself. Although other measures of financial return exist (e.g., return on equity, return on assets), BCR, ROI, and PP seem to be the most common measures and are most appropriate for measuring financial output of human capital investments. These data are the output of the process and represent an important part of analytics. Ultimately, many analytics projects lead to ROI and require a comparison of the benefits to costs.

Types of Analytics Projects

The variety of tasks, processes, and procedures involved in analytics is vast. Some analysts suggest that any type of analysis to understand, support, or improve human capital programs is an analytics project. However, it is helpful to think of projects as falling into five different but related categories. These categories are helpful because they represent typical existing studies that can easily be located, analyzed, and compared. Each category is described in detail in the following sections.

Sometimes only one of these analytics processes is used. For example, an organization may recognize a need to understand the financial value of a measure before investing in a solution or initiative. On the other hand, it may be important to show the ROI for a particular solution. This analysis includes demonstrating causation, converting data to money, and comparing the output to the cost of the solution. Regardless of the analytics project, these five categories should encompass whatever type of analysis is required.

Converting Data to Money (Type 1)

A tremendous push to understand the value of measures is evident in most organizations, and one of the best ways to understand value is to convert it to money. If it is something that needs to increase, such as engagement, executives want to know the monetary value of it. If it is something that needs to be eliminated or prevented, such as accidents or incidents, executives want to know the cost of each occurrence to understand the magnitude of the problem. One type of analytics project is to convert data to money. Some measures are easily converted, but others are "soft," which means they are more difficult to value and require a more advanced analytics process. Soft data items include the following:

- Job engagement
- Job satisfaction
- Stress
- Employee complaints
- Health status

- Ethics
- Teamwork
- Networking
- Customer satisfaction
- Reputation

For example, an electric utility company wanted to know the monetary value of the stress created as the industry became deregulated. Utility teams had to be more productive and efficient. This push for productivity caused excessive stress among team members, and the executives were interested in having a better understanding of the monetary value of the problem.[12]

The good news is that work has been done by organizations to convert some common soft data measures into money. A classic example is that of Sears, where an HCA project connected employee attitude to customer perception and then to revenue.[13]

Showing Relationships and Causation (Type 2)

This type of analysis involves understanding the relationship (or lack thereof) between variables and involves correlation and regression analysis. For example, a question of interest may be "Does increasing employee engagement increase the likelihood that employees will work more safely, be more productive, or reduce errors?" Analysis for these types of questions attempts to see not only whether a correlation exists but whether correlation indicates a causal relationship. Typical correlations that are being pursued through the use of analytics are as follows:

- Job satisfaction versus retention
- Job satisfaction versus attraction
- Job satisfaction versus customer satisfaction

- Engagement versus productivity
- Engagement versus safety
- Engagement versus sales
- Engagement versus quality
- Organizational commitment versus productivity
- Stress versus productivity
- Conflict versus productivity
- Culture versus productivity
- Ethics versus profit

The opportunities are limitless in terms of exploring relationships inside an organization. In addition, this step looks for causation that might not be based on mathematical relationships. Sometimes other methods can be used to explore the cause of a problem or determine what will influence an opportunity. These different techniques are listed in Table 14.2. An important point of this step is that the cause of the problem reveals the solution—the opportunity that needs to be developed.

Applying Predictive Models (Type 3)

Predictive models for projects are an extension of the relationship category. When relationships or connections are made, can they be used in a predictive way? The independent variable predicts the dependent variables. Here are some typical predictive relationships that have been established in organizations:

- Recruiting source predicts retention
- Selection test predicts safety performance
- Interviews predict absenteeism
- Values survey predicts early turnover
- Health-risk status predicts absenteeism

Table 14.2. Analysis techniques.

- Diagnostic questionnaires
- Statistical process control
- Focus groups
- Brainstorming
- Probing interviews
- Problem analysis
- Job satisfaction surveys
- Cause-and-effect diagram
- Engagement surveys
- Force-field analysis
- Exit interviews
- Mind mapping
- Exit surveys
- Affinity diagrams
- Nominal group techniques
- Simulations

- Absenteeism predicts productivity
- Benefits participation predicts retention
- Compensation predicts retention

Again, the opportunities are limitless in terms of developing these models. Sometimes the model involves a chain of measures so that one measure predicts another, and then that variable predicts another. The predictive model from Sears mentioned earlier connects job satisfaction to revenue growth. In this example, an increase in job satisfaction will predict improvement in customer satisfaction, which will predict a growth in revenue for the store. Results from the project show that a 5-point improvement in the total job satisfaction drives a 1.3-point improvement on a customer satisfaction survey, which drives a 1.5 percent improvement in revenue growth. The profit margin is applied to the sales growth to develop a value-added dollar figure. By way of this model, improvements in job satisfaction become a predictor of profit in stores.

Conducting Impact and ROI Analysis (Type 4)

A dominant type of analytics project involves showing the impact and ROI of a specific human capital program. These types of studies describe the reaction, learning, application, impact, and ROI for a particular solution. Executives find it helpful to understand the value of particular solutions. Most analytics projects lead to solutions. Impact and ROI studies are usually reserved for those programs and projects that are expensive, important, and command executive attention. They can cover a variety of areas:

- Recruiting/selection
- Training/learning/development
- Leadership/coaching/mentoring
- Knowledge management
- Organizational consulting/development
- Policies/procedures/processes
- Recognition/incentives/engagement
- Change management / culture
- Technology/systems/IT
- Green/sustainability projects
- Safety/health programs
- Talent retention solutions
- Project management solutions
- Quality / Six Sigma / Lean Engineering
- Meetings/events
- Marketing/advertising
- Communications / public relations
- Public policy / social programs
- Risk management / ethics / compliance
- Flexible work systems
- Wellness and fitness programs

All Roads Lead to ROI

It is helpful to understand the importance of impact and ROI in the minds of the executives who fund a variety of human capital projects and programs. In discussions with these executives, the focus often shifts or evolves to the ROI issue. For example, an organization has invested a tremendous amount of money on employee engagement. Engagement is being measured with an employee engagement survey. Executives may ask, "What is the value of having more engaged employees?" or "If engagement scores increase, what outcomes can we expect?" These questions suggest that executives are interested in the monetary value. This is a Type 1 analytics project.

In order to answer the question, engagement program owners would have to connect engagement to money—typically through an easy-to-value, hard data measure. The data may show that engagement is connected to gross productivity, which can be defined as revenue per employee. If engagement has been moved from a lower level to a higher level, the gross productivity movement can be pinpointed. These data are easily converted to money. Adding the profit margin shows the actual monetary contribution of the improvement in job engagement. This is a Type 2 analytics project. If the relationship is operationalized, after testing and validation, this is now a Type 3 project.

After showing the productivity improvement connection, the next question is, "So what is the ROI?" Answering this question requires comparing the monetary benefits of improvements in gross productivity connected to engagement with the fully loaded cost of the engagement solution. This ROI analysis is a Type 4 human capital analytics project. Quickly, a request for Type 1 leads to Type 2, which leads to Type 3, and finally Type 4, the ROI. Sometimes executives, when reviewing a potential program for improving job engagement based on the initial assessment of the score, may ask for a value of forecasted ROI before they get started. This more detailed project would be a Type 5 human capital analytics project, a ROI forecast. Obviously, after the project is implemented, this would also require a Type 4 analysis, which shows ROI on a follow-up basis. When discussing almost any solution or human capital analytics project with executives, they often ask, "So what happens if we do it? What is the impact? What is the monetary value? What is the ROI?" All roads lead to ROI.

Forecasting ROI (Type 5)

Sometimes when major projects or programs are implemented, it is helpful to understand the potential payoff for the program before it is implemented. This assessment involves forecasting the impact that will be driven by the program, converting it to monetary value, and comparing it to the proposed cost of the solution. A challenge with forecasting is to be as accurate as possible so that the forecast can be realistic and used for decisions. Of course, if a forecast is conducted as a requirement, follow up and make sure that the forecast has been achieved. Many major programs are now regularly subjected to forecasting:

- Wellness and fitness programs
- Flexible work systems

- New compensation arrangements
- New benefits structures
- Organizational development projects
- Transformational projects
- Talent retention projects
- Talent management projects
- Leadership development projects
- Change projects

Big Data

The last decade has seen a tremendous number of discussions, articles, books, and speeches about "big data." What is big data? Big data does not have an absolute, precise definition, but it has some common characteristics. One definition is offered as follows: Big data defines a situation in which data sets have grown to such enormous sizes that conventional information technologies can no longer effectively handle either the size of the data set or the scale and growth of the data set. The primary difficulties are the acquisition, storage, searching, sharing, analysis, and visualization of the data.[14] IBM, for example, suggests that the data generated by people and organizations within two years generates an amount equivalent to the data generated in all the previous years combined. This is exponential growth, and it can bring tremendous challenges in analyzing the data. Fortunately, computing power is now available to handle these large quantities of data systematically and efficiently.

What are the characteristics of big data? The first characteristic is size. Certainly large data sets—with records in the thousands, hundreds of thousands, or millions—fall into the big data category. Small data sets, involving a few hundred data points, would be considered in a smaller category. Big data also reflects the types of data. Some data are qualitative and others quantitative. Another issue is the fact that the data are often messy because they are not entered properly. With the various types of data, there are accuracy issues, accessibility issues, and clean-up issues that must be addressed in order to turn messy data into usable data sets for analysis. Finally, there is the speed of the data generation. The data set changes rapidly, and incoming data are often more useful than old data in analysis.

Big and Not-So-Big Data Items

Huge data sets are common. For example, close to fifty billion pieces of content are added to Facebook each month, YouTube users watch more than two billion videos per day, Twitter users perform thirty-two billion searches a month, more than 2.5 billion text messages are sent each day, five billion mobile phones are in use around the world, and Google processes close to ten billion searches a year. Obviously, these are big data items.[15] Within most organizations, data sets are not at that scale—but they are still large. Every organization has data about employees, transactions, customers, and external data sets that effect the organization. For example, Wal-Mart has almost two million employees in the United States. Even in human capital, big data projects are beginning to become commonplace. Lowes Home Improvement stores developed a correlation between employee engagement and store sales.[16] Nationwide Building Society in the United Kingdom took on a project to demonstrate a link between employee commitment, customer satisfaction, and business performance by correlating data collected from employee surveys, customer feedback, and sales figures.[17]

However, not all projects fall into the big data category—in fact, most analytics projects will probably not involve big data. For example, when an insurance company explored the possibility of employees working at home, 350 employees volunteered for the project. The company set up home offices with all the technology, data access, and data security that would replicate what was currently in the company's offices. This relieved the company from requiring more office space, and the payoff of this project was not only a reduction in office expenses but improvements in productivity and retention. Because this project involved collecting data from only 350 people, though, it is not considered a big data project.[18] Another project involved a large fashion retailer implementing a leadership development program for four thousand store managers. The analysis was to determine the success of a program with a sample of one hundred managers. These managers were involved in a program that required prework through e-learning, live classroom modules, coaching, and virtual tools in the follow-up process. The evaluation, all the way to ROI, represents a significant analytics project, but is not considered to be big data.[19]

Issues

Big data presents many opportunities but also many challenges. One of the challenges is that it requires more sophisticated technology, special platforms to handle big data options, and the computing power to go along with it. Big data also requires expertise that is often beyond the capabilities of the human resources function. Specialists are essential to make it work. Because big data is messy, it requires much clean-up. Sometimes, the amount of time it takes to clean up big data to make it usable is not worth it. Big data also often ignores the causation between connecting variables. For example, the two projects described previously involved relationships between variables. What is needed is not only significant correlation but also causation, and these two projects addressed the causation issue. Big data advocates, however, suggest that causation is not a major issue; they claim that if you run enough big data analytics with all the variables, the strongest correlations will often suggest causation. This may or may not be the case. Because big data sets require so much work to analyze, it might be wiser to address the issue of causation directly.[20] Finally, the use of big data often ignores the whole issue of sampling. Sampling is a critical part of viable fiscal analysis, and much of the human capital analytics will involve working with small samples.

Even with these challenges, big data is an important part of the process. Having made the distinction between big data and not-so-big data, we will now discuss the analysis that is used with both.

The Development of the Human Capital Analytics Model

Although much progress has been made, human capital analytics is not without its share of problems. The mere presence of the process creates a dilemma for many organizations. When an organization embraces the concept and implements a human capital analytics practice, the management team usually anxiously awaits results, only to be disappointed when they are not readily available. For the process to be useful, it must balance many issues, such as feasibility, simplicity, credibility, and soundness. More specifically, three major audiences must be pleased with the practice to accept and use it:

- Team members who design, develop, and conduct the projects need a simple, user-friendly process.
- Senior managers, sponsors, and clients who fund, initiate, and support projects need a credible outcome based on a conservative process.
- Researchers, professors, and critics who must support the analysis need a proven process that is logical, reliable, and valid.

To satisfy the needs of these three critical groups, the process must meet ten essential criteria for an effective human capital analytics model:

1. The process must be *simple*—devoid of complex formulas, lengthy equations, and complicated methodologies.
2. The process must be *economical* and must be implemented easily.
3. The assumptions, methodology, and techniques must be *credible*.
4. From a research perspective, the process must be *theoretically sound* and based on generally accepted practices.
5. The process must *account for other factors* that have influenced output variables.
6. The process must have the *flexibility* to be applied to a wide range of situations.
7. The process must be *applicable with all types of data*, including hard data (output, quality, costs, and time) and soft data (job satisfaction, engagement, and customer satisfaction).
8. The process must *include the costs of the solution*, when costs are needed.
9. The actual calculation must use an *acceptable ROI formula*.
10. Finally, the human capital analytics process must have a successful *track record* in a variety of applications. In far too many situations, models are created but never successfully applied. An effective HCA process should withstand the wear and tear of implementation and should get the results expected.

Because these criteria are considered essential, a human capital analytics process should at least meet the vast majority of them, if not all. The bad news is that many processes do not meet these criteria. The good news is that the human capital analytics model and process presented in Figure 14.4 meets all the criteria.[21]

Define the Problem/Opportunity

The first step is to define the problem, making sure that the business measure or measures linked to the project are clearly defined or the phenomenon is clearly described. The issue here is to clearly describe a problem or opportunity that must be addressed to make the project successful. Sometimes, initial problems or opportunities are presented to the human capital analytics team in vague terms. The challenge of this step is to make sure that it is a problem worth solving or an opportunity worth pursuing.

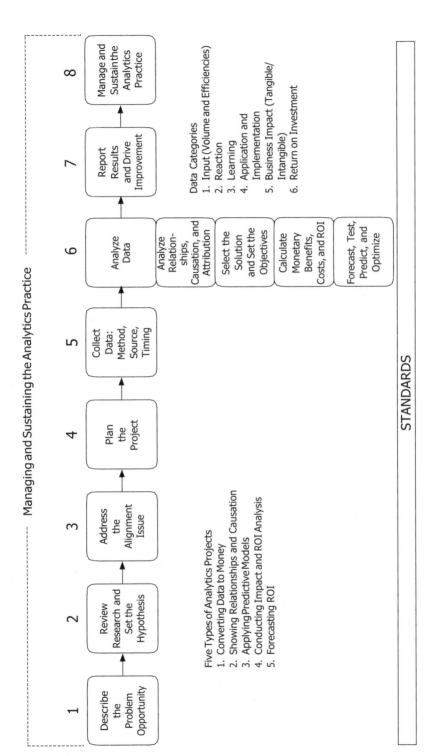

Figure 14.4. Model for making analytics work.

Review Research and Set the Hypothesis

When the problem is clearly defined, the question is, What do we expect to occur? For example, is job satisfaction related to attraction? Does job engagement relate to an increase in sales? These expectations are established as a hypothesis or, sometimes, multiple hypotheses. A hypothesis can be written mathematically, but it is often stated in simple terms to executives. The key is to anticipate expectations early in the process.

Address the Alignment Issue

Alignment ensures that the project is connected to important business measures throughout its implementation. Chapter 4 introduces the alignment of needs with objectives and evaluation. A human capital analytics project fits into the model at some point, as alignment can occur in several levels. Although this issue is addressed in step one, the alignment process keeps the focus. It may require detailed analysis, whereas other times it may be a quick conclusion based on the data. Alignment is critical at the business level, where specific business measures are identified in the beginning.

Plan the Project

Any analytics project will need a plan, maybe several of them. Planning is critical to ensure all key issues in the study are addressed, including making initial assumptions of how the project will unfold. Of the four types of plans, the first is the data collection plan, describing methods of data collection, sources of data, and timing of data collection. The second plan, the analysis plan, indicates what particular types of analyses are planned and how they will be used in the project. The third plan is the communication plan, detailing how the results will be reported to a variety of audiences and important topics with HCA projects. The fourth plan is the classic project plan that indicates the timing of the project from the beginning until the results are communicated and actions are taken. Proper investment in these four plans will make the entire project much easier.

Collect Data

Every human capital analytics study will involve collecting data. Data collection ranges from monitoring the data in the system to using questionnaires, interviews, focus groups, and observation. This step involves all the methods from the plan, which are now fully initiated.

Analyze Relationships, Causation, and Attribution

When trying to understand a problem, it is necessary to isolate the true cause from all the other factors, which moves beyond correlation. This step involves quantitative methods such as hypothesis testing and experimental design or qualitative methods such as problem solving or brainstorming. When a solution is implemented and improvement in a business impact measure has occurred, the question is how much of the improvement is actually connected to the solution. This critical step of attribution isolates the effects of different processes from the solution. It is necessary for accuracy and credibility. Several methods are available to accomplish this step.

Select the Solution and Set the Objectives

This analysis can come at different times, but at some point, a solution is needed. It could come early, after using descriptive statistics, or it can come after detailed analysis points to what exactly caused the problem. The solution is implemented to improve one or more impact measures. A variety of tools and processes will be used to ensure that this is the proper solution to address the problem or opportunity in the most economical way. An important part of this step is to set the objectives at different levels.

Calculate Monetary Benefits, Costs, and ROI

Sometimes a project involves converting data to monetary value. From a client perspective, the best way to understand a problem or an opportunity is to convert it to money, based on additional profits, reduced costs, or avoided costs. There are a variety of techniques available for converting data to money. This step is necessary if the project includes ROI analysis. When a solution is implemented, it is helpful to understand the impact of the solution in monetary terms, converting data to money at a later step in the process through a variety of techniques.

Sometimes it is necessary to develop the full cost of a particular human capital solution. For example, executives may ask for the total cost of wellness and fitness in terms of coordination, administration, equipment, facilities, programs, and even time for those who are involved in this process. These costs are necessary for a ROI calculation, in which the monetary benefits of the program are compared to all the costs. In either case, all costs must be included, both direct and indirect costs.

Forecast, Test, Predict, and Optimize

Sometimes the ROI forecast for a particular solution or the forecast of success from a predictive model may be needed. In today's climate, executives want to know whether a solution will work before it is implemented. This step also involves a predictive model at the impact level, testing the model for feasibility and accuracy, optimizing it, and exploring what can be done to maximize the impact and ROI.

Report Results and Drive Improvement

Any human capital analytics project involves many stakeholders. The challenge is to make sure that all stakeholders have the data and results, understand their role in achieving them, and know how to make improvements or adjustments. Some audiences need detailed information; others need brief snapshots. The key is to identify the appropriate audience, select the appropriate methods, and deliver a message that helps them achieve and understand the results. This final step includes driving improvements using results from the analytics project. These results are used to make adjustments. The key is to use the data to drive the improvement or the change desired and follow through to make sure that has happened.

Manage and Sustain the Analytics Practice

A variety of issues and events will influence the successful implementation of human capital analytics. Because this is such an important topic, specific topics or actions are presented later in this chapter:

- Meetings and formal sessions to develop staff skills with human capital analytics
- Strategies to improve management commitment and support for human capital analytics
- Mechanisms to provide technical support
- Specific techniques to place more attention on results

Human capital analytics can fail or succeed based on these implementation issues.

Human Capital Analytics Standards

Standards serve as the foundation for implementing the human capital analytics model. To ensure consistency across studies, the operating standards have been developed and tested in practice. The results of a human capital analytics project must stand alone and should not vary based on the individual who is conducting the study. The operating standards detail how each major step and issue of the process should be addressed. To date, sixteen standards have been developed:

1. Align projects to business measures.
2. Use the simplest statistics in the human capital analytics project.
3. When collecting and analyzing data, use only the most credible sources.
4. When analyzing data, select the most conservative alternative for calculations.
5. If no improvement data are available for a population or from a specific source, assume that little or no improvement has occurred.
6. Omit extreme data items and unsupported claims from the analysis.
7. Address causation in problem-solving analysis.
8. Use at least one method to isolate the effects of the solution.
9. Adjust estimates of improvement for the potential error of the estimate.
10. When a higher-level evaluation is conducted, collect data at lower levels.
11. When an evaluation is planned for a higher level, refrain from being too comprehensive at the lower levels.
12. Use only the first year of benefits (annual) in the ROI analysis for short-term solutions.
13. Use fully loaded costs for human capital analytics projects.
14. Define intangible measures as measures that are not converted to monetary values.
15. Communicate results of human capital analytics projects to all key stakeholders.
16. Use results of human capital projects to drive improvements.

These specific standards not only serve as a way to consistently address each step but also provide a much-needed conservative approach to the analysis. A conservative approach will build credibility with the executive audience.

Challenges and Opportunities

When human capital analytics practice is working, there are some potential challenges that can be quickly turned into very profitable opportunities. These challenges are also an important part of maximizing the value of the human capital analytics practice.

Culture and Analytics

Ideally, a human capital analytics practice is created because of a culture of analytics among the leadership of the organization. In most cases, it is the interest of the leadership of the organization, as they see the power of analytics in other functions, which has led to the creation of the human capital analytics practice. But this is not always the case. In some cases, it is the chief human resources officer who has convinced executives to fund the analytics practice. Either way, it needs to be supported by executives who see the value of having and using analytics. This leadership role is developed in many organizations and can be developed over a period of time.[22]

Analytical leaders are those who get involved in data and analytics in a big way. They often push for more data in analysis. They lead from the front, trying to role model the best practice. They recruit the smartest people and believe in accountability. They never give up. They set strategy targets, and they use analytics wisely. If this type of leadership is not already in place, the leader of the HCA practice must help develop that leadership. This will be accomplished by ensuring that the human capital analytics practice is fully functioning.

Intuition Versus Data-Based Decision Making

There has been much discussion about the value of intuition (sometimes referred to as "gut feelings") versus decision making based on data. Human capital analytics may push decision making entirely on the basis of data and not bring in intuition or gut feelings. This should not be the case. Both data and intuition are needed. In a recent study by the Corporate Executive Board that assessed five thousand employees according to their ability to balance judgment and analysis, 19 percent were found to rely on intuition, seldom trust analysis, and make decisions unilaterally. At the other extreme, almost 43 percent relied on value consensus from analysis over judgment. In the middle, 38 percent apply judgment to analysis, listen to others, and invite a variety of opinions.[23] The conclusion is that there is room for both. Data are an important part of the process and an important part of decision making, but they do not supplant or replace good judgment.

Optimization and Allocation

The goal of many human capital solutions is to optimize the effects on outcomes. As the ROI calculation is developed, these questions should be asked: What adjustments, changes, or other assumptions could be made so that the outcomes are enhanced? What levels of optimization can be achieved? The answers involve three different scenarios:

1. *Adjust the guiding principles.* The guiding principles, presented earlier, are conservative. Sometimes critics will argue that they are too conservative. Different assumptions can be made, without changing the standards, to see the effects of other scenarios. For example, for a short-term solution, one-year impact data are used. Sometimes, however, it is debatable whether a solution is long term or

short term. Multiple years may be entered to show how the ROI changes. This approach helps in understanding what may eventually occur as these standards are adjusted. It is important to report value using the standards and then report other scenarios, if different assumptions are made.

2. *Consider changing the benefits side.* In a ROI calculation, the impact measure is converted to money to produce the benefits for the numerator. Although in a predictive model or estimated forecast, the impact measures are specific, every model has room for improvement. It may be helpful to make adjustments to improve outcome measures to see the different effects they may have on ROI.

3. *Consider changing the cost side.* The denominator of the ROI calculation is the cost of the solution. The standard is that all costs are included, both direct and indirect. Although some of the indirect costs may be subject to debate, they should be included. One way to optimize the process is to examine ways to lower cost. If costs are lowered, obviously the ROI goes up, so adjusting these cost values shows different variations of the outcome.

Optimization can occur on a forecast to show what may be possible as different assumptions and changes are applied and the ROI is developed. On a postsolution ROI, changes in the inputs can be made. For example, changes in the design, development, and implementation of the solution can drive improvements. These changes show what can be done (and should be done) to make the results better, particularly when the initial results are disappointing. On a positive note, most solutions deliver positive ROI values, sometimes even high values. Optimization lets us examine what we must change to make ROI even more valuable.

With optimization comes the next stage: allocation. Optimization may tell you which programs add the most value, and it may mean that more resources need to be allocated to those programs. It may indicate the way in which programs are delivered to add the most value, and this may mean that allocations are more connected to that delivery system. Optimization is a natural driver to allocating the proper resources to optimize the output. When this is achieved, the human capital analytics practice is adding tremendous value to the organization and helping to drive some of the key business decisions.

How to Develop the Practice

Now comes the big question: "How do we actually develop the practice?" Although many human resources functions are well into this process, it is helpful to reflect on how the practice is developed. For those organizations already in the process, readjustment and review may be needed. The reality is that every human resources function will have part of this in development now, typically under the heading of research, evaluation, measurement, metrics, or another term. Reporting is taking place now, and technology is being deployed. But the push is for the human capital analytics function to make this a more powerful part of the process, and it is helpful to think of this evolution as preparing for the launch of the practice and then sustaining it after the launch. Here are eight things that must be done before the practice is launched and eight things that must be done after it is launched.

Before the Launch

Funding is usually provided to develop the practice before it is actually launched. The launch occurs when the notice is sent to executives that the capability and processes are in place to tackle critical issues in the HR area—that it is now open for business. But before that, eight steps must be taken:

1. *Build the team.* The human capital analytics team must be developed or acquired to provide the expertise necessary to make it work. The team often has four important skill sets:
   - Human resources
   - IT data systems
   - Operations and support
   - Statistics, math, and operations research

   The key is to have a good cross-section or balance of these skills. There can be too many analysts or not enough. Usually, the missing pieces are IT data systems experience and statistics, math, and operations research experience. A recent survey conducted by the ROI Institute and Vestrics showed that in current human capital analytics practices, 53 percent have HR staff in statistics, math, and operations research, and 58 percent have staff in IT.[24] The number of staff will vary with the organization and what is intended. The average staff is approximately three, with much variation depending on the size of the organization. The budget also varies, and it is often helpful to fix the budget as a percentage of the total human resources budget. The current average is between 2 and 3 percent, but it should be closer to 5 percent of the budget.

2. *Address the technology issues.* The first issue is selecting the platform to use to make the practice work. It could be a dedicated process available from SAP, SAS, SPSS, or Cognos, or it may be a standby process that has been around for some time, like Excel or Minitab. In the recent study from the ROI Institute and Vestrics, Excel was the number-one platform. The advantage of Excel is that you can build on current processes that are already in place and not have to invest a tremendous amount of money in a new platform. This step will also involve making sure that the systems and databases are accessible and can relate to each other properly. Unfortunately, with different legacy systems in use, data collection and integration may be a problem. This step is a huge challenge and often baffles teams as they start. With the help of IT, it must be tackled quickly so that work on HCA projects can get started.

3. *Review data issues.* This involves a quick review of the availability, accessibility, and integrity of the data. Sometimes, the HR team may not understand the data sets. This is where other functional areas, such as operations support, quality, and IT, can help ensure the data are accessible to the HR function. The quality of data may be out of their control, and HR may have to live with the data available to them, even if it is inadequate or incomplete.

4. *Review and adjust reporting.* Current reporting practices may need to be updated.

5. *Secure funding.* Some initial funding will need to be provided based on an estimate of what will be accomplished and the resources needed. That will be adjusted as the group delivers value.

6. *Select or develop an analytics model.* The model presented in this chapter is a systematic, conservative approach based on a logical framework, and it is used by hundreds of organizations.

7. *Create simple project-selection rules.* It is important to decide which projects to undertake. Dividing the projects into the five types detailed in this chapter is a helpful way to categorize projects and to see the value of them.

8. *Plan the process.* The process must have a project plan or a timeline of expectations and resources needed. The key is to not wait for perfection—waiting until all data are accurate or all technology speaks to each other—but to get things moving quickly.

After the Launch

The team must move quickly to deliver successes. The important issue is to be professional, engaged, capable, timely, efficient, and effective. This translates into eight important steps:

1. *Respond to the executives.* After all, the executives provided the funding, and they want to see results. If projects appear to take too many resources, they may be put off until later. The resources needed to make projects work need to be addressed, and it may be that the request is something that cannot be accomplished in a reasonable time frame. The key issue is to develop basic criteria around requests at this time.

2. *Look for high-value opportunities.* Some projects can deliver great value, and others cannot. Simple forecasting can often help reveal the value. If there is a huge retention issue for critical talent, you can bet that it is a high-value project.

3. *Start with business needs.* Every project should be related to a business need. These are impact measures usually involving key measures of output, quality, cost, and time. They are the important measures that will attract the attention of the executive group.

4. *Stay on track.* Although this is obvious, it often causes problems with teams. As they get started, they see other possibilities for other projects, one thing leads to another, and things can easily go astray down a bunny trail. The key is to stay on time and within cost, perhaps using project management tools to make it work.

5. *Position projects for action.* All this work is being done to deliver results and take action, and it should be positioned that way. A decision needs to result from each project.

6. *Focus on presenting results.* The presentation of the results is often undervalued and underdelivered. A compelling case for action needs to be made, and it may require a live briefing with the executive team. Beyond that, quick, easy-to-understand presentation techniques are useful, such as dashboard scorecards and one-page summaries with visualizations. The key is to not get bogged down in analysis that executives will not understand.

7. *Strive for quick successes.* *Quick* means that the team can do it in a reasonable time frame—certainly within the first year of the launch, though a few months would be better. *Successes* lead to actions that please the executives. The results from those actions are also important.

Unsuccessful human capital analytics practice	Successful human capital analytics practice
1. Sparse resources and inadequate funding	1. Fully funded with ample resources
2. Skill gaps exist among the team members	2. Highly skilled team with complementary skill sets
3. No model or systematic process	3. Proven approach and process
4. No clear way for selecting projects for analysis	4. A systematic way for selecting critical projects for analysis
5. Disorganized project teams	5. Great project management skills
6. Inefficient project teams	6. Efficient teams with on-time project completion
7. No consistent way of presenting results to executive team	7. Great presentations to executives, including live briefings
8. Projects not always positioned for action	8. Projects positioned for immediate actions and/or decisions
9. Few successes	9. Several major successes each year
10. Weak and uncertain manager support	10. Strong support from the management team
11. Weak and inconsistent executive commitment	11. Strong and consistent executive commitment
12. Weak credibility, influence, and respect	12. Strong credibility, influence, and respect

Figure 14.5. Human capital analytics practice success.

8. *Manage and sustain the practice.* As a summary, Figure 14.5 contrasts the differences between a practice that is doomed to failure and another destined for success. The key is to work on the right of the chart.

Implications for Human Capital Strategy

This force, the last of the twelve forces, is fitting to conclude with because it provides a vehicle for showing the value of addressing the other eleven forces. Using analytics and big data possibilities can make a huge difference. The team must develop a human capital analytics practice that is designed to deliver results and position itself for success quickly and consistently. To achieve this, these issues should be addressed in the human capital strategy:

- The creation and support of the HCA practice
- The development or adoption of an HCA model with standards
- The process for selecting HCA projects
- The funding formula for the practice
- How to build on successes with optimization and allocation

Notes

Preface

1. Telegraph Investor. "Winning: Jack Welch, Retired Chairman and CEO of GE, and Suzy Welch, Ex Editor-in-Chief of Harvard Business Review, Respond to Readers' Business Issues." Accessed April 2, 2015. http://www.telegraph.co.uk/finance/2942953/winning.html.

Chapter 1

1. "QUALCOMM Annual Report 2013." http://investor.qualcomm.com/secfiling .cfm?filingID=1234452-13-483.
2. Flamholtz, Eric G. *Human Resource Accounting*, 2nd ed. San Francisco: Jossey-Bass, 1985.
3. Cascio, Wayne. *Managing Human Resources: Productivity, Quality of Work Life, Profits*, 4th ed. New York: McGraw-Hill, 1995.
4. Sveiby, Karl Erik. *The New Organizational Wealth*. San Francisco: Berrett-Koehler, 1997.
5. Sullivan, Patrick H. *Value Driven Intellectual Capital: How to Convert Intangible Corporate Assets into Market Value*. New York: John Wiley & Sons, 2000.
6. Stewart, Thomas A. *Intellectual Capital: The New Wealth of Organizations*. New York: Doubleday, 1997.
7. Saint-Onge, Hubert. "Shaping Human Resource Management Within the Knowledge-Driven Enterprise." In *Leading Knowledge Management and Learning*, ed. Dede Bonner. Alexandria, VA: American Society for Training and Development, 2000.
8. Martin, Roger L. "The Rise (and Likely Fall) of the Talent Economy." *Harvard Business Review*, October 2014, p. 41.
9. Saint-Onge, "Shaping Human Resource Management."
10. Sullivan, *Value Driven Intellectual Capital*.
11. Stewart, Thomas A. "Intellectual Capital: Brainpower." *Fortune*, June 3, 1991, p. 44.
12. Kleiner, A. "The World's Most Exciting Accountant." *Strategy+Business*, June 1, 2004.
13. Mitchell, C., R. L. Ray, and B. van Ark. "The Conference Board CEO Challenge 2013." https://www.conference-board.org/retrievefile.cfm?filename=CEO-Challenge -Charts-and-Tables_FINAL1.pdf&type=subsite.
14. IBM. "Leading Through Connections: Insights from the IBM Global CEO Study." Accessed May 2012. http://www-935.ibm.com/services/us/en/c-suite/ceostudy2012.

15. Tracey, W. R. *The Human Resources Glossary*, 3rd ed. Boca Raton, FL: St. Lucie Press, 2004.

16. Stewart, T. A. "Taking on the Last Bureaucracy." *Fortune*, January 15, 1996.

17. Durfee, D. *Human Capital Management: The CFO's Perspective*. Boston: CFO Publishing, 2013.

Chapter 2

1. Andersen, Torben Juul, and Dana Minbaeva. "The Role of Human Resource Management in Strategy Making." *Human Resource Management* 52, no. 5 (September–October 2013): 809–827.

2. Favaro, Ken. "To the Nimble Go the Spoils." *Strategy & Business*, winter 2014, p. 64.

3. Surridge, Tanya. "Building the Business Case for Corporate Universities." Presentation at the Skills Africa Summit IRR, May 2005.

4. Eigenhuis, Ap, and Rob van Dijk. *HR Strategy for the High Performing Business: Inspiring Success Through Effective Human Resource Management*. London: Kogan Page, 2008, p. 31.

5. "CEO Perspectives: How HR Can Take on a Bigger Role in Driving Growth." *Economist*, August 19, 2012.

6. Charan, Ram. "It's Time to Split HR." *Harvard Business Review*, July–August 2014.

Chapter 3

1. Zeynep, Ton. "Why 'Good Jobs' Are Good for Retailers." *Harvard Business Review*, January–February 2012.

2. "100 Best Companies to Work For." *Fortune*, March 2015, p. 149.

3. Krantz, Matt. "Radio Shack Files for Bankruptcy." *USA Today*, February 6, 2015.

4. Kemp, R. C. *Benchmarking: The Search for Industry Best Practices That Leads to Superior Performance*. Milwaukee, WI: ASTC Quality Press, 1989.

5. Freiberg, Kevin and Jackie. *Guts! Companies That Blow the Doors off the Business-as-Usual*. New York: Doubleday, 2004.

6. Levering, Robert, and Milton Moskowitz. "The 100 Best Companies to Work For: With Labor in Short Supply, These Companies Are Pulling Out All the Stops for Employees." *Fortune*, January 10, 2000.

7. Phillips, Jack J. and Patricia P. *Proving the Value of HR: How and Why to Measure ROI*, 2nd ed. Alexandria, VA: Society for Human Resource Management, 2012.

Chapter 4

1. "Yale New Haven Health Annual Report 2011." http://yalenewhavenhealth.org/about/ynhhsar2011.pdf.

2. Phillips, Jack J. and Patti P. *Proving the Value of HR*, 2nd ed. Alexandria, VA: Society for Human Resource Management, 2012.

3. Phillips, Patricia P. "Case Study: Skill-Based Pay, Southeast Corridor Bank (SCB)." In *Managing Talent Retention: An ROI Approach*, ed. Jack Phillips and Lisa Edwards, 352–367. Pfeiffer, 2009.

Chapter 5

1. http://www.tata.com.
2. Ready, Douglas A., Linda A. Hill, and Robert J. Thomas. "Building a Game-Changing Talent Strategy." *Harvard Business Review*, January–February 2014.
3. Martin, Kevin, and Jay Jamrog. *Enabling Sustained Growth Through Talent Transparency*. Institute for Corporate Productivity (i4cp) research report, 2014.
4. Phillips, Jack, Patti Phillips, and Gene Pease. *Making Human Capital Analytics Work*. ROI Institute and Vestrics research report, October 2014.
5. Davenport, Thomas H., Jeanne Harris, and Jeremy Shapiro. "Competing on Talent Analytics: What the Best Companies Know About Their People and How They Use That Information to Out Perform Rivals." *Harvard Business Review*, October 2010, p. 52–58.
6. DiRomualdo, Tony, Kevin Martin, and Jay Jamrog. *Building a Change-Ready Organization: Critical Human Capital Issues*. Institute for Corporate Productivity (i4cp) research report, 2013.
7. "100 Best Companies to Work For." *Fortune*, March 2015, p. 145.
8. Ready, Hill, and Thomas, "Building a Game Changing Talent Strategy."
9. Deloitte Research. *It's 2008: Do You Know Where Your Talent Is? Why Acquisition and Retention Strategies Don't Work*. Deloitte Development, 2004.
10. Ibid.
11. Berger, Lance and Dorothy R. *The Talent Management Handbook: Creating Organizational Excellence by Identifying, Developing, and Promoting Your Best People*. New York: McGraw-Hill, 2004.
12. Spencer, Lyle M., Jr. "How Competencies Create Economic Value." In *The Talent Management Handbook: Creating Organizational Excellence by Identifying, Developing, and Promoting Your Best People*, ed. Lance and Dorothy R. Berger, 64. New York: McGraw-Hill, 2004.
13. Feintzeig, Rachel. "U.S. Struggles to Draw Young, Savvy Staff." *Wall Street Journal*, June 10, 2014.
14. Johnson, Mike. *Talent Management: Getting Talented People to Work for You*. London: Prentice Hall, 2002.
15. Harris Interactive. "The Harris Poll 2013 RQ Summary Report: A Survey of the U.S. General Public Using the Reputation Quotient." February 2013.
16. Michaels, Ed, Helen Handfield-Jones, and Beth Axelrod. *The War for Talent*. Boston: Harvard Business School Press, 2001.
17. Burke, Eugene, Conrad Schmidt, and Michael Griffin. "Improving the Odds of Success for High-Potential Programmes." CEB/SHL Talent Measurement, Talent Report 2014.
18. Phillips, Jack J. *Managing Employee Retention: A Strategic Accountability Approach*. Woburn, MA: Butterworth-Heinemann, 2003.

Chapter 6

1. "100 Best Companies to Work For." *Fortune*, March 2015, p. 145.
2. Quicken Loans. Accessed April 15, 2015. http://www.quickenloans.com/press-room/fast-facts/our-isms/.

3. Ray, Rebecca L., Patrick Hyland, David A. Dye, Joel Kaplan, and Adam Pressman. *DNA of Engagement: How Organizations Create and Sustain Highly Engaging Cultures*. The Conference Board research report, October 2014.

4. Morgan, Jacob. *The Future of Work: Attract New Talent, Build Better Leaders, and Create a Competitive Organization*. Hoboken, NJ: Wiley, 2014.

5. *2012 Global Workforce Study*. Towers Watson research report, 2012.

6. Ray, Rebecca. *Employee Engagement in a V.U.C.A. World*. The Conference Board research report, 2011.

7. Ibid.

8. Herzberg, Frederick. "One More Time: How Do You Motivate Employees?" *Harvard Business Review*, January 2003.

9. Myers, M. Scott. *Every Employee a Manager: More Meaningful Work Through Job Enrichment*. New York: McGraw-Hill, 1970.

10. Smith, Patricia C., Lorne M. Kendall, and Charles L. Hulin. *The Measure of Satisfaction in Work and Retirement: A Strategy for the Study of Attitudes*. Chicago: Rand McNally Psychology Series, 1969.

11. Ray, Rebecca, Gad Levanon, and Tom Rizzacasa. *Job Satisfaction 2013 Edition: At Least We're Working; Maybe That's Enough*. The Conference Board research report, 2013.

12. Kahn, William A. "Psychological Conditions of Personal Engagement and Disengagement at Work." *The Academy of Management Journal* 33, no. 4 (December 1990): 692–724.

13. Harter, K., F. L. Schmidt, and T. L. Hayes. "Business-Unit-Level Relationship Between Employee Satisfaction, Employee Engagement, and Business Outcomes: A Meta-Analysis." *Journal of Applied Psychology* 87 (2002): 268–279.

14. *State of the Global Workplace*, Gallup research report, 2013.

15. *State of the American Workplace*, Gallup research report, 2013.

16. Ray, Rebecca, Brian Powers, and Peter Stathatos. *Employee Engagement: What Works Now?* The Conference Board research report, 2012.

17. Ibid.

18. Mitchell, Charles, Rebecca Ray, and Bart van Ark. *The Conference Board CEO Challenge 2014: People and Performance*. The Conference Board research report, 2014.

19. Harter, James K., Frank L. Schmidt, Sangeeta Agrawal, and Stephanie K. Plowman. *The Relationship Between Engagement at Work and Organizational Outcomes*. Gallup research report, 2013.

20. Harter, James, Sangeeta Agrawal, Stephanie Plowman, and Jim Asplund. *Employee Engagement and Earnings per Share: A Longitudinal Study of Organizational Performance During the Recession*. Gallup research report, 2010.

21. *State of the Global Workplace*. Gallup research report, 2013.

22. *2012 Global Workforce Study*. Towers Watson research report, 2012.

23. *Using Continual Engagement to Drive Business Results*. Watson Wyatt Worldwide research report, 2009.

24. "Best Place to Work Awards." Great Place to Work. Accessed January 12, 2014. http://www.greatplacetowork.com/best-companies.

25. Ray, *Employee Engagement in a V.U.C.A. World*.

26. Nayar, Vineet. *Employees First, Customers Second: Turning Conventional Management Upside Down*. Boston: Harvard Business School Press, 2010.

27. *State of the Global Workplace*. Gallup research report, 2013.

28. Harris, Stacey. *Measuring the Business Impact of Talent Strategies*. Bersin & Associates research report, 2010.

29. Phillips, Patti P., Jack J. Phillips, and Rebecca Ray. *Measuring the Success of Leadership Development: Quantify Your Program's Impact and ROI on Organizational Performance*. Alexandria, VA: ASTD Press, 2015.

30. Phillips, Patti P. and Jack J. *Measuring ROI in Learning and Development: Case Studies from Global Organizations*. Alexandria, VA: ASTD Press, 2012.

31. Ray, *Employee Engagement in a V.U.C.A. World*.

32. *State of the American Workplace*. Gallup research report, 2013.

33. Rizzacasa, Tom, and Sherlin Nair. *The Happiness Premium: What Companies Should Know About Leveraging Happiness in the Workplace*. The Conference Board executive action report, 2013.

34. Reiss, Robert. "Tony Hsieh on His Secrets of Success." *Forbes*, July 1, 2010. http://www.forbes.com/2010/07/01/tony-hsieh-zappos-leadership-managing-interview.html.

35. Congdon, Christine, Donna Flynn, and Melanie Redman. "Balancing We and Me." *Harvard Business Review*, October 2014.

36. Waber, Ben, Jennifer Magnolfi, and Greg Lindsey. "Work Spaces That Move People." *Harvard Business Review*, October 2014.

37. CCIM Institute. "Ten Trends in Office Design." *CIRE Magazine*, March–April 1999. http://www.ccim.com/cire-magazine/articles/10-trends-office-design.

38. Waber, Ben, Jennifer Magnolfi, and Greg Lindsey. "Work Spaces That Move People." *Harvard Business Review*, October 2014.

39. Lohr, Steve. "Taking a Stand for Office Ergonomics." *New York Times*, December 1, 2012.

40. Phillips, Patti P. and Jack J. *Measuring ROI in Employee Relations and Compliance: Case Studies in Diversity and Inclusion, Engagement, Compliance and Flexible Working Arrangements*. Alexandria, VA: Society for Human Resource Management, 2014.

41. Ibid.

42. Phillips, Phillips, and Ray, *Measuring the Success of Leadership Development*.

43. Phillips, Jack J. and Patti P. *Proving the Value of HR: How and Why to Measure ROI*, 2nd ed. Alexandria, VA: Society for Human Resource Management, 2012.

Chapter 7

1. Bhalla, Vikram, Jean-Michel Caye, Andrew Dyer, Lisa Dymond, Yves Morieux, and Paul Orlander. *High-Performance Organizations: The Secrets of Their Success*. Boston Consulting Group research report, September 2011.

2. Schein, E. H. "Organizational Culture." *American Psychologist* 45, no. 2 (1990): 109–119.

3. Thomas, Howard, Richard Smith, and Fermin Diez. *Human Capital and Global Business Strategy*. Cambridge: Cambridge University Press, 2013.

4. Nalbantian, Haig R., Richard A. Guzzo, Dave Kieffer, and Jay Doherty. *Play to Your Strengths: Managing Your Internal Labor Markets for Lasting Competitive Advantage*. New York: McGraw-Hill, 2004.

5. Pulakos, Elaine D., Rose A. Mueller-Hanson, Ryan S. O'Leary, and Michael M. Meyrowitz. *Building a High-Performance Culture: A Fresh Look at Performance Management*. Alexandria, VA: Society for Human Resource Management, 2012.

6. Aon Hewitt. "The Status of Variable Pay Systems. U.S. Salary Increase Survey 2014–2015." *Workspan Magazine*, November 2014.

7. Anthony, Scott D., Davis S. Duncan, and Pontus M. A. Siren. "Build an Innovation Engine in 90 Days." *Harvard Business Review*, December 2014, p. 61–68.

Chapter 8

1. Evans, Lisa. "What 3 Companies Are Doing to Keep Employees Healthy." *Entrepreneur*, March 15, 2013. http://www.entrepreneur.com/article/226041.

2. American Hospital Association Committee on Performance Improvement (Jeannette Clough, Chairperson). *Hospitals and Care Systems of the Future.* American Hospital Association research report, September 2011.

3. *Value in Healthcare: Current State and Future Directions.* Healthcare Financial Management Association research report, June 2011.

4. Bisognano, M., and C. Kenny. "Leadership for the Triple Aim." *Healthcare Executive*, March–April 2012, p. 80–83.

5. Goldsmith, Marshall, and Mark Reiter. *What Got You Here Won't Get You There: How Successful People Become Even More Successful.* New York: Hyperion, 2007.

6. Squires, David A. "The U.S. Health System in Perspective: A Comparison of Twelve Industrialized Nations." Commonwealth Fund publication 1532 Vol. 16.

7. Munro, Dan. "Annual U.S. Healthcare Spending Hits $3.8 Trillion." *Forbes*, February 2, 2014. Accessed December 29, 2014. http://www.forbes.com/sites/danmunro/2014/02/02/annual-u-s-healthcare-spending-hits-3-8-trillion/.

8. Kaiser Family Foundation. *2013 Employer Health Benefits Survey.* http://kff.org/private-insurance/report/2013-employer-health-benefits.

9. Pilzer, Paul Z., and Rick Lindquist. *The End of Employer-Provided Health Insurance: Why It's Good for You, Your Family, and Your Company.* Hoboken, NJ: Wiley, 2015.

10. "WIN Weight-Control Information Network." *National Institute of Diabetes and Digestive and Kidney Disease (NIDDK).* Accessed December, 27, 2014. http://win.niddk.nih.gov/statistics.

11. Pilzer and Lindquist, *End of Employer-Provided Health Insurance.*

12. Centers for Disease Control and Prevention. "Smoking-Attributable Mortality, Years of Potential Life Lost, and Productivity Losses—United States, 2000–2004." *Morbidity and Mortality Weekly Report* 57, no. 45 (2008): 1226–1228.

13. Weber, Lauren. "Wellness Programs Get a Health Check: Designed to Motivate Workers to Get in Shape, Employers Tread Carefully with Toughened Plans." *Wall Street Journal*, October 10, 2014. http://www.wsj.com/articles/wellness-programs-get-a-health-check-1412725776.

14. Weber, "Wellness Programs Get a Health Check."

15. Kaiser Family Foundation, *2013 Employer Health Benefits Survey.*

16. Pilzer and Lindquist, *End of Employer-Provided Health Insurance.*

17. Kaiser Family Foundation, *2013 Employer Health Benefits Survey.*

Chapter 9

1. Dropbox. "About Us." Accessed April 17, 2015. https://www.dropbox.com/about.

2. Guynn, Jessica. "Dropbox Thinks Outside the Box on Diversity." *USA Today*, November 6, 2014. http://www.usatoday.com/story/tech/2014/11/05/dropbox-diversity/18473517.

3. "Disruptive Demographics." AgeLab MIT. Accessed December 28, 2014. http://agelab.mit.edu/disruptive-demographics.

4. Murray-Bailey, Melissa. "What Millennials Want." *Talent Management Magazine*, February 2014.

5. Gratton, Lynda. *The Shift: The Future of Work Is Already Here*. London: Harper-Collins, 2011.

6. Institute for Women's Policy Research. "Pay and Equity Discrimination." Accessed April 3, 2015. http://www.iwpr.org/initiatives/pay-equity-and-discrimination.

7. Sandberg, Sheryl. *Lean In: Women, Work, and the Will to Lead*. New York: Knopf, 2013.

8. Swartz, Jon. "Facebook's Sandberg Wants to Lead the Women's Movement." *USA Today*, March 11, 2013.

9. Ibid., 2A.

10. Reiss, Robert. "Top Women CEOs on How Bold Innovation Drives Business." *Forbes*, November 17, 2014. http://www.forbes.com/sites/robertreiss/2014/11/17/women-ceos-advise-to-start-with-mission-boldly-innovate-to-drive-business-outcomes-and-manage-pls.

11. Baig, Mehroz. "Women in the Workforce: What Changes Have We Made?" *Huffington Post* (blog), December 19, 2013. http://www.huffingtonpost.com/mehroz-baig/women-in-the-workforce-wh_b_4462455.html.

12. Zenger, Jack, and Joseph Folkman. "Are Women Better Leaders than Men?" *Harvard Business Review*, March 15, 2012. http://hbr.org/2012/03/a-study-in-leadership-women-do.

13. Barsh, Joanna, Susie Cranston, and Rebecca Craske. "Centered Leadership: How Talented Women Thrive." *McKinsey Quarterly*, September 2008. Accessed April 2, 2014. http://www.mckinsey.com/insights/leading_in_the_21st_century/centered_leadership_how_talented_women_thrive.

14. Malone, Thomas. *The Future of Work: How the New Order of Business Will Shape Your Organization, Your Management Style and Your Life*. Boston: Harvard Business School, 2004, p. 171–172.

15. Roberts, Sam. "Most Children Still Live in Two-Parent Homes, Census Bureau Reports." *New York Times*, February 21, 2008. Accessed April 22, 2015. http://www.nytimes.com/2008/02/21/us/21census.html?_r=0.

16. Vaillant, George E., Charles C. McArthur, and Arlie Bock. "Grant Study of Adult Development, 1938–2000." http://hdl.handle.net/1902.1/00290.

17. "The Decline of Marriage and Rise of New Families." PewSocialTrends.org, November 18, 2010. http://www.pewsocialtrends.org/2010/11/18/the-decline-of-marriage-and-rise-of-new-families/6.

18. Winters, Mary-Frances. "Trend 7: The New Global Workforce: Female, Young, and Old, Non-White." *Profiles in Diversity Journal*. Accessed January 3, 2015. http://www.diversityjournal.com/10217-10217.

19. Mourino-Ruiz, Edwin. *The Perfect Human Capital Storm: Workplace Challenges and Opportunities*. North Charleston, SC: CreateSpace Independent Publishing Platform, 2014, 11.

20. Kerby, Sophia, and Crosby Burns. "The Top 10 Economic Facts of Diversity in the Workplace." Center for American Progress, July 12, 2012. http://www.americanprogress.org/issues/labor/news/2012/07/12/12/11900/the-top-10-economic-facts-of-diversity-in-the-workplace.

21. Associated Press. "Trust in Elected Leaders Falls Sharply." January 20, 2014. Accessed April 3, 2015. http://profit.ndtv.com/news/davos/article-trust-in-elected-leaders-falls-sharply-global-survey-378148.

22. Fox, Justin. "The Economics of Wellbeing: Have We Found a Better Gage of Success than GDP?" *Harvard Business Review*, January–February 2012.

23. Thomas, R. Roosevelt. *Building a House for Diversity*. New York: AMACOM, 1999.

24. Baytos, Lawrence. *Designing and Implementing Successful Diversity Programs*. Englewood Cliffs, NJ: Prentice Hall, 1995.

25. Hubbard, Edward E. *The Diversity Scorecard: Evaluating the Impact of Diversity on Organizational Performance*. New York: Routledge, 2014.

26. Thomas, *Building a House for Diversity*.

27. Martin, Jean. "Seven Imperatives for Diverse and Inclusive Organizations." *Strategic HR Review* 12, no. 3 (2013): 151–152.

Chapter 10

1. Graham, Jefferson. "A Nose for Apps as Well as News." *USA Today*, March 13, 2013.

2. Casey, Judi. "The Impact of Technology on Our Work and Family Lives." *Huffington Post*, October 2, 2012. http://www.huffingtonpost.com/judi-casey/the-impact-of-technology-_b_1932974.html?.

3. "Smartphone Users Worldwide Will Total 1.75 Billion in 2014." E-Marketer, January 16, 2014. http://www.emarketer.com/article/Smartphone-Users-Worldwide-Will-Total-175-Billion-2014/1010536.

4. Burkitt, Frank. "A Strategist's Guide to the Internet of Things." *Strategy and Business Magazine*, November 2014, p. 51.

5. Cearley, David. "Gartner's Top 10 Strategic Technology Trends for 2015." *Forbes*, October 21, 2014. http://www.forbes.com/sites/gartnergroup/2014/10/21/gartners-top-10-strategic-technology-trends-for-2015.

6. Rotman, David. "How Technology Is Destroying Jobs." *Technology Review*, June 12, 2013. http://www.technologyreview.com/featuredstory/515926/how-technology-is-destroying-jobs.

7. "Impact of Technology on Communication." *Buzzle*. Accessed January 4, 2015. http://www.buzzle.com/articles/impact-of-technology-on-communication.html.

8. Crowley, Mark C. "How Google Humanizes Technology in the Workplace and You Can, Too." *Fast Company*. Accessed January 3, 2015. http://www.fastcompany.com/3028812/bottom-line/how-google-humanizes-technology-in-the-workplace-and-you-can-too.

9. Wilson, James, P. J. Guinan, Salvatore Parise, and Bruce D. Weinberg. "What's Your Social Media Strategy?" *Harvard Business Review*, July–August 2011, p. 24.

10. Elkeles, Tamar, Patti P. Phillips, and Jack J. Phillips. *Measuring the Success of Learning through Technology*. Alexandria, VA: ASTD Press, 2014.

11. Hunt, Steven. "The Role of Technology in the Evolution of HR." TLNT, March 17, 2011. http://www.tlnt.com/2011/03/17/the-role-of-technology-in-the-evolution-of-hr.

12. "71% of Americans Care Deeply about Their Online Privacy amid Recent Privacy Concerns." Businesswire.com. July 29, 2014. Accessed January 4, 2015. http://www.businesswire.com/news/home/20140729006077/en/71-Americans-Care-Deeply-Online-Privacy-Privacy#.VR7pSvnF8gk.

13. McGrath, Maggie. "Target Data Breach Spilled Info on as Many as 70 Million Customers." *Forbes*, January 10, 2014. Accessed January 3, 2015. http://www.forbes.com/sites/maggiemcgrath/2014/01/10/target-data-breach-spilled-info-on-as-many-as-70-million-customers/.

Chapter 11

1. Hagerty, James R. "A Toy Maker Comes Home to U.S.A." *Wall Street Journal*, March 11, 2013, p. 31. Used with permission.
2. http://simple.wikipedia.org/wiki/Globalization.
3. Steger, Manfred B. *Globalization: A Very Short Introduction*. Oxford, UK: Oxford University Press, 2013.
4. Ibid., p. 95.
5. Cohen, Patricia. "Oxfam Study Finds Richest 1% Is Likely to Control Half of Global Wealth by 2016." *New York Times*, January 19, 2015. Accessed January 25, 2015. http://www.nytimes.com/2015/01/19/business/richest-1-percent-likely-to-control -half-of-global-wealth-by-2016-study-finds.html?_r=0.
6. Britt, Andi, and Nina Kreyer. "Leading Beyond Borders: Insights and Case Studies from IBM's Global Chief Human Resource Office Study." *Strategic HR Review* 10, no. 4 (2011): p. 18–25.

Chapter 12

1. Friedman, Thomas. *Hot, Flat, and Crowded: Why We Need a Green Revolution— and How It Can Renew America*. New York: Farrar, Straus and Giroux, 2008.
2. Hewlett-Packard Development Company. "HP 'Closed Loop' Ink Cartridge Recycling." Accessed April 7, 2015. http://www8.hp.com/us/en/hp-information/ environment/hp-closed-loop-ink-cartridge-recycling.html#.VSKYI_nF8gk.
3. A Southern Company. "Energy Innovation: Smart Energy: Smart Choices: Earth-Cents." Accessed April 7, 2015. http://www.southerncompany.com/what-doing/ energy-innovation/smart-energy/smart-choices/earthcents.cshtml.
4. Klein, Naomi. *This Changes Everything: Capitalism Versus the Climate*. New York: Simon & Schuster, 2014.
5. "Definition of Green Building." Accessed April 7, 2015. http://www.epa.gov/green building/pubs/about.htm.
6. Phillips, Patricia P. and Jack J. *Measuring the ROI in Employee Relations and Compliance: Case Studies in Diversity and Inclusion, Engagement, Compliance, and Flexible Working Arrangements*. Alexandria, VA: Society for Human Resource Management, 2014, p. 61.
7. Remarks as prepared for Duke, Mike. "New Commitments to Drive Sustainability Deeper into Walmart's Global Supply Chain." Accessed April 7, 2015. http://news .walmart.com/executive-viewpoints/new-commitments-to-drive-sustainability -deeper-into-walmarts-global-supply-chain.
8. Walmart. "Our Story." Accessed April 7, 2015. http://corporate.walmart.com/ our-story/.
9. Phillips, Patricia P. and Jack J. *The Green Scorecard: Measuring the Return on Investment in Sustainability Initiatives*. Boston: Nicholas Brealey, 2011.
10. Winston, Andrew. *Green Recovery: Get Lean, Get Smart, and Emerge from the Downturn on Top*. Boston: Harvard Business Press, 2009.
11. Phillips, Patricia, and Jack J. Phillips. *The Green Scorecard*. Boston, MA: Nicholas Brealey, 2011, 18.
12. Winston, Andrew S. *The Big Pivot: Radically Practical Strategies for a Hotter, Scarcer, and More Open World*. Boston: Harvard Business Review Press, 2014.

13. MIT Sloan School of Management. "Peter Senge Brings His Deep Expertise on Systems Thinking and Collaborative Leadership to the Mit Sloan Sustainability Curriculum." Accessed April 7, 2015. http://mitsloan.mit.edu/sustainability/profile/peter-senge.

14. Schendler, Auden. *Getting Green Done: Hard Truths from the Front Lines of the Sustainability Revolution.* New York: Public Affairs, 2009.

15. Moody-Stuart, Mark. *Responsible Leadership: Lessons from the Front Line of Sustainability and Ethics.* Sheffield, UK: Greenleaf, 2014.

16. Werbach, Adam. *Strategy for Sustainability: A Business Manifesto.* Boston, MA: Harvard Business School Publishing, 2009.

17. Eccles, Robert G., and Michael P. Krzus. *One Report: Integrated Reporting for a Sustainable Strategy.* Hoboken, NJ: John Wiley & Sons, 2010.

Chapter 13

1. Ellehuus, Christoffer. "Transforming Business Leaders into Talent Champions." *Strategic HR Review* 11, no. 2 (2012): 88.

2. Phillips, Patricia P., Jack J. Phillips, and Rebecca Ray. *Measuring the Success of Leadership Development.* Alexandria, VA: ATD, 2015.

3. Drucker, Peter. "What Makes an Effective Executive?" *Harvard Business Review,* June 2004. http://hbr.org/2004/06/ what-makes-an-effective-executive/ar/1; Goleman, Daniel. "What Makes a Leader?" *Harvard Business Review,* November–December 1998. http://hbr.org/2004/01/what-makes-a-leader/ar/1.

4. Collins, Jim. "Level 5 Leadership: The Triumph of Humility and Fierce Resolve." *Harvard Business Review,* July–August 2005. http://hbr.org/2005/07/level-5-leadership-the-triumph-of-humility-and-fierce-resolve/ar/1.

5. *CEO Challenge 2011: Fueling Business Growth with Innovation and Talent Development.* The Conference Board research report.

6. Smallwood, Norm. "Why Leadership Development in Asia Is Better than in Europe." *Harvard Business Review,* March 8, 2010. https://hbr.org/2010/03/why-leadership-development-in-asia/.

7. Hansen, Morten T., Herminia Ibarra, and Urs Peyer. "The Best Performing CEOs in the World." *Harvard Business Review,* January 2010. http://hbr.org/2010/01/the-best-performing-ceos-in-the-world/ar/1.

8. *ASTD State of the Industry Report (SOIR),* American Society for Training & Development, 2010.

9. *Employee Engagement Report 2011: Beyond the Numbers: A Practical Approach for Individuals, Managers and Executives.* BlessingWhite Inc. research report, January 2011.

10. Sinar, Evan, Richard Wellins, Rebecca Ray, Amy Lui Abel, and Stephanie Neal. *Ready-Now Leaders: Meeting Tomorrow's Business Challenges; Global Leadership Forecast 2014/2015.* The Conference Board and DDI research report, 2014.

11. Hallenbeck, George, Pushp Deep Gupta, and J. Evelyn Orr. "Getting Started with Assignmentology: A Case Study." Korn/Ferry International. Accessed April 7, 2015. http://www.kornferry.com/media/lominger_pdf/Assmntlgy.pdf.

12. Lamoureaux, Kim, and Karen O'Leonard. *Leadership Development Factbook 2009: Benchmarks and Analysis of Leadership Development Spending, Staffing and Programs.* Oakland, CA: Bersin & Associates, 2009.

13. Ibid.
14. *Report of the 2010 Best Companies for Leadership Study.* Hay Group. Accessed July 10, 2011. http://www.haygroup.com/BestCompaniesForLeadership/downloads/2010 _Best_Companies_for_ Leadership_Report.pdf.
15. "Sixth Annual Hay Group Study Identifies Best Companies for Leadership." Hay Group, January 25, 2011. http://www.haygroup.com/ca/press/details.aspx?id=28966.
16. Derven, Marjorie, and Kristin Frappolli. "Aligning Leadership Development for General Managers with Global Strategy: The Bristol-Myers Squibb Story." *Industrial and Commercial Training* 43, no. 1 (2011): 4–12.
17. Useem, Michael. "Four Lessons in Adaptive Leadership." *Harvard Business Review,* November 2010. http://hbr.org/2010/11/four-lessons-in-adaptive-leadership/ar/1.
18. Sinar, Evan, Richard Wellins, Rebecca Ray, Amy Lui Abel, and Stephanie Neal. *Ready-Now Leaders: Meeting Tomorrow's Business Challenges; Global Leadership Forecast 2014/2015.* The Conference Board and DDI research report, 2014.
19. Heifetz, Ronald, Alexander Grashow, and Marty Linsky. "Leadership in a (Permanent) Crisis." *Harvard Business Review,* July–August 2009. http://hbr.org/2009/ 07/leadership-in-a-permanent-crisis/ar/1.
20. Hill, Linda. "Where Will We Find Tomorrow's Leaders?" *Harvard Business Review,* January 2008. http://hbr.org/2008/01/where-will-we-find-tomorrows-leaders/ar/1.
21. Cappelli, Peter, Harbir Singh, Jitendra V. Singh, and Michael Useem. "Leadership Lessons from India." *Harvard Business Review,* March 2010. http://hbr.org/2010/ 03/leadership-lessons-from-india/ar/1.
22. Komm, Asmus, John McPherson, Magnus Graf Lambsdorff, Stephen P. Keiner Jr, and Verena Renze-Westendorf. *Return on Leadership: Competencies That Generate Growth.* Egon Zehnder International and McKinsey & Company research report, 2011.
23. Phillips, Jack J., Patricia P. Phillips, and Rebecca L. Ray. *Measuring Leadership Development: Quantify Your Program's Impact and ROI on Organizational Performance.* New York: McGraw-Hill, 2012.
24. Stern, Gary M. "Company Training Programs: What Are They Really Worth?" *Fortune,* May 27, 2011. http://management.fortune.cnn.com/2011/05/27/company -training-programs-what-are-they-really-worth.
25. Gardner, Nora, Devin McGranahan, and William Wolf. "Question for Your HR Chief: Are We Using Our 'People Data' to Create Value?" *McKinsey Quarterly,* March 2011.
26. Stern, "Company Training Programs."
27. Kincaid, Stephen B., and Diane Gordick. "The Return on Investment of Leadership Development: Differentiating our Discipline." *Consulting Psychology Journal: Practice and Research* 55, no. 1 (winter 2003): 47–57.
28. Lawler, Edward E., III, Alec Levenson, and John Boudreau. *HR Metrics and Analytics: Uses and Impacts.* Los Angeles: Center for Effective Organizations, 2004.
29. Schein, Lawrence. *The Business Value of Leadership Development.* New York: The Conference Board, 2005.
30. Avolio, Bruce J., James B. Avery, and David Quisenberry. "Estimating Return on Leadership Development Investment." *The Leadership Quarterly* 21 (2010): 633–644.
31. Schwartz, Anne. "Leadership Development in a Global Environment: Lessons Learned from One of the World's Largest Employers." *Industrial and Commercial Training* 43, no. 1 (2011): 13–16.

32. Davenport, Thomas H., Jeanne Harris, and Jeremy Shapiro. "Competing on Talent Analytics." *Harvard Business Review*, October 2010. http://hbr.org/2010/10/competing-on-talent-analytics/ar/1.

33. Bryant, Adam. "Google's Quest to Build a Better Boss." *New York Times*, March 12, 2011. http://www.nytimes.com/2011/03/13/business/13hire.html?pagewanted=all.

Chapter 14

1. "Fortune's Workplace Recognitions Put Scripps in National Media Spotlight." Accessed April 1, 2015. http://www.scripps.org/news_items/5180-fortune-s-work place-recognitions-put-scripps-in-national-media-spotlight.

2. "Scripps Health Selected among Nation's Top 10 Health Systems." News Release, June 21, 2010. Accessed April 1, 2015. http://www.scripps.org/news_items/3717 -scripps-health-selected-among-nation%E2%80%99s-top-10-health-systems.

3. Bock, Laszlo. *Work Rules! Insights from Inside Google That Will Transform How You Live and Lead.* New York: Hachette Book Group, 2015.

4. Bhalla, Vikram, Jean-Michel Caye, Andrew Dyer, Lisa Dymond, Yves Morieux, and Paul Orlander. *High-Performance Organizations: The Secrets of Their Success.* Boston Consulting Group research report, September 2011.

5. Phillips, Jack J. *Investing in Your Company's Human Capital: Strategies to Avoid Spending Too Little—or Too Much.* New York: AMACOM, 2005.

6. Ray, R. L., C. Mitchell, A. L. Abel, and P. Phillips. *The State of Human Capital 2012: "False Summit: Why the Human Capital Function Still Has Far to Go."* McKinsey & Company and The Conference Board research report number R-1501-12.RR.

7. Fitz-enz, Jack, Patricia Pulliam Phillips, and Rebecca Ray *Human Capital Analytics: A Primer.* The Conference Board research report R-1500-12-RR, 2012, 15.

8. LaValle, Steve, Eric Lesser, Rebecca Shockley, Michael S. Hopkins, and Nina Kruschwitz. "Big Data, Analytics, and the Path from Insights to Value." *MIT Sloan Management Review* 62, no. 2 (2011): 21–32.

9. Fitz-enz, J. *The New HR Analytics: Predicting the Economic Value of Your Company's Human Capital Investments.* New York: AMACOM, 2012.

10. Price, T., H. Nalbantian, B. Levine, and L. Chen. *Making the Case for Scaled Management of Human Capital: Valuing Workforce Strategies in Facility Services; Human Capital Analytics @ Work Volume 1.* The Conference Board research report, 2014.

11. Davenport, T. H., J. G. Harris, and R. Morison. *Analytics at Work: Smarter Decisions, Better Results.* Boston: Harvard Business School, 2010.

12. Phillips, Patricia Pulliam, and Jack J. Phillips. *Proving the Value of HR: ROI Case Studies,* 2nd ed. Birmingham AL: EBSCO Media, 2010, 31–62.

13. Rucci, A. J., S. P. Kirn, and R. T. Quinn. "The Employee-Customer Profit Chain at Sears." *Harvard Business Review,* January–February 1998, p. 82–97.

14. Ohlhorst, Frank. *Big Data Analytics: Turning Big Data into Money.* Hoboken, NJ: John Wiley, 2013.

15. Davenport, Thomas H., and Jinho Kim. *Keeping Up with the Quants: Your Guide to Understanding and Using Analytics.* Boston: Harvard Business Review Press, 2013.

16. Pease, Gene, Boyce Byerly, and Jac Fitz-enz. *Human Capital Analytics: How to Harness the Potential of Your Organization's Greatest Asset.* Hoboken, NJ: John Wiley, 2013.

17. Baron, Angela. "Measuring Human Capital." *Strategic HR Review* 10, no. 2 (2011): 30–35.

18. Phillips, Patti P., and Jack J. Phillips. *Measuring ROI in Employee Relations in Compliance: Case Studies in Diversity and Inclusion, Engagement, Compliance, and Flexible Working Arrangements.* Alexandria, VA: Society for Human Resource Management, 2014.

19. Phillips, Patti P., Jack J. Phillips, and Rebecca Ray. *Measuring the Success of Leadership Development: Step-by-Step Guide for Measuring the Impact and ROI of Leadership Development.* Alexandria, VA: ASTD Press, 2015.

20. Mayer-Schönberger, Viktor, and Kenneth Cukier. *Big Data: A Revolution That Will Transform How We Live, Work, and Think.* Boston: Houghton Mifflin Harcourt, 2013.

21. Davenport, Thomas H., and Geanne G. Harris. "Leading the Way Toward Better Business Insights." *Strategic HR Review* 9, no. 4 (2010): 28–33.

22. Shah, Shvetank, Andrew Horne, and Jaime Capellá. "Good Data Won't Guarantee Good Decisions." *Harvard Business Review*, April 2012.

23. Phillips, Patti P. and Jack J. *Making Human Capital Analytics Work: Measuring the ROI of Human Capital Processes and Outcomes.* New York: McGraw-Hill, 2014.

24. ROI Institute and Vestrics. "1st Annual Human Capital Analytics Study: Making Human Capital Analytics Work." October 2014. Accessed April 2, 2015. http://www.roiinstitute.net/human-capital-analytics-study-released/.

Index

Note: Italicized page numbers refer to figures.

About the Authors

Jack and Patti Phillips bring significant experience to this book. Together they have more than forty years of actual business experience, with much of that in the human resources area. For example, Jack spent fifteen years as head of HR in organizations, including a Fortune 500 firm. Patti headed up HR in a smaller firm. Together Jack and Patti have won several awards for their work, particularly in the human resources area. Jack has appeared on the cover of *Human Resource Executive Magazine*, highlighting his work while he was the head of HR for one organization. The Society for Human Resource Management gave Jack its highest award for creativity, recognizing his work in bringing accountability to human resources. The American Society for Training and Development has recognized Jack's work with its highest award of "Distinguished Contribution to Workplace Learning and Development." The International Society for Performance Improvement has recognized Jack by electing him president of the organization.

Jack and Patti have written more than twenty-five books in the HR area, including books that focus on investing in human capital, proving the value of human capital, and human capital analytics, among others. Together they routinely make presentations at international conferences around the world, speaking on the topics of human resources and human capital, especially accountability in human resources and the importance of investing in human capital.

With the ROI Institute, consulting often takes them directly to top executives, including chief human resources officers. Collectively, Jack and Patti have taught more than twenty thousand managers and executives about the importance of human capital and accountability in the human capital investment.

Finally, they have conducted research into understanding the different human capital issues. Both of their PhD dissertations (and master's theses) have focused directly on this issue, and their research work extends through the ROI Institute. Their combination of practical experience, insightful research, extensive writing, and consulting practices create an ideal background and experience for this new publication.